POLITICAL SOCIOLOGY

POLITICAL SOCIOLOGY

Satish Mittal
Sushil Kumar Saxena

Commonwealth

Political Sociology

ISBN : 978-81-311-0376-0

Edition : 2021

Published by :

COMMONWEALTH PUBLISHERS
4831/24, Prahlad Street,
Ansari Road, Darya Ganj,
New Delhi - 110002
Ph. : 23275511, 23257835
Fax : 91- 011- 23257835
e-mail : commonwealthbooks@gmail.com

Typesetting by :

Rishu Computers
Delhi

Printed at :
Roshan Offset Printers
Delhi

Preface

Political sociology is the study of the relations between state and society. The discipline draws on comparative history to analyse sociopolitical trends. Political sociology looks at how major social trends can affect the political process, as well as exploring how various social forces work together to change political policies. Political sociologists apply several theories to substantive issues. Three major theoretical frameworks are pluralism, elite or managerial theory and class analysis which overlaps with Marxist analysis.

This book introduces the key conceptual debates and approaches in contemporary political sociology, including the power relationship between the state and civil society and the impact of recent social changes on this relationship. Important and topical issues including globalisation, rise of new social movements, neo-liberalism, citizenship, political culture and political participation are also explored.

The book is the definitive introduction to the key processes that are changing the nature of politics and society in the modern world. The focus is on clarity, accessibility, and the needs of the student. An extremely well-written and engaging book, it takes an upbeat and argumentative style that brings the subject matter to life. It strikes the right balance between covering the core theoretical and conceptual issues associated with the subject while also adopting a central thesis that gives structure to the field and stimulates further enquiry.

Authors

Contents

1

Political Sociology in Modern Society

The contemporary global society is marked by a skewed distribution of resources and capabilities accorded to different groups in the world and therefore a skewed distribution of power and capacity. The contemporary global society is also a society in transition, in the sense that some fundamentals changes to the structure of world economy—namely, globalisation—are leading to new developments that have not been the purview of political sociology as conceived at the time of bounded nation-state units, the hallmark of the times when political sociology came of age. It is important to remember that the field of political sociology as conceived in those times was also a product of a certain social and cultural milieu— which shows up in the importance accorded to topics that flow from the heart of European philosophy and history.

The contemporary global society is marked by a skewed distribution of economic resources. It is true that as compared to any other time in human history many more people are living on earth. It is also true that as compared to any other time in human history many more people are living longer and healthier lives. Yet it is also true that the level of economic inequality among different population groups is also bigger than any other time in human history. The question of skewed distribution of economic and cultural resources in the language of political sociology is a question of who has power and how this power is exercised. Three different perspectives try to answer this question. The first perspective, the pluralist perspective, finds its origin in classical liberal ideas of Hobbes, J.S. Mills and Jeremy Bentham and in work of French aristocrat DeTocqueville. The liberal thought of Hobbes and Mills were concerned with protecting the rights of individuals in the context of English society of 17th and 18th century. For them it was individual liberty—defined in a narrow economic and individualistic basis—that was of foundation importance. Hobbes conceptualised the world in terms of a jungle where the only reason we do not cheat or hurt each other is because of the presence of the institution of state— the Leviathan. But then the problem becomes how to stop the state from taking over the whole sphere of existence.

The economic activities in particular were held by the thinkers like Mills and Bentham—whose ideas Marx ridiculed as the view of the bourgeois of the market street—to be sacrosanct and therefore outside the purview of state. The truth is that liberalism in its own time was a revolutionary idea. The ending of royal privileges and the need for individual social dignity—although this for J.S. Mills did not include non-property owners and colonised people—was the goal. The goal was to dethrone the clerical authority. For Mills and Bentham the reason for the existence of human beings and the state was to maximise pleasure and minimise pain, the idea that is known as utilitarianism.

In the modern world, this notion of liberal idea of power came to be encapsulated in the form of pluralist perspective. With the royal privilege destroyed and the clerics in retreat, the freedom to undertake commerce became dominant and the pluralist perspective echoes the individualist, liberal ideas. For pluralists, the society is not dominated by any one particular interest, but rather different people with similar interest come together and they play a part in the electoral process via which the ideas with most appeal to the populace gets into the government and therefore become applied to the society. For pluralists the process of elections as conceived in the present fashion is sufficient; power for them is not concentrated and is in fact dispersed throughout the society. DeTocqueville's construction of the local level of democracy among Americans in 1830s—as described in *Democracy in America*—who self-organised at local level and took initiative without any direction from government or any other centralising authority, forms the basis of this model of power. The most famous statement of modern pluralist thought is found in Robert Dahl's work, *Who Governs? Democracy and Power in an American City*, in which he studies the distribution of power in local politics in New Haven and argues that there had occurred in New Haven a historical. shift from "a system of cumulative inequalities in political resources to a system of non cumulative or dispersed inequalities in political resources". Pluralists extend this model to the polity at large and argue that there is no concentration of power.

They also down play the role of state; for them the state in the shape a minority (*homo politics* as Dahl had it) does not play an important role. Dahl terms most of the people in the society as *homo civics*, people who do not have much interest in the political affairs. The people who have an active interest in politics are characterises as *homo politics*. The population therefore is divided into two strata: apolitical statrum and political stratum. It is the second stratum—which does not require any special qualification for entrance such as wealth and education, except for an interest in politics—that people in government are selected from. The state then is a democratic state in the sense that it is elected by electoral process in which anyone can contend. People make the decisions and the words of Abraham Lincoln—"government of the people, by the people and for the people"—reflects the true nature of government. Democracy in this perception is defined as polyarchy, a system of limited democratic representation. For Dahl the idea of polyarchy is an improvement over the closed hegemonies of the authoritarian societies. William I. Robinson characterises this notion as "low intensity democracy" since it is associated with democracy in a formal rather than substantive sense. The notion of civil society in this perspective is the font from where the ideas that find representation in state arise. The state is not partial to any interest; it floats over all interest and its actions and policies are reflective of what the people at large want. Class and social movements do not exist in this language, because if they were real issues they will find a voice in the electoral process.

To begin with, this model is an idealised model of American society. This model does not even attempt to give a prescription to the world outside the United States. There are those who argue that American society is an exceptional society and that there is no existence of the notion of class in the American society because it does not requite the language of old world. It is a known fact that United States never had a strong socialist party and nor a strong socialist tradition. This for Seamier Martin Lipset had to with American exceptiones in the sense that America never had a feudal background so Americans were born conservatives and as well the limitations put on government from the beginning made Americans gravitate towards libertarianism and anarchism ideas than socialism. There are things that are truly different about America, but pluralism as a model does not even do justice to capturing how power is exercised, let along power on the global scale. The pluralist perspective applied to a global society will dictate that polyarchy is the answer for different parts of the world. Anywhere there is electoral process, which is nominally free, we have a polyarchy—which is all fine and well with the American government and as well as with capitalists who want to consolidate the present distribution of power in the world: in favour of those with money and power and against those lacking either capital and power. William I. Robinson in his perceptive work, *Promoting Polyarchy*, argues that polyarchy as a political program has been adopted by American foreign policy on the behalf of promoting interest of global capitalist fraction of the capitalist class.

Pluralist's notion of power, that they say exists in the world, is not complete. This conception of power—defined by Dahl as "the ability of A to make B do what otherwise B will not do"—is a relational one, that is visible in real world transactions. This model of power, as defined in this way, is focused on observable power—what Stiffen Lukes refers as one-dimensional notion of power. Lukes also points out that the one-dimensional power is about behaviour of making policy decisions about conflict of (subjective) observable interests. This kind of focus on what would be a model of behaviourism—which neglects the black box of consciousness—is a reflection of the electoral process that is central to Dahl's model.

As the United States preaches polyarchy to Middle East countries at this instance in global political situation—via its Greater Middle East Project—it is clear that they it does not want to let real substantive democracy come into play. Take, for example, of Egypt where supposedly American political pressure is bringing changes in the political structure. The supposed change that United States wants is the ability of different groups to be able to take part in elections and be able to get selected into government. So the visible conflict in the society is between Islamists and secularists (read American favoured)—but even when America is calling for changes in the political restructuring of Egypt, it is not asking for an open elections that will have the real conflicts of interests between the Mubarak regime and the Muslim brotherhood to come to the fore. While Mubarak has declared that he will allow other candidates to run against himself or the nominee of the ruling Nation Democratic Party nominee in the up coming presidential elections this year, in fact the desire of the Mubarak regime and the American side is very clear in actions of the ground: Mubarak has accepted that other people will run against him in the elections but he has attached an onerous and insuperable condition. Any candidate who would want to run the elections will have to get the signature of 50 members of the parliament (All but 10-15 of whom happen to be from another party); this then blocks out any chance for a real possibility that someone from Muslim brotherhood will run in the elections.

The state-civil society relations implied by pluralism are also partial in truth. For this perspective the state is but the clear representative of the democratic interests of the populace. And civil society therefore is truly represented in the state, which implies that there should not be antagonistic relation between the government and the civil society. It therefore makes no space for the social movements to in this equation. The only legitimate way of making one's voice heard is via organised lobby and pressure groups. In their reading, if people are not satisfied they can form a lobby or pressure group and influence the government. But for them there is no difference of a lobby group such as National Association of Manufacturers (NAM) and the Sierra club because each has an equal chance to be heard in the system. This, however, is patently false because the economic resources that a group such as NAM can bring to play are widely substantial from the resources that a group such as Sierra club can bring to play. Lastly, in relation to the differential economic resources, there is no sense of class differentials present in this perspective, which will be necessary to understand the contemporary global political and social situation. This then is a perspective that is very local to American society and it is even flawed when applied to that society.

The second perspective in political sociology that tries to answer the question of political power is the elite perspective. This perspective is based upon the work of Gaetano Mosca and Villfredo Pare to. Both these theorists held that societies are divided between elates and masses. This division comes from the differential abilities present in human beings. Those who end up elite have superior ability and those who remain in masses have lower abilities. These theorists point to the existence of a ruling group all through the human history as a factor supporting their theory. Pare to was so sure of his theory that he drew a curve that showed the distribution of elates and masses that parallel the curve of distribution of income among the population. Human nature, for these theorists, explains the persistence of elates and masses all through the history. Human nature for Pare to is an unchanging entity and therefore we have a universal presence of elates and masses throughout human history. Pare to explained the persistence of this division in terms of irrational behaviour of human psyche—in terms of "deep resides". He divided the population into two groups: those with "instinct for combination" and those with "instinct for aggregates". Those in the first group possess ability to make combinations and are cunning in their reason and they end up as elates. Those in second group are borne to resist change and have devotionals to stability. The combination of these two factors—the Machiavellian foxes and lions—keep society in stability. While the elite theorists are known for their critique of both liberal democracy and Marxism, one of them at least sees a limited role for liberal democracy. Mosca sees a limited liberal democracy as a mechanism for the circulation of elates since the elections will move those born in masses that have the ability of elite. This 'circulation of elates' will give the system an appearance of stability.

The second idea that is at the heart of elite perspective is that complex organisation need leadership to insure effective functioning. In this context of work of Robert Michaels in *Political Parties* put forward the "iron law of oligarchy". For Michaels, one "who says organisation, says oligarchy". Michaels studied the German Social Democratic Party to see how he can explain the concentration of power in the hand of a few people. His intention was critical, but he came to the conclusion that any organisation turns into an oligarchy because of the requirement of concentration of power in the hands of a small number of people—the elite—for effective running of any organisation. This kind of idea is also entertained by Marxism, as can be seen from the Lenin's idea of "dictatorship of proletariat" in *State and Revolution*, in which the working class is to be lead through the transition from capitalism to communism via the dictatorship of proletariat, which will wither away as people become prepared for communism.

As from the case of Soviet Union, this did not work as the dictatorship of proletariat become another kind of elite rule. Max Weber also drew attention to the process of bureau-cratisation that gets in the way of real democratic rule. For Weber, the only break out the "iron cage of bureaucracy" was to be provided by charismatic personality. In *Capitalism, Socialism and Democracy*, Schumpeter also talks about democracy as a system that inevitably leads towards elite rule because it bureaucratises the process of selection of leaders. The democratic process then become only a way for selecting as to who will rule them. The modern variant of the elite theory are found in the work of C. Wright Mills who in *Power Elite* argues that American society is ruled by elates from three different fields: military, corporate and political. Further work in Domhaff's Who *Rules America? Power and Politics* continues Mills tradition of democratic elite theory but with an increasing focus on class.

The notion of notion of power in the elite perspective is identified with the second-dimension of power in Steven Lukes' work, which assumes that there is a hierarchical relationship between groups in which the group in power is able to further its interest in not only the sense of the one dimension of power—that is by making an actor do something that the actor would not do otherwise—but also in the sense of being able to exercise political power by keeping certain issues off agenda. This perspective is identified with managerialism by Afford and Fried land in *Powers of Theory*, because it the power is concerned with the way structures of organisation allow the exercise of power by elite. The power flows from the organisation of structure via which decisions are made. In this sense the centralisation and the institution of bureaucracy becomes a central point of exercise of power.

The state then in this perspective is something that stands above the society to exercise in a non-partial manner that is for the good of the system. The bureaucrats in this model have independence from the economic elates. Echoing Weber, there is not only one basis for the socialite power. Class, which is understood in a different fashion than the Marxist notion of class, while an important factor is not the sole source of social power, and in addition to class, status and political party are other basis of power. The state in this system reflects two views: the sectional interest and structure of the interests of the dominant group—the elates—in the society and the functional interests of keeping the system going by making decisions that are important for the working of the system. Therefore the centralisation and rationalisation of the state are accompanied by the increasing coercive power of the elates against rebellious population.

The nature of democracy in this perspective is limited to an understanding of democracy in which is understood as a result of elite competition. Further democracy is understood to keep the circulation of elates going and in some more generous version of this perspective—namely, Mosca—democracy is a way by which individuals born among the masses can rise to become part of elates. Democracy here works to co-opt the populace. The political imperative that marks this system is one of reform and reaction. It is no accident that most of the major figures of this perspective found attraction in fascism. Pare to was sympathetic to fascism and Michaels left socialism for the fascist work under Benetino Mussolini. The state and civil society relationship in this perspective are organised around inter-organisational authority and conflict. The conflict is managed and resolved in this perspective and politics—which allows for the management of conflict—plays a central role in the world-view of this perspective. Given that the state is an autonomous entity in this perspective, the civil society and social movements do not get any importance, because the state can resolve the questions of importance without partiality to any one side.

This is an interesting perspective that works very well in some aspects on the global political situation today. The understanding of the growing role of state in surveillance and the control of human bodies can be understood via this perspective. This perspective also could be used to explain the persistence of inequality and evil in the world. It exists, because it is in human instincts to be unequal—and therefore those with ability can move up and become part of the elite and others will have to be content with being part of masses who will be looked after yet dictated to by state. There is a fundamental level of justification of inequality built into this system. At the national level, the absence of whole groups of peoples from the elite structures points to the problem with this perspective. For example, the lack of representation of minorities in the political power structure can be construed as if the whole of the population lacks in some of the capabilities that are needed in the elates. The elite perspective though if applied to the selection of ruling elates in the United States is not able to answer the question of whether it is possible for someone to be able to rise to a power of political prominence or even within the prominent political structure without a level of economic affluence? It seems as if anyone who runs in the elections has deep pockets. Another related question is whether the bureaucrats making decisions that are autonomous of the interests of the capitalists in their work? On this point, there are a number of instances where it could be argued that a managerial state makes decisions that seem to go against elite interests in the first instance. If elite perspective was the ruling paradigm in the world, the power hierarchy of the world would be made up of bureaucrats who made decisions about what the best way for maintaining the system—and this would have meant that there was more stability in the system.

The third approach to global political situation is the Marxist perspective in political sociology. The Marxist political sociology is based upon the work of Karl Marx who stressed that throughout the human history—except in the prehistoric times—there have always existed two classes of people, the oppressors and the oppressed. The oppressed are the ones who sell their capital to make a living and oppressors are the ones who own the means of production. Men make their own history but not the conditions of their own choosing—this sums up how Marx views the relationship of work to the making of history. The social conditions and relationships, according to this perspective, prevailing in a given society reflects its organisation of the mode of production. Different modes of production represent different relationships: the feudal mode of production has the master-slave relationship and the capitalist mode of production has capitalist-workers relationship. In works such as *Capital* Marx worked out the centrality of labour to the production of profit under capitalism. For Marx, the organisation of political life is to be understood in relation to the class relationship between its population. Whenever the mode of production becomes more productive than the social organisation that is present in the society, a revolution takes place and brings into being a new mode of society. For both Marx and Engels, as they argue in *The Communist Manifesto*, the history of all societies hitherto has been a history of class struggle and therefore under capitalism the struggle is between the bourgeoisie and the proletariat. The bourgeoisie's power over the proletariat is because of the formers control over the means of production.

The notion of power in Marxist approach flows from the control of economic resources. For Marx the economic differences within the civil society are manifest in the structure of state and the dominance in the realm of economic field implies dominance in the power in terms of state. Those who control capital in the society therefore also control the institution. In *The Communist Manifesto* Marx identities the state as the "executive committee of the bourgeois"—that is, it serves the interests of capitalists in a very straightforward way. Anything that benefits capitalists gets done by the state and anything that benefits the working class is not done by the state of its own volition but is rather forced by the working class if they are strong enough. But it has also to be said that this is not the only way Marx understands state. There are other times in which he gives more leeway to the way state acts.

The notion of power—a structural one—implied by the Marxist theory is captured in the three-dimensional model of power as captured by Steven Lukes in *Power: A Radical View*. The third degree of power is concerned not solely with what is on the agenda as is the case with pluralist perspectives or as to what is kept of the agenda as is the case of elite theory, but it deals with the latent issues along with observable issues and also with how some potential issues are kept out of politics by sectional interests. In Grammes's work on hegemony in *Selections from the Prison Notebooks* he is concerned with how the working class—even though it is suffering from exploitation at the hands of the capitalists—does not revolt in keeping with Marx's prediction of revolution. The answer for this for Gramsci is to be found in the way the civil society becomes the place where sectional interests are able to change the cultural modes of thinking via their deployment of hegemony eliciting mechanisms.

According to Gramsci, hegemony—the consent to leadership by the capitalist class—is established not in the narrow repressive way but also in ideological way. So the state was not only involved in the establishment of hegemony in repressive terms but more importantly in the ideological sense. Therefore for the resistance to this the real stagy will involve a war of position in the civil society, whose importance between state and economy was established by Gramsci within Marxists, and this will be a slow and long process, one that would need the involvement of organic intellectuals in creating alternative hegemony via cultural work. Gramsci is refreshing because he is saying that a society cannot be just changed by taking over the institution of state, as was the Lenin's program in Soviet Union. In so doing, Gramsci lays the foundation for an alternative understanding of why the revolution did not happen in the advanced industrial revolution, which was Marx's idea of how the transition from capitalism to communism will unfold. It is also important to realise here that this kind of work was later extended by the Frankfurt school scholars who centred culture in their analysis of capitalist societies. In recent times, the ideas of Robert Cox in *Production, Power and World Order: Social Forces in the Making of History*—who builds upon Gramsci's work—are interesting because he argues for understanding power at the global level by examining the "state-civil society" complexes not only in a given nation, but in an international field of power in which some states have maximum degree of external autonomy, and others are dominated by these states with maximum external autonomy.

The Marxist debates around the institution of state are perhaps the most important debates over the institution of state in any of these three approaches. Classical Marx's position—although he gave different stresses to it—was that state acted as the executive committee of the bourgeois. Therefore what was in the favour of the bourgeois was also in the favour of the state. But the debates between Ralph Miliband and Nicos Poulants as were the modern markers in increasing the understanding the nature of state. For Miliband who follows the instrumentalist approach in *The State in Capitalist Society*—that is, the state is an instrument of capitalist power pure and simple—and therefore argues that all the actions taken by the state are in favour of the ruling class. But Nicos Poulants as faults Miliband for thinking of the state as an 'empty space' and not as a social relationship. He argues that state has "relative autonomy" from the capitalist class and even though it the state might in the short term take act against what might be the interest of capitalist class in the last instance it will take the side of capitalist class. Fred Block in his article, "The Ruling Class

Does Not Rule" argues that the state is not concerned with working for each single capitalist but that in fact the role of the state is to maximise the accumulation of profit and therefore not each single action in case of individual capitalist should be seen as a signification of state's intent.

The idea of democracy favoured by this approach is also different from the other conceptions. The democracy here is not limited to the procedural and formal one or as something that is to be managed by the elates within a liberal democracy. The democracy in this approach is a real measure of economic as well as cultural equality for all the population. Democracy thus takes on the sphere of economy, state and the civil society. Marxists argue that for a democratic system we need to ensure that there is equal opportunity for the development of capacities of each individual from day one. There should be select few who can afford nice cars and schools from day one and others who cannot even afford to go to school. If only does the state provide free education for the children of the poor on par with the rich, argued Marxists, then only can we have a chance at a the establishment of a real democracy. But as studies such as Bourdieu's in *Distinction: A Social Critique of Value of Judgment* show, the markers of class are embedded within the family background so deep that the first institution of socialisation—the family itself—cancels out the impact of equalisation of education upon the possible establishment of a democratic education. The social movements that arouse out of the Marxist approach were class based and therefore they demanded actions to improve the economic and social position of workers. But since the defeat of the Soviet experiment, the labour movement the world over has suffered a strong blow.

The truth is the contemporary political situation in the world is marked by the shadows of 1989. The death of Soviet experiment in the graveyard of authoritarianism and the victory of capitalism marked the end of an era and the beginning of another. While Fukuyama wrote paeans to the victory of liberal democracy at the end of history, new ramblings were rising inside the very developments that were responsible for the fall of the Soviet Union. The world of today marked at it is by globalisation is not the same which was analysed by the classical perspectives of political sociology—pluralism, elite theory of class perspective. The rise of international trade and the corresponding need for a political structure that facilitates the process of trade and as well the movement of capital and goods across nation-state boundaries has impacted the world political dynamics. The increasing importance of trans-national institutions—such as the International Monetary Fund (IMF), World Bank (WB), World Trade Organisation (WTO), Group of Eight (G-8), Organisation for Economic Cooperation and Development (OECD) and Asia Pacific Economic Cooperation (APEC)—for political coordination of this system of increasing global trade has led to a focus on issues that cannot just be explained by reference to the notions of power and politics conceived in the political sociology literature. There is a need for a rethink in the basis concepts of political sociology. Since most of the concepts of political sociology come from the time when the world economy was divided into neat and bounded boxes of nation-states, the present conjuncture in the world political situation cannot be completely grasped by the concepts of political sociology.

Take, for instance, the concept of globalisation and its impact upon the institution of state. There three four basic positions that can identified in the impact of globalisation in the state. First, there are those who argue that the role of state is weakening under globalisation and the importance of trans-national institutions is increasing. This position has been called the hyper-globalism position, because it sees the role of nation-state as weakened and therefore it focuses on the trans-national. As part of global capitalism school, William I. Robinson's work, A Theory of Global Capitalism: Production, Classes and State in a Trans-national World, can be seen as a representation of this perspective. HE argues that "the apparent declining ability if national state to intervene in the process of capital accumulation and to determine economic policies reflects the new found power that capital acquired over the nation-state and popular classes..." and that "real power in the global system is shifting to a Trans-national space that is not subject a 'national control". Others of view that the nation-state as being weakened by this perspective include Kenichi Ohmae, who argues that the "global civilisation" will be the product of the changes brought about by globalisation and that nation-state is history. Second, there are those who argue that the world has seen a higher level of globalisation in the previous epoch and therefore the institution of nation-state is not weakening and in fact the process of globalisation is being controlled and shaped by nation-state This group is known as the skeptics. Third, the last group is made of those who are known as trans-formationalists who argue that the world is undergoing complex changes and although the role of nation-state is changing it is not yet okay to argue that its role has weakened.

In terms of democracy, the political situation in the contemporary times is marked by the absence of any real representation by majority of population in their own political systems. In most of the western democracies, there is certainly a much higher level of formal democracy today than in the past. The level of political participation in formal elections is also healthy, with the sole exception of the United States where political participation at the national level are very low and political culture is heavily dominated by irrational elements. Outside the western world, formal democracy has spread via the third wave of democracy . The biggest mark of this was the fall of Soviet Union and the conversion of the Eastern Europe to formal democracies in 1989. This then is the victory of capitalism that has made it possible for the capitalists to dominate the world political, economic and cultural scene like never before. The discourse of formal democracy has serviced the designs of the powerful countries and by extension the forces that stand behind these nations—the capitalist class.

The United States' discourse of support for democracy is about extension of the market and its logic into all parts of the globe and into all facets of human life, without regard for popular democratic ideals. William I. Robinson's path breaking *Promoting Polyarchy: Globalisation, US Interventionism and Hegemony* is the best work to capture the deployment of low intensity democracy for controlling the popular forces around the world. The low intensity is being used to make consumers of the people the world over, thereby superseding other more organic identities that people have. The invasion of Iraq and the gunboat democracy that we are seeing today shows the desperate nature of capitalist rule and its interest in consolidating formal democracy, which is integral to the capitalist system in our epoch. If one juxtaposes Venezuela next to the case of Iraq, one can really see the sordid nature of how capitalist power works. Despite coups and repeated attempts of overthrown Chives, the capitalist interests represented by the United States government cannot bring them to accept that Chives has the popular support of a solid majority of Venezuelans.

The resistance to exploitation that is part and parcel of capitalism, nonetheless, continues. The fall of the Soviet Union in 1989 was blow to the social movements and class movements that opposed capitalism. The nature of protest and rebellion has changed in the world over. But there is no end of history yet, as protest, rebellion and politics has come back on agenda again. In terms of social movements, there has been a differentiation in the number and types of social movements active in the world. The social movements that held sway in the past, such as the class based movements have suffered a loss of strength in the aftermath of the Soviet demise. The rise of the new social movements in Europe in 1980s has centred the issue of culture. Whereas the social movements before 1980s were based mostly around the issues of class, the NSMs stressed the quality of life issues. In this way, a number of questions that were limited to the class dimension were reconsidered to become questions of quality of life questions and a number of other agendas that were not represented in the class movements were brought forth.

Ronaldo Ingelhart has suggested that the rise of movement like the NSMs (New Social Movements) signify the movement of societies to a set of post-material values, in that the ideas beyond material ideas—which guided the class based opposition to large number of people—have become central to populace' life. This then shows up in their desire to think of politics in terms of quality of life issues rather than in material terms. This has meant proliferation of movements that range from identity-based movements to peace movements and the environmental movement.

But the NSMs are movements that are more present in the advanced industrial countries than in the global south. There is still space in the global south for the kinds of actions that are still concerned with the issues of material well being and economic justice. The rise of an energised global civil society has also made its mark on the global scene. The work of Kick and Sikkink in *Activists beyond Borders* and Jackie Smith in *Trans-national Social Movements and Global Politics: Solidarity Beyond State* shows the increasing engagement of global civil society with social justice issues beyond nation-state boundaries.

2

Elite Theory in Political Sociology

The origins of Elite theory lie most clearly in the writings of Gaetano Mosca, Vilfredo Pareto and Robert Michels. Mosca emphasised the ways in which tiny minorities out-organise and outwit large majorities, adding that "political classes" – Mosca term for political elates – usually have "a certain material, intellectual, or even moral superiority" over those they govern. Pareto postulated that in a society with truly unrestricted social mobility, elates would consist of the most talented and deserving individuals; but in actual societies elates are those most adept at using the two modes of political rule, force and persuasion, and who usually enjoy important advantages such as inherited wealth and family connections. Pareto sketched alternating types of governing elates, which he likened, following Machiavelli, to lions and foxes. Michels rooted elates ("oligarchies") in the need of large organisations for leaders and experts in order to operate efficiently; as these individuals gain control of funds, information flows, promotions, and other aspects of organisational functioning power becomes concentrated in their hands. Emphasising the in escapability and also the relative autonomy of elates, all three men characterised aspirations to fully democratic and egalitarian societies as futile.

Many democrats and social radicals have rejected this "futility thesis". They have sought to demonstrate that particular elates are not those with superior endowments or organisational capacities, but merely persons who are socially advantaged in power competitions. Adherents of this view have argued that the existence of elates can be terminated either by removing the social advantages that some people enjoy or by abolishing the power concentrations that spur competitions among them – remedies that often go hand-in-hand. There are no historical instances, however, where these remedies have been successfully applied in a large population for any significant length of time.

The writings of Mosca, Pareto, and Michels constitute a paradigm from which a general theory of elates and politics might be derived. But efforts to produce such a theory have not been conspicuously successful. Linking elates causally to major regularities in politics remains elusive; there is no accepted typology of elates and no accepted specification of the circumstances and ways in which one elite type replaces another; political interactions between elates and non-elite population are captured only piecemeal. Nevertheless, political scientists and sociologists pay much attention to elates and their key roles in democratic transitions and breakdowns, revolutions, political regimes of all kinds, mass movements, democratic politics, globalisation, and many other political phenomena.

ELITES

Elites derive from a fundamental and universal fact of social life, namely, the absence in any large collectivise of a robust common interest. While it is true that most large collectivised rest on a base of social and cultural understanding, these tend to be ambiguous and rough. The satisfaction some of their members seek are only partly compatible with the satisfaction sought by other members. Members constantly claim statuses and other valued goods for themselves, their kin, friends, and allies that other members do not accept as fully legitimate. Acceding to these claims is often more a matter of judging that it is dangerous or inexpedient to resist them than of recognising that the persons and groups making the claims have some right to do so. In large collectivised common interest is fairly minimal and must always be supplemented by authoritative decisions that dissenters and opponents dare not or find it inexpedient to resist.

Common interest is even more limited as regards the detailed features of any large collectivise functioning. Its operations involve day-to-day decisions and, thus, allocations and re-allocations of tasks and statuses. Merely for a large collectivise to survive, „intelligent and „objective decisions that transcend individual interests must regularly be taken. But there can seldom be any firm consensus among a collectivise members about the rightness of these decisions. This is partly because only a few are in positions that afford a relatively comprehensive view of the collective effort and its present location in time and space relative to its goals. Yet such a view is usually necessary for knowing if a particular decision is "right". Moreover, the need for constant decision-making deprives members of the time they would need to reach agreement about how their interests apply to current problems and needs. Even a relatively unimportant decision changes the line-up of influence for the next decision so that the details of a collectivity structure and needs are always different today from what they were yesterday. This means that any incipient consensus among its members necessarily focuses on yesterday's structure and needs.

These aspects of collectivities give to elites their importance in political and social theory. Collectivities of any size and complexity require decisions by persons who happen to be strategically located in them. Because such collectivities are concentrations of power in the wider society, their top decision-makers have disproportionate socialite power and influence, and they nearly always enjoy disproportionate privileges and protections. If we call these persons elites we casay that large and complex collectivities necessarily create elites. In this sense only are elites an inherent feature of societies; all other reasons for the existence of elites are less persuasive and more debatable. Recognising this is not, however, merely to echo Michels dictum that "Who says organisation says oligarchy." For oligarchy, aristocracy, and other euphemisms for elites imply or impute specific structural and behavioural features. Whether elites are cohesive, conspiratorial, self-conscious, and so on is answerable only through empirical investigation. While elites are the inescapable consequence of conflicting interests in all large and complex collectivities, their configurations vary according to political and social circumstance.

Elites may be defined as *persons who, by virtue of their strategic locations in large or otherwise pivotal organisations and movements, are able to affect political outcomes regularly and substantially*. Put differently, elites are persons with the *organised capacity* to make real political trouble without being promptly repressed. They consist not only of prestigious and "established" leaders – top politicians, important businessmen, high-level civil servants, senior military officers – but also, in varying degrees in different societies, relatively transitory and less individually known leaders of mass organisations such as trade unions, important voluntary associations, and politically consequential mass movements. "Counter-elites" are subsumed by this definition because they clearly have the organised capacity, although perhaps mainly through negation, to affect political outcomes regularly and substantially.

It is important to stress that this is a limited and specifically political definition of elites. It is restricted to persons who are at the top of the pyramid or pyramids of political, economic, and social power. It does not consider all those in a society who enjoy high occupational, educational, or cultural statuses to be elites in a political sense. As defined, national political elites are not large in number. Geraint Parry has observed that the entire British elite could be seated with ease in a soccer stadium. Using strict organisational and positions criteria, as well as data about sizes of elite networks, some researchers have estimated that the national political elite in the United States numbers perhaps ten thousand persons, maybe half this number in medium-sized countries like France, Australia or Germany and about fifteen hundred in small countries like Denmark and Norway. This last estimate of fewer than two thousand persons is probably the most plausible for all countries during the early modern historical period and all but the most populous developing countries today.

Elites and Political Stability

The presence or absence of stable political institutions is one of the major differences between political systems that can be explained on the basis of differences between elites. It is unusual for political power to be institutionalised effectively, as it has been for many years in Great Britain, the United States, the Netherlands, Sweden, Switzerland, and a few other Western countries. Stable political institutions are marked by the *absence* of irregular seizures of government executive power or obvious military influence in policymaking through threats of military intervention. Every four years since 1789 a president has taken office in the United States on the basis of election and has served out a term, unless dying in office, as the more or less effective head of the American political system. In Britain over an even longer time span prime ministers and cabinets have regularly succeeded each other as the chief political authority in accordance with principles and rules that, in spite of being largely informal, are well known.

The personalised manipulation of political institutions through individual and direct control of military and police forces has been, and is, much more common. Typically, there is a distinct elite group that effectively commands organised coercive forces and is prepared to arbitrate political decisions no matter what existing institutions prescribe. It is of little consequence analytically whether this group centres on a traditional monarch, a civilian coalition tied closely to professional military commanders, or it is an overt military junta. What is consequential analytically is that elites, no matter what their partisan inclinations may be, see power as personalised and directly dependent on the support of organised coercive forces. Elites critical of current social organisation, for whatever reason, necessarily view political change in terms of removing or altering the group that effectively commands those forces. In their eyes and the eyes of their opponents, power flows from gaining at least temporary control over the principal means of coercion. Attempts to seize government executive power by force are seen by all as plausible, even probable, eventualities.

This is the basic aspect of a *disunited elite*. For long periods, as in Spain, Portugal, and Latin America during the nineteenth and most of the twentieth centuries, governance oscillates between "dictatorial" and "democratic" poles. These oscillations are transitory and circumstantial manifestations of the political system inherent instability so long as most elite persons believe that the hold on government power is subject to sharp and sudden changes. The historical record shows overwhelmingly that politics in most countries normally approximate an unrestrained struggle among mutually distrustful elites to defend and advance their interests with little regard for cost or propriety.

Of supreme interest in political analysis, therefore, are the relatively few countries in which political instability is not the order of the day. For, as noted, a few countries have displayed patterns of institutionalised authority and procedure that have been respected and perpetuated over long periods. In them, irregular seizures of government power by force are unknown and informed observers consider such seizures highly unlikely. Elite theory holds that these deviant cases are explicable *only* in terms of elite behaviour. More specifically, the historically normal situation of political instability has been abrogated in countries only when a *united elite* has formed.

There are, however, two markedly different types of united elites and, consequently, two quite different forms of political stability. One type is an *ideologically united elite*, which is marked by the uniform profession of a single and defined ideology by all or nearly all elite persons. These persons consistently avoid taking conflicting positions in public about current policies and political beliefs; they foster the image of a single and homogeneous leadership group. But given the conflicting interests that exist in any society, this image is more apparent than real. To some extent it arises from the determination of uppermost leaders imbued with a specific ideology to afford no opening for the intrusion of "unsound" outsiders into policymaking. But even for elite insiders the ideological uniformity is in part coerced. Behind the public profession of more or less complete agreement about current policies and goals – behind the expression of a single and defined ideology – there exists an apparatus of power sufficient to force all or most current and aspiring elite persons to harmonise their public statements with the views that are currently orthodox. Defining what is orthodox is the task of a few individuals in the highest elite positions, and adhering to this orthodoxy obviously blocks the expression of divergent interests.

The content of the single ideology that marks an ideologically united elite is of little analytical importance. It must probably be sufficiently diffuse and removed from present conditions to permit flexibility in interpreting always changing realities. It must probably be focused on some future, imaginary social condition toward which society is allegedly moving. It must, in short, be substantially utopian. But analytically speaking, whether the ideology describes a future classless society or one in which eternal salvation or pastoral contentment for all will be realised is of little consequence for the enforced unity that prevails among elite persons. Because the only permissible public position for organising endeavours is defined and monopolised by those in power, political institutions can be centralised to a degree unknown elsewhere. Individuals and groups who want to alter those institutions can be identified easily, and they possess few means with which to appeal for public support. Evidence indicates that, once established, institutions operated by an ideologically united elite are stable for long periods.

The other type of united elite, a *consensually united elite*, does not depend on all elite persons taking essentially the same political position in public. There is no single and defined ideology to which all must adhere. Instead, persons with power and influence take clearly divergent positions on public matters. These positions often accord with opposing ideologies, as in the long conflict between conservatives and liberals within British and Swedish elites during the nineteenth century, and the subsequent conflict between liberals and socialists within the same elites during the first half of the twentieth century. The striking aspect of these conflicts is that they occur under a set of rules that is nowhere comprehensively codified but is tacitly and widely understood to remove serious personal danger from elite contests and competitions. These informal rules emanate from a structuring of power that gives all or most elite persons and groups sufficient access to decision-making so that it is in their collective interest to avoid seriously disruptive actions and keep the political situation manageable. Although elite members disagree and oppose each other in limited struggles for ascendancy, power is distributed so that all or most can have influence on political decisions sufficient to deter them from translating their oppositions into attempts to seize government power by force. Political institutions are, accordingly, stable for long periods.

Origins of Elite Types

Ideologically united elites originate in revolutionary circumstances that enable a movement dogmatically expressing a specific ideology or creed to suppress and supplant previously existing elites. Examples are Russia 1917-1921, Italy 1922-1925, Germany 1933-1934, North Korea 1946-1948, China after 1949, Cuba 1959-1961, and Iran 1979-1981. Ideologically united elites may also originate when an external power possessing such an elite imposes its clone on a conquered or otherwise subordinated country, as in East Germany and Eastern Europe following World War II. By contrast, consensually united elites sometimes originate through dramatic changes in the situations and attitudes of the key groups that have constituted a disunited elite. This involves an *elite settlement* in which warring elite camps manage to bring their major disputes to a close and establish a basis for mutual trust. The first historical instance of an elite settlement occurred in England „Glorious Revolution of 1688-1689, and it is worth recalling its basic features.

English elites had been bitterly and deeply disunited, as evidenced by the Civil Wars and Interregnum between 1642-1660. In 1660 the monarchical system was restored, albeit with some shifting of positions and blurring of lines between the previously warring elites. Thereafter one main elite camp, the Tories, sought to exploit their association with the monarchy, while the other main camp, the Whigs, maintained its anti-monarchical stance. The Tories were thoroughly identified with the religious doctrine and institutions connected to the Church of England. But when in 1685 the birth of a son to James II, who professed both Roman Catholicism and an absolutist version of monarchical power, made an indefinite Catholic succession to the throne likely, the Tories were as discomfited as their Whig rivals. Fearing a resumption of civil war, key leaders of the two elite camps conspired to invite the successful military intervention of the Dutch *stadtholder*, William of Orange, and the elite camps subsequently agreed, in early 1689, to establish William as king under terms that effectively guaranteed them joint political influence. Occurring in a predominantly agrarian society where the elite stratum was necessarily small and exclusive, these events marked the beginning of the limited and restrained political contests with understood informal rules that have characterised the British polity ever since.

Consensually united elites have also originated in the attainment of independence by former colonies in which local or "native" elites have been able to practice a restrained home-rule politics while waging long, in some cases violent, struggles for independence. As illustrated by elites in Britain North American colonies, both American and Canadian, local elites in partially self-governing colonies may develop a high enough level of mutual trust when resisting the colonial power interventions and seeking independence that they are consensually united from the date of independence or the grant of full home rule. In addition to the U.S. And Canada, this was the experience of elites in Australia and New Zealand during the latter part of the nineteenth century, and of white South African, Indian, and Malayan elites during the twentieth century first half. It is worth noting that Dutch elites became united in this manner before and during their successful struggle for independence from Spain late in the sixteenth century, although full integration of the seven Dutch provinces did not occur until after the Napoleonic Wars.

In cases where consensually united elites formed as an outgrowth of colonialism, colonial governments had active representative institutions that afforded elites a considerable practice of limited and restrained politics. But this was not the situation in the Latin American colonies of Portugal and Spain, where, moreover, there was little clear understanding of territorial boundaries when independence was gained. Consequently, military leaders and local political bosses (*caudillos*) tended to predominate in Latin America at independence and for long periods thereafter. Nor were the political experiences of elites under colonial rule and when struggling for independence propitious for the formation of consensually united elites in more than a few of the scores of ex-colonies that achieved independence during the decades following World War II. Except in India, Malaya (later Malaysia), Senegal, and no more than a handful of other ex-colonies, such as Jamaica and Barbados, independence brought with it disunited elites and long-lasting political instability.

To summarise, there have been two ways in which disunited elite became consensually united historically: (1) through basic and sudden elite settlements in societies at relatively low levels of socioeconomic development; (2) through colonial home rule and struggles for independence where local elites had already received, or received in the course of those struggles, experience in political bargaining and restrained competitions. Neither origin appears relevant to the situation of most disunited elites in today world. A necessary condition for an elite settlement appears to be a level of socioeconomic development lower than that of most developing countries with disunited elites today. At higher development levels elites are probably too numerous and closely tied to particular non-elite interests to be able to fashion a settlement. Colonial dependency is obviously a condition necessary for creating a consensually united elite through home rule and independence struggles, but it is a condition that is no longer seriously present. These observations raise the question of whether there may be a third way in which consensually united elites form.

In countries that have transited to democratic elections, the opposing camps and factions making up a disunited elite may begin to converge if some of the opposing elites form a broad political coalition that mobilises enough voters to win the elections repeatedly. This enables the coalesced elites to dominate government executive power and obtain the greater security that derives from this domination. An elite convergence may continue if factions hostile to the winning coalition conclude that seizing power by irregular means is not a realistic possibility and they must beat the winning coalition in election contests if they are to escape permanent political subordination. This means acknowledging the value of elections and promising to accept their results. An elite convergence may be considered complete when the formerly hostile and losing factions gain government executive power in an election and then govern in a way that is respectful of established institutions and tacit live-and-let-live reciprocities with the previously dominant elite coalition. As happens more clearly and quickly in elite settlements, through convergences elites gradually reach an underlying consensus about the norms of restrained political competition so that political institutions become stable.

Elite convergences occurred in several European countries and in Japan during the twentieth century second half. All were at a relatively high level of socioeconomic development and general prosperity when the convergences took place. The four clearest cases were France once General de Gaulle associates formed a winning electoral coalition after his return to power in 1958; Italy once the "organic" Christian Democrat - Socialist winning coalition took clear shape in 1963; West Germany after several victories by the Christian Democrat – Christian Socialist – Free Democrat winning coalition formed in 1953; Japan once the Liberal Democrats and centrist parties constituted a winning coalition starting in 1964. In each of these countries, dissident and hostile elite camps eventually came to see that they had no real political alternative to moderating their stances in order to compete effectively in elections, and in each what had previously been a disunited elite gradually became consensually united – by 1981 in France when the previously dissident Socialists won power and governed with moderation, during 1979 in Italy when the "revolutionary" Communist Party cooperated with the dominant Christian Democrats to repress extra-parliamentary terrorist groups; in West Germany when the dissident Social Democrats entered into a "grand" governing coalition with their previous nemesis, the CDU-CSU coalition; and in Japan once the Socialist Party jettisoned its Marxist baggage during the mid-1980s.

Elite Theory and Democracy

Although an elite theorist's personal preference may be for democratic politics, he or she does not believe that in most countries and circumstances a practical and stable form of democratic politics can be achieved. Meaningfully democratic institutions and practices depend upon the type of elite that a society has. No type of elite is compatible with the full democratic ideal, and only one of the three types is reasonably compatible with the stable democratic politics that are practised in Western countries and a few others today. However, none of the three elite types is *reliably* conducive to even this limited form of democracy.

The most common political situation, that of disunited elites, has the basic feature of institutional instability. While institutions operated by some part of a disunited elite may at times have a formally democratic facade, the institutions are hardly worth much promotion or defence because they are unlikely to survive a serious political crisis. Commonly, any substantial increase in normal political tensions leads, with or without a military coup, to a more authoritarian and repressive government. Although such a government may eventually mellow or even be replaced by a more democratic one that has the tacit consent of the elite veto group associated with the military, this improvement is likely to be merely an interval in a succession of more or less repressive governments. As noted, historical evidence is overwhelming that disunited elites and the unstable institutions they create persist through most vicissitudes and that each government is in practice one permitted by those who happen to control military and police forces.

The circumstances in which disunited elites become ideologically or consensually united are unlikely to appeal to people with democratic sentiments. An ideologically united elite does not allow competitive politics, and where it exists meaningful actions motivated by democratic sentiments are nearly impossible. The basic settlements in which a few consensually united elites originated historically had as their principal features substantial elite autonomy from mass pressures together with the sacrifice of deeply held political principles for which opposing elites and their supporters had long stood. The colonial origins of consensually united elites involved empires that are odious to convinced democrats and are, in any case, no longer feasible politically and economically. Where opposing camps in a disunited elite have gradually converged, those who have most liked to consider themselves genuine democrats have found themselves consistently in the minority, while more conservative and traditional persons who are part of the majority to which the winning coalition appeals are inclined to merely pretend that they are democrats. Moreover, although a consensually united elite may emerge via an elite convergence and open the way to a more widely accepted and stable democratic regime, the process depends on socially radical groups becoming disillusioned with their democratic ideals.

It is also the case that the regime created and operated by a consensually united elite may not, in fact, be very democratic. It can be based, as in most historical cases, on a highly restricted suffrage. Even temporary dictatorship or the long dominance of a high-handed chief executive is possible so long as the elite remains internally trusting and is prepared to cooperate in removing the dictator or chief executive if he or she becomes seriously incapacitated or incompetent. Fundamentally, practical democracy depends on the ability of a consensually united elite to keep political tensions moderate. Where such an elite exists the problem for people imbued with democratic ideals is deciding how much public attention they should try to centre on issues that they consider morally right but that are also potentially explosive. The champions of such morally charged issues are likely to find that members of a consensually united elite distort, partially suppress, or simply confuse the issues if doing so seems necessary to maintain institutional stability. Morally charged issues will be subject to "benign neglect" if elites conclude that the issues have reached a threshold of articulation and antagonism beyond which political stability is endangered.

Should those who cannot get the hearings that they believe their moral causes deserve acquiesce in such elite actions? If it is correct that consensually united elites are ordinarily quite capable of managing political tensions, the question is without significance. Yet, suppose that the elite cannot quite do this in the face of embittered demands and vehement mass demonstrations. On the assumptions of the approach to elites outlined here, this would break up the elite and in all probability create a disunited elite with the usual consequence of covert or overt military rule and the suppression of political dissent. Would it be right for staunch democrats to help bring this outcome about on behalf of a high moral cause? The answer is obvious.

Elite theory teaches, in other words, that a mature and experienced advocate of democracy must always settle for a political order that is considerably less than ideal. An elite that is consensually united, or one that approaches this condition, is necessary for practical democracy. Only such an elite will effectively manage conflicting interests whose open and dogmatic expression would create disastrous internal conflict. Where an elite does this over the course of many years, representative political institutions guided by reasonably competitive and influential elections are possible, although not inevitable. But where groups within the elite fully and openly reflect and express and conflicting non-elite interests, then at some point political freedom for considerable numbers of elite and non-elite persons alike will be suppressed or the polity will not survive. Elite theory rejects the fashionable but fatuous notion that the most desirable political system is one in which the divergent interests of a population are clearly represented and forcefully articulated at the elite level. Posing "a real choice, not an echo" in practical democratic politics threatens to weaken a consensually united elite and concomitant institutional stability. Recognising this, proponents of elite theory cannot properly feel compelled to pursue the democratic ideal in all circumstances and at all costs.

Elites and Revolution

There is no agreed definition of revolution that attaches the term to a clearly specified political event or process. It is sometimes used to mean almost any irregular and forcible seizure of power, thereby covering the many coups and sporadic uprisings that occur where elites are disunited. "Revolution" is also often used to label civil wars and wars of liberation that centre on dynastic, ethnic, regional, or religious divisions. This definition vagueness makes it a matter of subjective judgment whether to call a regime, movement, or violent conflict "revolutionary" – a judgment that is, indeed, frequently made after the fact, as happened with the so-called Cuban Revolution that established the Castro regime. When they were fighting the Batista dictatorship, Castro insurgents portrayed themselves as, and were widely believed to be, liberal and populist, not revolutionary. It was only after a year or two in power that Castro and his associates proclaimed themselves "revolutionaries" and a Cuban Revolution was widely perceived. By not distinguishing between many kinds of violent upheavals, "revolution" has lacked the precision required of a concept that can be utilised seriously in an elite theory of politics.

There is, however, one special kind of upheaval with features that are objectively different from those of coups, civil wars, secession, and popular outbursts. This is an upheaval that begins when normal government authority, most manifest in disciplined military and police forces, suddenly and dramatically collapses. During the shorter or longer interval that follows, maintaining order against riot or pillage becomes highly problematic until government authority and military and police discipline are either restored or built anew by some victorious group. One cannot say that an elite of any of the three types exists during this interval. Power resides, as radicals like to say, "in the people" or, more precisely, in persons who assemble fairly spontaneously, usually under arms, and respond to immediate propaganda and oratory with mass actions. Such assemblages typically include bodies of rank-and-file troops who have either liquidated their officers or are simply ignoring officers orders.

An upheaval of this kind eventually brings a substantially different body of persons to elite status, and it changes political and especially economic institutions in fundamental ways. But before such sweeping alterations become apparent, whoever attempts to restore or construct a semblance of organised power in the area where government authority has collapsed usually comes under attack from areas to which the government collapse did not extend. To survive this attack, the new power organisers must quickly create some degree of bureaucratic centralisation accompanied by disciplined military and police units. Sooner than later, the popular assemblages that have held forth are policed and suppressed. When this happens, the observer can again speak of a regime operated by one or another type of elite. In the English and French upheavals of 1642-1645 and 1789-1794, respectively, the new elite was again disunited. But after the upheaval in Russia, 1917-1921, the elite was ideologically united as a consequence of the victorious Bolsheviks tight organisation and doctrinal coherence during the upheaval.

If for purposes of conceptual order and terminological consistency "revolution" refers only to an upheaval involving the collapse of government authority and an ensuing interval when coercive power is located in more or less spontaneous popular assemblages, it is a rare and unlikely event. A revolution in this sense can probably occur only in societies at low levels of socioeconomic development, that is, largely agrarian or peasant societies. In more bureaucratic societies at higher development levels the widespread collapse of government authority and disciplined military and police forces seems even more implausible today than it did when proponents of revolution counted, for the most part mistakenly, on large numbers of citizen-soldiers turning on governments after hardships and defeats in large-scale warfare. Moreover, advances in military technology, especially nuclear weaponry, suggest that wars fought by mass armies may now be relics of history.

Whether or not they are any longer likely, do revolutions in the present sense of the term bring political improvements? From the standpoint of democratic and liberal criteria, the answer is an emphatic No. Because of the searing enmities and political scars they create, revolutions never eventuate in consensually united elites. Their consequences are either disunited or ideologically united elites, neither of which is congenial to reliable democratic practices. Although much has been heard from persons outraged by what they regard as fundamental moral deficiencies of contemporary political regimes, not least Western democracies, the sweeping "revolutionary" changes that these persons have demanded lie well beyond what elite theory depicts as possible; they are just dreams and wishful thoughts that are from a liberal and democratic standpoint deeply imprudent.

Elites and Non-Elites

How does elite theory treat non-elite population and link them to elites? The bulk of Pareto million-word *Treatise* was an attempt to answer this question and it is self-evident that no satisfactory answer to it can be offered here. The question requires conceptualising a dynamic relationship between elites and non-elites in which, under specifically conditions, elites override non-elites, but under different and equally specifically conditions non-elites override elites. Where elites prevail, a theory must be content to specify the *outer limits* of possible elite behavioural and, thus, of political outcomes. Where non-elites prevail, political outcomes can be forecast with greater certainty. Specifying the changing predominance of elites and non-elites theoretically is, therefore, the crucial task.

To illustrate how this might be tackled, consider the proposition that at low levels of socioeconomic development a leftist or levelling propensity is potentially widespread among non-elites. In extreme political circumstances, this propensity may eventuate in a revolutionary collapse of government authority and military discipline of the kind just discussed. But such levelling revolutions appear possible *only* in an early phase of development, and even then they are exceedingly rare: the English, French, and Russian revolutions are the classic instances and all three occurred in pre-industrial conditions. Much more normally in pre-industrial societies, bodies of peasants and artisans are not greatly aggravated by the encroachments of elites, and their fundamentally leftist or levelling propensity is not strongly activated. Non-elite propensities become more inflamed, however, when societies reach the industrial stage of development. In this stage, manual industrial workers, who are numerous, hold consistently to egalitarian sentiments and a hostile view of elites, clearly articulated by the powerful trade unions and leftist parties that mobilise them. Bureaucratic and service workers, who are also numerous, tend to accept the presence of elites even if they do not condone all of their actions and features. Diminished and now more or less comparable numbers of artisans and ex-peasants, who in industrial conditions typically own small farm properties, are ambivalent about elites and elite actions: they resent elite interferences in their farming and artisan endeavour but are inclined to support those elites who seek to check levelling forces. In extreme political circumstances, an anti-egalitarian and possibly "fascist" upheaval aimed at crushing levelling forces is possible: northern Italy in the 1920s; Weimar Germany in the late 1920s and early 1930s; Spain in the late 1930s; strong fascist movements in Austria, Belgium, France, and most other European countries during the interwar period. Normally in industrial societies, however, the large numbers and political influence of non-manual bureaucratic and service workers, augmented by ambivalent artisans and ex-peasants, are sufficient to prevent strongly egalitarian mobilisations of manual industrial workers from gaining government power. If elections are held, the latter are simply outvoted. Finally, the pervasiveness of non-manual bureaucratic and service workers in socioeconomic development post-industrial stage rules out the dramatic levelling and anti-levelling political changes that are possible in earlier stages of development.

There is an important caveat. In societies that are latecomers to socioeconomic development and in a handful of mostly small societies with large petroleum reserves it is clear that today production and communication technologies greatly accelerate the conversion of work-forces from an overwhelmingly peasant and artisan composition to one that consists predominantly of bureaucratic and service workers. In these accelerated and technologically more sophisticated circumstances, manual industrial workers are at once fewer in relative numbers and, perhaps because of their smaller numbers and more sophisticated work tasks, their outlooks appear to be less intransigently egalitarian and hostile toward elites. The main political problem in societies coming late to socioeconomic development may, consequently, reside less in the composition of their rapidly changing work forces than in the inability of these work social practices.In labelling African states as weak, fragile or even failed, we are applying the socio-logical definition of the state in a normative way. Social practices which are based on traditional reciprocity turn into corruption and nepotism, and the informal distribution of social resources appears as an illegal strategy. In particular, states with strongly donor-dependent economies have to please the expectations of two different audiences. The big man entrepreneur must take into consideration both the formal norms of the supply side and the social norms of his local constituencies. The dynamics of contemporary state-formation have to be sought in these structural contradictions, which provide a framework in which current state-builders act. What does this mean for the field of applied policies?

State-Building and International Intervention

In a recent article, Francis Fukuyama argued for ''Stateness' First'. He discerned in contemporary interventionist policies a contradiction between state-building and the promotion of democracy, between, on the one hand, the monopolisation of physical force in the hands of the state and, on the other hand, the building of public and legal institutions which can constrain the state's power monopoly. Indeed, applying the categories of historical sociology, contemporary state formation is characterised by a confusion of the (chrono-) logic of the two phases of the monopoly mechanism. In cases such as Afghanistan and Iraq, institutional features of the second phase – constitutions, elections, representative bodies – were implemented before achievement of the first phase, the establishment of a legitimate state monopoly of physical force. Oriented toward the normative image of the modern state, current state-building processes tend to invert the social logic of European state formation, in which the coercive formation of state monopolies preceded both the juridification of political authority and the enhancement of state capacities.

Contrary to European state formation, post-colonial state-builders achieved a form of 'negative sovereignty', a formal legal entitlement which actually hides the lack of empirical statehood, that is, the social content related to the definition of the mod-ern state. The de-colonisation process established statehood only as a form of external representation, as a formal territorial and legal framework of international politics guaranteed by the world state system and by international law. Behind the facade of modern state institutions, however, social practices of a quite different nature have continued. The synchronisation of the state as an institution and as daily social practices, as in Elias' model of the civilising process, is still under way. From this perspective, 'fragile states' are not a new phenomenon at all. On the contrary, measured by the standard of the ideal image of modern statehood, most post-colonial states have been defective states from the beginning. In many of them a legitimate monopoly of physical force has not yet been achieved, and the so-called new wars of our times are therefore less an expression of state decay than an indication that the 'classical' European path to modern statehood has been derailed.

If at all, the term 'state decay' applies to some states of the former socialist world. There, relatively firm monopolies of physical force had been established, yet in some cases the second phase of Elias' monopoly mechanism ended in the at least temporary dissolution of the first. In these cases, the simultaneous introduction of grand schemes of political and economic liberalisation eroded the core institutions of the state rather than brought about the blessings commonly associated with the democratic state. Contemporary state formation does not seem to be following the state-building logics which historical sociology abstracted from the European experience.

Looking at current state-building in Afghanistan, Iraq or the territories of the former Yugoslavia. In these territories, a multiplicity of actors are involved in taking over a broad range of tasks, from combating and disarming militias to the building of political, social and economic institutions. Although oriented towards the image of the state, these 'new protectorates' only dimly remind us of forms of legal political authority which we can call a state. Rather, we are confronted with a kind of 'controlled anarchy', with fragmented political arrangements in which various international, trans-national, regional, national and local interests and competence overlap. For all these actors, the image of the state serves as a central normative reference while they follow their own goals on the ground. Whether these complex social arrangements will ever lead to viable states nobody knows.

The lesson we can learn from historical sociology is to understand state formation as an ongoing and open-ended process. State formation is characterised by both successful state-building and state decay, and in European history too, more states may have disappeared than became established according to our modern image of the democratic state. Both phases of the monopoly mechanism are extremely fragile and war-prone periods of institution-building and social transformation. What decides success or failure is contextual and cannot be derived from the abstract concepts of sociology. In Afghanistan, for instance, the Taliban were the first political force ever to come close to establishing a factual state monopoly of force over Afghan territory. From the perspective of historical sociology, that is, they successfully built up the core institutions of modern statehood. Their fall was not due to contradictions in the inner logics of state-building, but a result of the historical political context in which they acted. Due to political interests and normative demands on the international level, state-building in Afghanistan had to start again from scratch, involving a new coalition of old and new actors. Given this general contingency of the historical context, contemporary state-builders are facing the same general uncertainty as their European predecessors, namely that even their intended actions will have unintended outcomes. This applies also to policies of international interventions whose political rationale and public justification cannot be found in sociological reasoning or long-term state-building strategies guided by scholarship. The decision-makers in both state agencies and non-governmental organisations are not driven by sociological grand schemes, but by their own organisational interests and the dominant issues of everyday politics.

forces to provide employment for large parts of swollen and mostly young non-elite population.

The illustrative point, in any case, is that non-elite configurations, sketched here as distinct work force compositions and concomitant mixes of orientation toward elites, rule out certain elite actions and political outcomes at different stages in socioeconomic development, but they do not determine what elites will do and what political outcomes they will produce. Thus, early in socioeconomic development non-elites tend toward a hostile view of power exercises by elites, and their impoverished situations give non-elites little reason to fear a general levelling of existing hierarchies. If elites are exceptionally incompetent or unlucky, a collapse of government authority that triggers a levelling revolution is possible.

But elites may circumvent this by couching effective appeals for non-elite support in terms of religious and other traditional beliefs. In socioeconomic development industrial stage, a shift to fascist rule is possible, although entrenched elites may circumvent it by holding elections in which levelling forces simply lack sufficient numbers to prevail. What is not possible in industrial societies – in other words, what is precluded by the non-elite configuration – is a successful levelling revolution, and, *pace* Marx, none has occurred. Meanwhile, industrial societies appear to prevent sudden and deliberate settlements of basic elite disputes because their relative complexity makes the elite stratum large and not sufficiently autonomous from non-elites. Elite actors are numerous and many give their primary allegiance to the partisan interests of the mass organisations and movements they head. Negotiating behind the political stage to compromise principled interest positions that elite factions have repeatedly taken when mobilising non-elite support and then getting followers to accept such compromises is unlikely. Forming a winning political coalition that successfully defends existing hierarchies is the more plausible option for elites in industrial societies.

Elites in Post-industrial Conditions

How do elites and non-elites affect each other in Post-industrial conditions? By the 1970s all of the Western countries that were experiencing these conditions – the Anglo-American, Scandinavian, and Benelux countries, plus West Germany and perhaps Austria - had consensually united elites and stable political institutions. Disunited elites in several countries that were just then reaching the Post-industrial stage of development were becoming more consensually united – French, Italian, Japanese, Greek, and Portuguese elites via convergences; Spanish elites via a dramatic elite settlement in the wake of the *Franquist* regime.

Initially, Postindustrial conditions seemed to accentuate the political stability that consensually united elites produce. This was because the preponderance of bureaucratic and service workers blurred class lines and weakened customary partisan alignments among non-elites. Consequently, elites needed less recourse to ideologies, such as socialism and liberalism, in order to justify their statuses, policy positions, and governing actions.

Elite political discourse shifted to discussing affluence and the welfare state as solvents of historic discontent and problems. Observers avidly discussed the „end of ideology, a thesis that is probably best seen in hindsight as rationalising blandly optimistic views of the Postindustrial landscape, especially as viewed by sub-elite commentators. With high productivity and nearly full employment, the absence of serious economic downturns, a shrunken working class acquiring middle-class life styles, and no other large and obviously discontented collectivities in sight, there was the appearance of considerable harmony among non-elite population. Elites, accordingly, adopted a more blatantly managerial posture and they voiced a complacent belief that mere „fair treatment of individuals and groups would ensure social progress and tranquility.

With the passage of time, however, the greater non-elite harmony and elite complacency that appeared to be the principal political effects of Postindustrial conditions diminished. Increased crime, narcotics use, and other deteriorating social conditions became apparent in many cities; a seemingly intractable form of poverty spread in urban slums and rural backwaters; and many young people with essentially privileged family backgrounds displayed considerable alienation and discontent. These trends suggested that Postindustrial conditions could be more difficult politically than they first seemed.

Postindustrial conditions are in important respects the terminus of socioeconomic development. They complete the conversion of work forces that consisted overwhelmingly of peasants and artisans at development outset into work forces pervaded by bureaucratic and service personnel. It is quite unlikely that some further stage of development, conceived in terms of new basic kinds of work and new work force components, lies beyond Postindustrial conditions. If this is so, it must be asked whether Postindustrial societies can over the longer haul remain viable politically without the sense of progress and spread of hope that development engendered historically. Crudely put, can Postindustrial societies "stagnate" indefinitely in their non-elite configuration without suffering major political upheavals?

One concern is the increased empathy between elites and non-elites that occurs in Postindustrial conditions. The preponderance of bureaucratic and service work intermingles previously distinct social strata. Persons more frequently and routinely ascend to elite positions from non-elite origins and locations than happens in more rigidly stratified societies at earlier development levels. As a consequence, not a few persons holding elite positions in Postindustrial conditions see themselves as one of a kind with non-elites, among whom they frequently have intimate personal associates and for whom they have considerable empathy. These close and empathetic ties to non-elites help ensure that elite persons are better able to determine measures that at least partially assuage non-elite discontent and aspirations. But what may happen if it is not possible to assuage non-elites? Presumably, actions and measures ranging from deception to discouragement to outright repression will be more reviled by non-elites and harder for elites to take.

A still wider difficulty confronts elites in Postindustrial conditions. In all earlier stages of socioeconomic development political action was not generally required to keep most persons steadily engaged in the performance of necessary work. For the most part, internalised attitudes and customary social controls supplied by neighbours and work mates sufficed. In Postindustrial conditions, however, such close social controls, along with most religious and other traditional belief systems, attenuate greatly. In earlier stages of socioeconomic development, moreover, most persons worked diligently in order to stave off dreadful personal circumstances – dismissal, eviction, hunger, etc. – and a significant proportion worked without surcease because they could plausibly believe that by doing so their strong personal ambitions could be realised. In these earlier societies only a small number of specially favoured persons – mainly the offspring or friends of the rich and powerful – were un motivated to work in disciplined ways and were inclined toward a self-indulgent, if perhaps aesthetically satisfying, leisure.

It is easy to see that the proportion of people who are un motivated for steady work increases markedly in materiall affluent and empathetically indulgent historical moments, to a period of technological stagnation. Gold stone's emphasis on the significance of the steam engine, and the science and engineering culture that fostered its invention and development, provides a more specific explanation of the rise of the West. than more general theories of rationalisation, bureau-cratisation, institutionalisation, capitalisation, or modernisation. Indeed, Gold stone demonstrates that much of what is cited as unique to the West can be found in many regions of the world at different points in history. The steam engine, however, was the first really powerful technology in that it transducer fire into mechanical motion, a dream pursued by a number of engine scientists in the seventeenth century, including William Petty. Though the steam engine represented a departure from previous technologies, its invention is not surprising when viewed in the context of over a century of experimental engine science, the engineering culture it fostered, and the material technologies it spawned.

Three crucial dimensions of the modern science idea can be distinguished:

— mechanical philosophy (the grand unifying concept),

— ingenuity (a cognitive culture of intellectual and technological inventiveness), and

— experimentation (the concept of how to practice natural philosophy).

Experimentation implies an overarching engine science that places material technologies at the heart of natural scientific inquiry. Engine science requires the integration of natural philosophy, engineering, and mathematics *in practice*. The result is a culture of inquiry in which the conceptualisations of theory are tied to the manipulations of engineering and the operations of mathematics.

This new culture of inquiry is importantly defined by the role of material engines in the key epistemic practices of measuring, scoping, graphing, and manipulating. The four forms of material engine that correlate with these practices are meters (barometer, hydrometer, etc.), scopes (telescopes, stethoscopes, etc.), graphing technologies (cartographic instruments), and chambers (e.g., hydraulic and pneumatic technologies). These are *epistemic engines,* because they generate objects of inquiry, institutionalise and structure practices of inquiry, and drive the research agenda.

In doing so, they become what Labour calls "obligatory passage points" in scientific inquiry Attention to these technologies facilitates a comprehensive and naturalistic understanding of science as a very specific cultural complex of discourses, practices, and material culture. And though the specific technologies employed in statecraft may differ from those in natural inquiry, analogous practices of scoping, metering, graphing, and manipulating can be identified. Geological surveys and censuses, for instance, can be understood as terra-scopes and socio-meters. The point is to view the specific technologies in terms of the wider practices of engineering culture that straddle science and government in the modern period. Practices are the linchpin between discourses and materiality, because they participate in both.

Science-State Relationship

The understanding of the state in international politics has its roots in Max Weber's classical definition of modern statehood. With reference to the violent history of European state-building, Weber defined the central feature of modern statehood as 'the monopoly of the legitimate use of physical force within a given territory'. In Weber's words, the war-prone formation of state monopolies of physical force was a long-lasting process of 'political expropriation' in which all political communities other than the state had gradually been deprived of the means of coercion. However, the establishment of state monopolies of physical force should not be conceptualised merely in terms of power relations through which power-holders carry out their will despite any resistance from the subordinated. In order to establish consolidated states, the factual monopoly of the use of physical force has to be considered legitimate by both rulers and ruled. Stable systems of political authority do not rest on a monopoly of coercion alone: this state monopoly also has to be anchored in the cultural order of society. A political order needs legitimacy.

Long-lasting political institutions require a stable set of rules, which, in normative and cognitive ways, regulate the social conduct of rulers and ruled. In referring to the inner justification of systems of domination, Weber precisely distinguished political authority from mere power relations by resort to the notion of legitimacy. His concept of legitimacy is intended to give an answer to the question of when and why people obey. According to Weber, modern statehood rests on legal or rational authority, i.e. belief 'in the legality of enacted rules and the right of those elevated to authority under such rule to issue commands'. He sharply distinguished this modern authority based on formal legal procedures from pre-modern or traditional forms of authority, which rest on personal ties and the 'established belief in the sanctity of immemorial traditions and the legitimacy of those exercising authority under them'.

In the 1930s, Norbert Elias critically took up Weber's core definition and conceptualised European state formation as a 'civilising process.' In doing so, he applied a double perspective: The civilising process, seen from the aspects of standards of conduct and drive control, is the same trend which, when seen from the point of view of human relationships, appears as the process of advancing integration, increased differentiation of social functic. s and interdependence, and the formation of ever-larger units of integration on whose fortunes and movements the individual depends, whether he knows it or not.

In his theory of the civilising process, Elias put together the macro-sociological aspects of state formation and the micro-sociological consequences of this process, that is, the ways in which the evolution of the modern state has shaped social practices. Combining Weber with Freud, he defined the immanent link between the macro- and micro-levels as the conversion of outer constraints into self-restraints, and concluded that the formation of modern states has been reflected in increasingly differentiated patterns of self-control on the part of the individual. The pacifying institutional setting of modern statehood was accomplished by a particular normative restriction of the public behaviour of individuals. In this sense, state structures and social practices are inseparably knitted together, and the maintenance of public order relies on both functioning state institutions and forms of social action that are able to transform legal authority into daily practices.

In historical terms, however, this civilising process has not been 'civilised' at all. On the contrary, Elias traced the origin of both the internal pacification of society and the autonomy of the modern individual back to an unrestricted and violent process of elimination in which any individual or small group struggled among many others for resources that had not yet become monopolised. In mainly abstracting from the history of France, Elias differentiated between two distinct phases in the emergence of the modern state monopoly of physical force:

1) In the first phase, a factual monopoly of physical force is established. An increasing number of people lose direct access to the means of force, which progressively become centralised in the hands of a few and thus placed outside open competition.

4

Political Culture and Democratisation

The notion of political culture came from German sociology, where it had a long and diverse lineage by the early 20th century. The German tradition did not coalesce into a single coherent definition of culture; rather, different authors emphasised different characteristics of culture: as the sum total of all socialite norms and practices, a legacy of history, norms or accepted ways of thinking and acting, a set of psychological orientation, a system that organises society, or something that humans create and pass along to the next generation. This holistic understanding of political culture resonated well with the national/ethnic stereotypes and racism that were widespread in the West in the first decades. Cultural theories have fallen out of favour more than once since the Second World War—partly because of their dalliances with racism and ethnocentrism—but reformulated versions have been proposed periodically.

Today a variety of cultural approaches can be found in political science. The dominant version of political culture since the 1960s has been a behavioural approach that borrows from psychology and uses survey research and experiments. Nevertheless, other kinds of cultural theories survive that owe more to anthropology and the earlier German tradition. The anthropological view, most famously described by Clifford Geertz, holds that culture is a property of a whole society, or subgroups within society, but in any case not of individuals.

Culture consists of both attitudes and behaviours, especially those that have become stable and routine and unquestioned. Culture is therefore is relatively static, in this view. Culture is also rich and complex: there are many attitudes and behaviours. Furthermore, these cultural elements cohere, united by their own internal logic. In this view, individuals may deviate from cultural norms, but the culture exerts pressure on them to conform. For this reason, individuals cannot be fully understood apart from the culture in which they live. This approach calls for *verstehen*, which in German simply means "understanding," but in English-language academic circles has come to mean an empathic, deep understanding of the culture by a perceptive scholar who knows it intimately enough to see it through the eyes of its members.

This approach emphasises the *meaning* of words and actions to the actors themselves. Several authors have claimed to describe cultures that are distinctively favourable or unfavourable for democracy. For example, Howard Wiarda has repeatedly argued that Latin American societies have a "corporatism" culture influenced by the teachings of St. Thomas Aquinas and the hierarchical organisation of the Catholic Church. This corporatism culture carries values antithetical to individualism, pluralism, and capitalism, all of which have been associated with political democracy. Another example is Lucian Pye's *Asian Political Culture*, which derives various orientation to political authority – some compatible with democracy, others not – from thick descriptions of family structure and child-rearing practices in seventeen Asian countries.

One common criticism of this anthropological approach, or at least of its extreme stereotype, is that it exaggerates the homogeneity of a society. Societies, especially large ones on the scale of nations, always contain subgroups with their own subcultures, and these often contain individual dissenters. Another common criticism is that while a static version of culture may be very useful for explaining political stability, it provides no leverage for explaining political change. A third weakness is that this approach forces the social-scientific community to trust the subjective judgment of self-appointed expert interpreters of a culture, as it would be difficult or impossible for other researchers to replicate the expert's field experience, even if they had access to extensive documentation. Nevertheless, it is probably true that this approach yields more detailed, accurate, and insightful portraits of a culture than a battery of survey questions can. A recent reformulation, inspired by later work in critical anthropology, rectifies some of the drawbacks. The "semiotic practices" approach does not assume that cultures are uniform or static or internally coherent. Rather, culture is the ongoing process in which individuals "make meaning" by engaging in political activity. In this view, culture becomes a hive of constantly evolving activity that is means different things to different participants. This approach strives for even more fine-grained and exhaustive descriptions of a culture, which demand even more skill and effort to collect and analyse texts, conversations, and practices.

At the opposite extreme lies the behavioural approach to culture, inspired by psychology. In this approach, culture is merely the aggregation of individuals' attitudes and (in some applications) behaviours. Culture does not exist except in the minds of individuals, although for some purposes it may be useful to describe the culture of a group, society, or nation by referring to the collective distribution of attitudes or an average attitude. This approach takes as little as possible for granted concerning the uniformity, stability, and coherence of attitudes. It may be that certain attitudes are dominant, that various attitudes go together because they are constrained by underlying value orientation, and that these patterns are stable or slowly changing; but in this approach, these are hypotheses to be tested, not features that can be safely assumed or asserted, even after extensive "soaking and poking" by an insightful expert. The best way to understand culture, according this approach, is to conduct rigorous survey research. Sometimes researchers also conduct psychological experiments. One early example of this approach with relevance for democratisation was *The Authoritarian Personality*, a project that began as a study of anti-Semitism in 1943 but eventually led to a scale measuring a "right-wing authoritarian" personality presumed to be supportive of fascist regimes. On the democratic side, the landmark study was *The Civic Culture*, which used public opinion surveys in five countries to identify a cluster of attitudes that the authors believed to be most propitious for stable democracy. Both studies suffered fierce criticism on methodological grounds, much of which was justified. However, because their mistakes inspired others to do better, they founded what is now a vast body of survey research on political culture and democratisation.

Whether an anthropological or a psychological approach is better depends on one's purpose. If the goal is to provide a rich, "thick" description of a small, relatively homogeneous community, then the prolonged immersion that anthropological approaches require is likely to lead to better insights. But if one's goal is to develop and test fairly general ideas about the impact of political culture on democratisation, then survey research and statistical analysis are indispensable. Beyond the study of small, homogeneous communities, the psychological approach is superior overall to any anthropological approach. By making questionnaires more comprehensive and more in tune with how people really think, survey research can approach thick description;

Postindustrial conditions. It is useless to ignore this by holding that modern technology greatly reduces the need for human labour. Responsible work is not readily parcelled out in little pieces in any society. Some tasks must still – and presumably must always – be performed with care, diligence, and forethought, and those who perform them will not allow a large body of essentially idle people, however decorative they may be, to receive substantial rewards for their idleness. This disjunction between the diligent and the idle signals a growing clash between segments of non-elite population in Postindustrial societies, although it is uncertain if this clash will have a magnitude that consensually united elites are unable to manage.

Limits of Elite Theory

Elite theory's predictive pretensions are necessarily modest. Elite behavioural cannot be inferred, let alone projected, from knowledge of non-elite configurations and propensities. For instance, neither the creation nor persistence of a consensually or an ideologically united elite is discernibly linked with non-elite propensities. The probability of a united elite of either kind forming and creating stable political institutions can only be guessed at from knowledge of recent elite history. Does this history display long and costly, but essentially inconclusive, warfare between disunited elite factions who, in consequence, may be disposed toward a basic settlement of their disputes? Have elites recently suffered a defeat so grave that the way may be open for a well-organised but previously peripheral group to seize and consolidate power in revolutionary circumstances? The difficulty is not merely that elite behavioural is poorly understood; it always contains enough elements of arbitrariness, capriciousness, or simple lack of obvious explanation to defy deterministic explanation. Thus, while societies have displayed similar non-elite configurations during socioeconomic development, no such regularities in the behaviours and configurations of their elites can be identified. Any theory that recognises this disjunction between elites and non-elites must allow considerable leeway for political accident and unpredictable political choice, so that its explicative claims must be quite modest.

It must also be recognised that elite theory is distasteful to many because it rules out the more ideal aims and outcomes that are regularly voiced by intellectuals, mass movement leaders, and even loosely predicted by social scientists. Elite theory has no place for idealised visions of democracy or social revolution, nor does it have a place for the spread of new values that dispose human beings toward a consistent and thorough altruism. Human conflicts inevitably dilute social cohesion and constitute political problems that elites must manage as best they can. However well or poorly they accomplish this task, elites are the central actors in politics, but the theory that centres on them is unlikely to have many enthusiastic adherents.

3

Sociology of State Formation

The idea of the modern state is variously institutionalised, ideological, philosophical, and scientific. In the context of these wider discourses, the modern state-idea is articulated with respect to at least six key centres of gravity: discourses of legitimacy (e.g., Hume's concept of "natural liberty"); discourses of political representation (who should be represented and by what mechanism); discourses of nation (the "nation-state" idea); discourses regarding the proper scope of government authority (e.g., with respect to the economy, political liberties, etc.); discourses of security (including generalised health and safety); and discourses of design (schemes for governing land, the built environment, and the population). The focus of this study is on discourses of design, for it is there that ideas in science and government most clearly intersect. But it should be noted that a focus on design necessarily provides a route to discussions of the other five centres of gravity, for most matters concerning the modern state-idea ultimately become matters of design and craft, social and political engineering, and security.

Designing States

The French revolutionaries of the late eighteenth century were among the first to suppose that one could wipe the political slate clean and engineer a state from the bottom up on the basis of an entirely new and abstract design. Their attempt, like that of the Bolsheviks in the early twentieth century, stumbled and failed, partly because the inertia of the existing conditions called forth the application of brute force, a strategy that from the outset betrayed and corrupted the very values the revolutionaries claimed their designs sought to realise. The English took a somewhat different approach, in which a strong tradition of localism, an ideology of self-government, a peculiarly modern worship of indigenous antiquities, and a more empirically oriented idea of science than one finds in Cartesian France shaped an engineering culture that sought to build into what already existed rather than erase older forms in the name of an overly abstract rational plan.

When Ireland was completely mapped in the second quarter of the nineteenth century, enormous effort was made to research the oldest and most "authentic" civic boundaries and place-names, and their inscription on the new map affirmed continuity with antiquity. The English and French cases demonstrate how the business of engineering the modern state in different contexts drew upon divergent designing ideas, sometimes highly abstract and "rational," other times resembling those of the *bricoleur*. These ideas about the state were, one might say, "internal" to its construction. There were others who sought to understand the state from the "outside," from the perspective, in particular, of the social, political, and economic sciences. The distinction, once again, involves a centre of gravity rather than an absolute or categorical separation, but the point of the distinction is to make possible a reflexive stance, one that places social-scientific conceptualistic of the state on the same level as those articulated by the state engineers. The interests of social scientists are generally quite different from those of state engineers, but that is not

2) In the second phase, this relatively private control over the monopoly of physical force tends to become public, i.e. it moves from the hands of state-makers into a political setting of legal institutions and appointed rulers under the control of the public.

While the first phase of the monopoly process is associated with absolutist and authoritarian forms of rule, the second phase deposes coercive state-makers and establishes structures of legal political authority. The two phases conceptualise the transition from traditional to rational authority in the emergence of the modern state. Consequently, state formation comprises not only the establishment of the monopoly of physical force, but also the transition of the normative and institutional order on which this monopoly rests from personal rule towards democratic governance.

From the perspective of 'state-builders', however, this transition of forms of authority was never intended. On the contrary, sociology conceptualised the formation of the modern democratic state as the non-intended outcome of the intended actions of European state-builders. In his article 'War Making and State Making as Organised Crime', Charles Tilly compared the early European state-builders with 'criminal' racketeers. Their interest was not in building states, but in acquiring material resources through coercive action. Accordingly, Elias' first phase of the monopoly mechanism could be understood as a system of protection and extraction, leading to the accumulation and monopolisation of the means of physical force in the hand of state-makers. The second phase Tilly described as a long-lasting process of negotiation between state-makers and the emerging capitalist bourgeoisie in which 'the pursuit of war and military capacity, after having created national states as a sort of by-product, led to a civilisation of government and domestic politics.'

In terms of global state formation, this long-lasting negotiation process can be traced in the legalisation of state-society relations, which was accompanied by a gradual increase in the state's capacities. The modern state and democratic social practices developed through the expansion and growing density of written formal law, framing the specific social space within which civil society could emerge. In this context, Jürgen Habermas identified four particular steps of juridification:

1) The establishment and consolidation of the monopolies of physical force and of taxation in the absolutist state.
2) The break with the personal monopoly of power in the absolutist state in constitutional monarchies by legally anchoring state power in political institutions and civil law.
3) The bourgeois revolutions initiated the nationalisation of the state monopolies, eventually bringing about the democratic nation state, with its separation of juridical, legislative and executive powers.
4) The formation of the welfare state tamed the autonomous dynamics that spring from the accumulative logic of the economic system and incorporated a variety of social functions into the domain of modern statehood.

Modern State—Image and Social Practice

Political scientists summarised this legacy of historical sociology and European state formation in an ideal type of the modern state. In institutional terms, statehood is defined as a centralised form of representative government based on electoral procedures and a set of administrative, policing and military organisations. The modern state claims the legitimate monopoly of physical force which state agencies exert over a certain territory and a relatively cohesive population that forms a community of citizens with political, social and economic rights.

In the academic field, this ideal type of state is primarily an analytical instrument to measure empirical statehood: it does not directly portray the 'real world' but represents an instrument of academic research. The definition, therefore, disregards both the historical length and the social and developmental steps which eventually resulted in this form of modern social contract between state-builders and society. Yet this image of the state has travelled from the social sciences into the conceptual world of political actors and societies at large. It has acquired a normative quality, telling us what a state ought to be. It is a globally relevant ideal of political order according to which we imagine the modern state as a transcendental and neutral power, a democratically controlled arbitrator standing above social conflicts. With this image of the state in mind, we judge political action in accordance with distinctions such as legal/illegal, formal/informal or public/private in order to measure and judge social action.

In reality the modern state is both an abstract and coercive macrostructure and a network of interdependent social actions in everyday life. Modern statehood consists of two dimensions: historically developed and relatively stable institutional structures, and culturally defined social processes. The institutional structure gives societies politically isomorphic forms. In this sense, the sociological definition of the national state developed into a formal blueprint for the political organisation of societies. Modern statehood is a central feature of world culture, and its ideal image has been formalised in most state constitutions. Ye t the second perspective, the state as social practice, characterises the actual social content of statehood as forms of permanent interaction and ephemeral social groupings. On this level, we can observe a complex and often amorphous tangle of social actions of which we make sense in reference to the ideal image of the state. Apparently, the rules of statehood as an organisational pattern and the logic of social practices do not necessarily correspond. In particular, the post-colonial state is characterised by competing and conflicting organising principles and social practices. This contradictory interface between the state as institution, image and social practice becomes particularly transparent when we soon in on individual political leaders.

Franchise Madder, for instance, analysed African statesmen as 'political entrepreneurs', a reference to both the symbolic and material sides of legitimate rule. In accumulating economic, political and social resources, the political 'big men' act through a system of personalised power in the name of the abstract institution of the state. In this way, these statesmen represent both the patriarchal chief of an extended network of personal ties (traditional authority) and the head of a formally institutionalised system of rule (legal authority). The contradictions in their position are apparent in three strategies of social action that are necessary for their political survival. In order to extract resources from international and trans-national donors, they have to pretend that they are acting according to the standards of modern statehood, that is, following the rules of good governance which emanate from the normative image of the state. As political entrepreneurs, however, they apply strategies of personal enrichment in accumulating external and internal resources within their networks of personal ties. Finally, they must meet the normative expectations of 'traditional' African societies for a redistribution of their resources within a system of clients. Caught in this pattern of often contradictory organisational and social constraints, the 'big man entrepreneur' must act according to a hybrid normative setting, containing elements of both the universal image of the state and the particularised values of local but survey research has valuable advantages that anthropological approaches can never equal. Only survey research takes samples that are demonstrably representative of a population, eliminating the need to rely on the authority of one observer. Only survey research can reveal how a population is distributed among different attitudes—a great improvement over asserting that the culture is homogeneous or admitting that it is heterogeneous without revealing the sizes of the subgroups. Only survey research can rigorously test a claim that certain attitudes cohere in a more fundamental structure. Only survey research can tell us whether certain attitudes or patterns really are stable. And only survey research, in combination with probability theory and statistics, can estimate how confident we can be that a sample is representative, that a subgroup is of a certain size, that an underlying cultural dimension exists, or that attitudes are changing or stable.

The fundamental difference between the anthropological and psychological or statistical approaches to political culture is that the latter holds that the attributes of a culture should not be asserted by an authority or merely assumed; rather they should be demonstrated with evidence. This principle applies to descriptions of individual attitudes, claims about the structuring of attitudes, relationships between attitudes and behaviour, and claims that any aspect of a culture is dynamic or static. Before the 1990s, lack of data made it practically impossible to demonstrate trends or stability in political culture beyond a handful of countries and topics. However, repeated waves of surveys—especially the U.S. National Election Studies, the Euro Barometer, and the World Values Surveys—have begun to make such generalisations possible. Unfortunately for the anthropological approach, these studies cast doubt on the alleged stasis of political culture. In fact, much of this research has been devoted to explaining patterns of change such as the decline of institutional trust and the emergence of post-materialist values.

Macro-Macro Studies

The kind of political culture research that is most obviously relevant for democratisation examines associations between national averages of individual-level attitudes and levels of democracy, the duration of democratic regimes, or the probability of regime transitions. Almond and Verba's *The Civic Culture* inaugurated this line of research. This study of the United States, Britain, Germany, Italy, and Mexico argued that democracy was most likely to thrive and survive where citizens possess a "civic" culture. Such a culture is a balance of "participant" traits, which incline citizens to take an interest in politics and participate in elections and other activities that make democracy work, and "subject" traits, which incline citizens to respect the law and the authority of the state and the government. Because this was the first cross-national survey project, it was path-breaking for its time but amateurish by today's standards. Critics pounced on it for using unrepresentative samples, asking invalid questions, overestimating the stability of attitudes and underestimating the impact of short-term political events, and drawing unwarranted connections between cultural patterns and regimes; in general, for reaching conclusions not justified by the evidence. But it hinted at what would be possible if such research were done more rigorously, and therefore inspired innumerable other studies.

In subsequent decades, comparative survey research became much more rigorous and abundant. Consequently, social scientists gained the ability to describe attitudes, trends, and relationships with much greater confidence. And as knowledge of political culture improved and trends became evident, theories about the impact of culture on democratisation evolved considerably. In *The Crisis of*

Democracy, Crozier, Huntington, and Watanuki argued that slow economic growth and high inflation were eroding the capacity of governments in the U.S., Western Europe, and Japan at the same time that citizen demands on government were increasing. They predicted that the growing gap between expectations and performance would eventually undermine confidence in leaders, institutions, and democracy itself. Some scholars predicted that many advanced democracies would fail within a few decade. One of these predictions did come true: confidence in institutions did decline, even outside wealthy Western countries. In most countries, confidence or trust in "government," legislatures, courts, politicians, civil service, armed services, police, and especially political parties fell from the 1970s to the 1990s. There were signs of widespread deterioration in other symptoms of civic culture as well: electoral turnout, party membership, generalised social trust, and face-to-face participation in voluntary associations.

Nevertheless, Western democracies did not fail, and support for democracy is strong, if not stronger than before. It has been suggested that this paradox can be explained by the moderation of inflation and by the conservatism of the 1980s, which lowered expectations of government. But these reasons are incompatible with declining trust in institutions. Two other arguments are more convincing. First, Rose, Mishler, and Haerpfer's comparisons of post-Soviet countries suggest that no matter how unpopular politicians, parties, and democratic institutions become, democracy will not break down unless some alternative regime has *greater* legitimacy. If true, this means that in the West, support for democracy remains strong partly because the collapse of Communism left it without a rival. Second – and contrary to Almond and Verba's embrace of some degree of the "subject" orientation and the *Crisis of Democracy* school's fear of disorder – there is a growing consensus that a certain amount of distrust in government is actually healthy for democracy. The growing numbers of "critical citizens" who question elite authority, shun traditional forms of participation, and invent new ways to associate, act collectively, and make their demands heard may be improving the quality of democracy by making representatives more responsive and accountable to the public. This explanation is also consistent with the fact that many formal democracies in the Third World are "illiberal" or "hollow" because, being less economically developed, they have fewer critical citizens.

The culmination of research in this vein is Inglehart and Welzel's *Modernisation, Cultural Change, and Democracy: The Human Development Sequence* (2005). This ambitious book proposes a sweeping theory of cultural change and democratisation, based on a quarter-million survey interviews in up to 81 countries from 1981 to 2001. Using factor analysis, Inglehart and Welzel identify two fundamental dimensions that structure national-average attitudes across countries. The first is the preference for traditional authority vs. Secular-rational authority. The second is an "emancipative values" dimension ranging from concern with basic economic or physical survival to an emphasis on elite-challenging self-expression. The authors also confirm the existence of various civilisations, defined by religion and colonial heritage, which tend to occupy distinct positions on these two dimensions.

For example, Confucian national cultures tend to be relatively secular and survival-oriented, Islamic national cultures tend to be traditional and survival-oriented, English-speaking national cultures tend to be relatively traditional and oriented to self-expression, and Protestant European national cultures tend to be secular and oriented to self-expression. Socialite values shift along both dimensions in response to economic transformations, in two phases. First, sufficient reason to treat the two asymmetrically. Indeed, as discursive formations, academic constructions of meaning often times exhibit an easily identifiable traffic with the ideas of state engineers. In this context an important effect of a critical reflexive stance is to question the idea of the state as an *actor,* an idea first fully elaborated by Hobbies and still central to discourses of state that emerge from both within and without the offices and chambers of government.

LIMITS OF THE ACTOR-STATE IDEA

While it makes sense to speak of the state as an actor in some contexts, the idiom has its limitations, because, states are complex and historically changing configurations of meanings and institutions, agencies, technologies and practices, and land, built environment, and people. While sovereign governments act in the name of states, they are not co-terminous with states. Indeed, to conflate "the state" with the "government" or its bureaucratic agencies is in effect to rob a people of a body politic that is importantly constituted through that people's very corporeal being, bestowing on a particular government or regime, at a particular moment in time, the image of the universally representative state-as-actor, philosophically conceived by Hobbes as the sovereign. When social scientists uncritical adopt the idiom *the actor-state,* they do not so much describe a political reality as become agents in the construction and institutionalisation of the Hobbesian state-idea, the idea that when the head of state acts, the state itself acts. John Mayor has noted the problem, acknowledging that states "are by no means really actors," despite the deeply institutionalised idea that they are.

Questioning the idea of the actor-state is not an idle academic exercise. Philip Abrams, one of the founders of historical sociology in Britain, has suggested that one of the crucial ways through which organised political subjection is effected in modern societies is by a particular and interested government presenting itself as the universal and disinterested organisation of the society as a whole. A particular political organisation thus presents itself as a unitary entity, speaking and acting in a unitary manner and in a highly personified form. Abrams alerted sociologists to this state-supporting discursive strategy in order to warn about the ease with which social-scientific discourses might unwittingly serve it. Yet his remedy, that sociologists reject the notion of the state as a "real" object and instead focus on the ways the state-idea is constructed and legitimised, directs analysis toward ideology rather than material forms. Problematising the personified actor state-idea need not, however, lead analysis in this idealist direction. While accepting that such a state-idea is central to the ideological project of legitimising organised political subjection, one need not be diverted from the ways the material environment is itself constituted as a force of moral and political governance. Like Abrams's analysis, Mayor's analysis of the state does not get us there, because he reduces the state to its "tendentious" culture, suggesting that its real foundation is a series of discursive "myths."

If treating the state-idea as *the* centre of gravity of *the state* leads us into idealism, an exclusive focus on the state-system is also problematic. Treating the state-system as though it is coextensive with the state as a whole circumvents analysis of the material forms of state power that do not reside in the apparatus of governing bureaucratic agencies. Faculty rejected such an analysis precisely because it implied the existence of another domain, that of civil society, which was set in opposition to the state, and this is one of the reasons he was "led to raise the question of power by grasping it where it is exercised and manifested,... Without considering, for example, the presence of a state which would exercise its sovereignty upon a civil society which itself would not be the depository of analogous processes of power." Faculty suggested that we should cut off the king's head in political theory, and work inspired by Facuity has seriously questioned the value of talking about the state as an actor. Such work has not generally done so, however, on the basis of an analysis of ideology. Rejecting the idea that power and ideology stop at the water's edge of knowledge, the work focuses on discourses of knowledge-power and the discursive rationalists of governance. Though centrally concerned with issues of science and power, "governmental studies" largely remain at the level of discursive "mentalities." This is true even though governmental studies emphasise the importance of science and technology in politics. As Mitchell Dean acknowledges, "thought" rather than practice is the centre of gravity of governmental studies.

Discourse, Practice, and Ideology

Without an analysis of the ideological aspects of discourse, maintaining an efficacious analytic distinction between discourse and practice is difficult. For instance, by presenting "medical police" as an essentially German or Continental phenomenon inherently at odds with English political discourse, Thomas Osborne dispatches it as irrelevant to English history. "Britain," he declares, "was a country without a tradition of police." Osborne arrives at this conclusion because his theoretical orientation takes discursive formations at face value. Accepting the central premise of English liberal discourse, that is, the idea of self-government, as a sufficient measure of social reality, he precludes empirical analysis of the role of government through police in eighteenth-century England. Yet as Karl Polanyi has demonstrated, the discourse of classical liberalism was crucially ideological, because there was "nothing natural about lassies fair." On the contrary, the "road to the free market was opened and kept open by an enormous increase in continuous, centrally organised and controlled interventionism."

This mismatch between discourse and practice is difficult to grasp without acknowledging the ideological aspects of discourse. Polanyi's insight is readily applicable to the history of the relationship between police and public health in England. Though the liberal discourse of nonintervention and self-regulation with respect to markets was extended into the domain of public health, that domain was, in fact, secured (to the extent that it was) by the expansion of the police power of government. This is an important point, because it counters the claim that medical police was a feature of English colonial government but not of English domestic government. Such arguments tend to down play the role of police in modern liberal state formation. Thus, while governmental studies provide a rich resource for understanding the development of liberal rationalities of government, much greater attention needs to be paid to actual practices of government. This is beginning to happen. Patriot Joyce, in his remarkable book *The Rule of Freedom,* navigates the discontinuity across discourses and practices with respect to liberalism and the modern English city, noting that liberal ideas of self-government have never fully displaced practices of police government.

Science, technology and State Formation

The effort to integrate the theoretical and methodological strategies of historical sociology with those of science and technology studies (STS) has, however, great potential for advancing explanation in both areas. The scientific, engineering, and technological culture that facilitated the Western takeover of the world is now being recognised for the power that it has been. Jack Gold stone, for instance, explains why the technological "effervescence" of modern Europe did not give way, as in other regions and at other industrialisation shifts the source of authority from religion and tradition to secular states, science, and technology. But often before this cultural shift is complete, postindustrial transformations (particularly the growth of the service sector) halt secularisation and promote the questioning of authority of any type. Any country's average position today in this two-dimensional cultural space is a function of which civilisation it started from and how far industrial and postindustrial transformations have shifted its values toward secular-rational authority and self-expression values.

Contrary to the modernisation theory of the 1960s, Inglehart and Welzel argue that secularisation has nothing to do with democratisation: secular culture is as compatible with Communism and fascism as it is with liberal democracy. Instead, the cultural tendency that really matters is the level of self-expression values. There is a logical connection between having a large proportion of citizens who value self-expression—who feel economically secure, independent from elite domination, and claim "the ability to make decisions and actions based on autonomous choices"—and the probability of a country having a democratic regime in which representatives respect citizens' demands. Inglehart and Welzel argue explicitly that the Linz-O'Donnell-Schmitter elite-bargaining frameworks for understanding regime change underestimated the impact of political culture:

> Democracy is not simply the result of clever elite bargaining and constitutional engineering. It depends on deep-rooted orientation among the people themselves. These orientation motivate them to press for freedom, effective civil and political rights, and genuinely responsive government – and to exert continual vigilance to ensure that the governing elites remain responsive to them.

Inglehart and Welzel present massive evidence and sophisticated analyses to support most of their key arguments. Their two fundamental dimensions are robust, i.e., they appear even when different sets of countries and different sets of variables are used. They show that the traditional–secular/rational dimension is associated more strongly with the degree of industrialisation, and the survival–self-expression dimension more with the degree of postindustrial transformation. They show that cultural zones cannot be reduced to economics or regime experience. They show that wealthier countries have tended to experience value shifts in the same direction and that these shifts are associated with increases in elite-challenging political activity. They distinguish between formal democracy and "effective" democracy, which incorporates information about elite integrity. They go to great lengths to show that self-expression values cause stable democracy but stable democracy does not cause self-expression values, while controlling for a variety of competing causes.

Nevertheless, the analysis is not airtight. Macro-macro comparisons generally are vulnerable to several criticisms. Inglehart and Welzel's book partially overcomes some of them, but not all, so it is still useful to evaluate their contribution while discussing five problems frequently encountered in other macro-macro analyses.

One of the biggest challenges in cross-national survey research is achieving conceptual validity. When surveys must be administered in different languages and different cultural contexts, where the meaning of words and symbols can vary in subtle ways, designing questionnaires that can measure what is demonstrably the same concept across many countries requires care, experience, and trial and error. *The Civic Culture* was harshly criticised for its failure to do this, for example, in its mishandling of the difficult-to-translate standard U.S. Question, "Do you think that quite a few of the people running the government are a little crooked, not very many are, or do you think hardly any of them are crooked at all?" One common tactic for dealing with this problem is simply to keep trying a variety of questions until a consensus develops that it validly measures what it purports to measure. A question is more likely to be valid to the extent that it elicits the answers that were expected from respondents, it is strongly correlated with questions designed to measure the same concept, and it is strongly correlated with factors that were expected to cause it and with phenomena that it was expected to cause. Another tactic, which has become very common in survey research, is to use factor analysis to create an index that measures a fundamental dimension captured imperfectly by multiple survey questions. Each question can be thought of as a reflection of both the concept that one wishes to measure and one or more contaminating ideas. The more questions one has that capture the concept of interest, even if each one is quite contaminated, the more feasible it is to isolate the variation in each one that reflects the concept from the contaminants. Factor analysis (or a common variant of it, principal-component analysis) is simply a statistical technique that reveals whether it is useful to reduce multiple questions or variables to a simpler set of underlying dimensions. The factor analyst still must use subjective judgment to interpret what the underlying dimensions are, but factor analysis is extremely useful for identifying how many dimensions there are and which variables reflect which ones.

Inglehart and Welzel's two dimensions are indices constructed from just this kind of factor analysis. Because interpreting dimensions requires as much art as science, they remain subject to challenge, especially when an analyst claims to have identified universal values that have the same meaning in all countries. For example, it is not obvious that all of the variables included in the index of self-expression values really belong there. Is rejection of science really part of self-expression? Toleration of homosexuality? A preference for female leaders? Describing one's own health as good? More generally, is "self-expression" the best label for the commonality in all these attitudes? Are "elite-challenging values," "individual autonomy," and "human development," different labels Inglehart and Welzel often attach to this same dimension, really interchangeable? Are all of these the same as "post-materialism," the label that Inglehart favoured for over 20 years before revising and reinterpreting his index? If not, why did the interpretation change? The dimensions Inglehart and Welzel identify are robust enough that there is little doubt that they are real, but there is some fussiness around the edges of the interpretation that has been imposed on them.

A second common problem in macro-macro comparisons is that it is hard to disentangle the impact of culture from that of other static or slowly changing country characteristics, such as institutions, geography, level of economic development (within a short time-frame), world-system position, or particular historical legacies. This problem is strictly insuperable when the data are cross-sectional: a "snapshot" of many countries at one instant in time. Unfortunately, for many years all comparative survey research was cross-sectional because there were no repeat surveys for large numbers of countries.

But even though public-opinion time series are now available for many countries, it is still difficult to distinguish the impact of cultural characteristics that change slowly from the impact of fixed effects or gradual trends that tend to move in a consistent direction. If many countries are simultaneously becoming more democratic, more prosperous, and shifting toward self-expression, then it is very hard to say with confidence whether it is the economy or culture that is driving democratisation. One of the great strengths of Inglehart and Welzel's study is that it is the first to take advantage of the three waves of World Values

Survey data from 1981 to 2001. This span of time is long enough to contain some dramatic cultural shifts and to contain changes in democracy and economic performance that do not necessarily parallel changes in culture. This makes it possible for the first time to estimate the relative impacts of culture and economic development on democratisation. By the standards of more advanced time-series research—for example, analyses of presidential approval ratings month by month over many years, which makes strong causal inferences possible—Inglehart and Welzel's research design is still primitive. It does not go beyond examining the impact of a change in culture (and control variables) in one period on changes in democracy in one subsequent period, across anywhere from 19 to 81 countries. It is still much more a cross-sectional analysis than a dynamic analysis. Nevertheless, it is a clear advance over other cross-national cultural research on democratisation in this respect.

A third weakness of cross-sectional research designs is that they say nothing about the direction of causation. Even if culture and regimes are strongly associated, cross-sectional analyses leave open the possibility that regimes shape culture, rather than culture shaping regimes. Indeed, this was a contentious issue in cultural research on democratisation as long as studies were cross-sectional, and some of the most rigorous analyses persuaded many political scientists that a democratic culture was a by-product, not a cause, of democracy. However, Inglehart and Welzel report a fairly sophisticated series of tests to show that the causal order is as they claim: economic transformations cause shifts in values, which then make countries become more democratic and remain so. More specifically, they rely on the notion (standard in quantitative analysis) of "Granger causality," which holds that one can infer causation when 1) the cause temporally precedes the effect, 2) one controls for any factor that might affect both the cause and the effect, and 3) one also controls for past values of the effect. In their most rigorous test, Inglehart and Welzel demonstrate that self-expression in the early 1990s has a significant impact on average levels of democracy in 1997-2002, controlling for socioeconomic resources and average levels of democracy in 1981-1986; but average levels of democracy in 1981-1986 have no significant impact on self-expression in the early 1990s, controlling for socioeconomic resources and self-expression values in 1981.

Studies that associate regimes with highly aggregated indicators of attitudes often suffer from a fourth problem. It is usually called the ecological fallacy, meaning the error of assuming that a relationship between variables at a higher level of analysis also holds at a lower level of analysis. The classic example is the positive association between the size of the Black population in Southern U.S. Congressional districts in the 1950s and the share of the vote won by segregationist candidates: the positive association at the district level does not mean that Blacks were voting for segregationists. One may also commit the opposite, individualistic fallacy of believing that a relationship among individuals must hold when aggregated to districts, states, nations, or any higher level of analysis. For example, the fact that observant Muslim citizens of countries on periphery of the Middle East tend to support democracy more than non-observant Muslims should not lead us to predict that Islamic countries tend to be democratic. The simple fact is that a relationship at the national level says nothing about the relationship at the individual level, and vice versa.

Davis and Davenport claim that the post-materialism dimension does not exist at the individual level (because some of its components do not covary), and that it cannot be valid at the cross-national level if it is invalid at the individual level. Seligson similarly argues that the apparent cross-national relationship between mean national self-expression values and democracy is spurious because there is no corresponding relationship between self-expression and support for democracy at the individual level. Inglehart mounts two somewhat contradictory defences against these charges

. On the one hand, he insists that political culture is a system-level (national) phenomenon whose relationship with democracy is appropriately studied at the system level. Critics who demand confirmation of the relationship at the individual level are committing the individualistic fallacy, he contends. On the other hand, he goes out of his way to report that some of the relationships he identifies at the system level also exist at the individual level, although much less strongly. If the relationship were purely a system-level phenomenon, this evidence would be irrelevant. Furthermore, his expositions of the theory behind these relationships frequently refer to the motives and behaviour of individuals.

In summary, Inglehart and Welzel present strong empirical evidence that countries with a high percentage of the population with self-expression values are very likely to be democracies, but the evidence prohibits them from claiming that there is a powerful dimension of survival vs. Self-expression values at the individual level within many countries, or that individuals who value self-expression do more, on average, to produce or sustain democracy than their fellow-citizens who care more about mere survival.

Finally, there is a related but more subtle problem in these macro-macro comparisons that has attracted little notice. Cross-national comparisons of means sacrifice information about variability within each case. In effect, they ask us to believe that all respondents hold the national mean attitude or that there is a purely random relationship at the individual level. To deal with this problem and the previous one, it would be advisable for scholars to use hierarchical linear modelling (also known as random-coefficients models), which takes intra-country variability into account when estimating cross-national relationships. Such models can also allow the relationship between two variables to be different (positive, negative, or anywhere in between) within countries than it is across countries. If researchers were to develop a good theory to resolve the ecological paradox, such models would allow them to test it.

Comprehensive Framework

This critique of macro-macro comparisons suggests that a fundamental problem with cultural theories of democratisation is that the alleged cause and the effect are on different levels of analysis. Culture (understood as individual attitudes) is a micro-level phenomenon, but democratisation is necessarily a macro-level phenomenon. Attempts to bring the two together in an explanation casually shift the level of analysis of either the cause or the effect. Micro-micro studies translate regime change or survival into individual level actions or attitudes, such as protest, voting, strikes, tolerance, trust, or regime support. The macro-macro studies aggregate individual attitudes into a national mean attitude. The latter is a defensible move, but it is certainly not the only way, and probably not the best way, to shift levels. It is the best way only if theory says that a) the impact of culture is a matter of degree: the larger the proportion of the population that has the attitude in question, the greater the impact on democratisation; and b) it does not matter which citizens have the relevant attitude: generals and beggars are interchangeable. Even if a theory made these assumptions explicit and justified them, it would be incomplete because it would not tell us how clusters of attitudes translate into behaviour by certain actors to bring about the regime outcome.

In order to avoid shifting levels, or even to know how best to shift levels, it is essential to develop theories that specify the causal mechanism linking culture to regime survival and regime change. At present we do not have such a theory, but we can describe several of its elements. First, a cultural theory of democratisation would have to connect attitudes to behaviour. Which attitudes produce which kinds of actions? How reliably? Under what conditions? Without an understanding of this linkage, we are left to imagine a population magically willing a regime into existence or oblivion. Second, a theory must identify which citizens are in a position to have a significant impact on the regime. The attitudes and actions of military officers, politicians, judges, police, guerrillas, and union leaders are clearly more consequential than those of ordinary citizens, especially if the latter are not politically active. Therefore, an adequate theory should focus attention on the actors whose subculture really matters. But the set of actors who are influential depends on the institutional context. So, third, a cultural theory of democratisation should be conditioned on the initial regime and the direction of the regime transition. More actors, especially mass actors, are relevant for the survival or breakdown of democracy than for the survival or breakdown of non-democratic regimes.

For the study of transitions to democracy, one would want to pay more attention to the official party if the initial regime is totalitarian, to the military if it is a military authoritarian regime, to the ruling family in a traditional monarchy, to parties and the legislature if it is an electoral authoritarian regime, and to the dictator's cronies if it is a sultanates regime. Each context requires a distinct variant of the theory, depending on who the most directly relevant actor is. Fourth, there are various pathways to regime change (or consolidation) within each context. A democracy can break down by military coup, presidential coup, civil war, revolution, or a more subtle slide into human rights violations, party proscription, manipulated elections, or other illiberal practices.

Different actors and behaviours are relevant for each one. Sixth, a theory should also distinguish among phases of a transition. Mass actors can play a leading role in a regime breakdown and their pacific behaviour is essential for its survival, but only elites can create the institutions of a new regime. A theory of the impact of culture on regimes should therefore be highly conditional. Each kind of transition requires a different variant of the theory for different contexts that focuses attention on different actors, behaviours, and attitudes.

Specifying the conditions under which culture could matter for regime change would be a substantial improvement, but an adequate theory should also tell us more about the dynamics of culture. The most common criticism of theories of political culture has been that culture is too static to explain political change. This criticism is directed more against the anthropological understanding of culture than against the individualistic behavioural view that prevails today.

But a behavioural understanding of culture is entirely compatible with a more dynamic and powerful causal role for attitudes. Breakdowns should be associated with declines in support for democracy among key actors, transitions to democracy should be associated with increasing support for democracy at least among some actors, and democratic consolidation requires, by definition, the spread and strengthening of regime support. An adequate cultural theory of regime change should incorporate and explain these attitudinal changes.

Such a theory would ideally show how the attitudes of the most directly relevant actor are influenced by the attitudes of other, indirectly relevant, actors. In some cases, for example, the most directly relevant actor is the military. Why do some top military officers sometimes reject democracy and carry out a coup? They are not completely isolated from the rest of society, so it would be good to know to what extent they are responding to, or anticipating, a rejection of the democratic regime by business elites, foreign powers, the middle class, or the Church. Or if the armed forces decide not to initiate a coup in spite of difficult structural conditions, it may be that they are constrained by the attitudes of these other groups in society. Theories of regime change that focus exclusively on elites may give culture too little credit if they ignore the broader cultural environment that influences elite actions. Influence can flow in both directions, however. The phenomenon known as leadership can be understood as elite influence on mass attitudes. For democratisation, therefore, it would be useful to know to what extent the positions of elites (executive, party leaders, business leaders, the military, leaders of ethnic or religious groups) move mass opinion for or against democracy.

It is also important to understand how different kinds of attitudes are interrelated. Certain attitudes seem to be closely connected to behaviours that would affect regime change and stability, such as support for the incumbent regime and government or the rejection of violence. But other attitudes, such as moderation, political trust, social trust, tolerance, and evaluations of government performance, may affect these attitudes and gradually move them toward a threshold of regime change. A good cultural theory should make these connections explicit. It should also identify non-attitudinal factors that directly affect attitudes that are relevant for regime change. These could include generation-defining events such as the Great Depression, wars, Waterage, and the 9/11 attacks; learning; crime; and corruption scandals. Whose attitudes are affected? Which attitudes are affected? How quickly? How long do these effects last? All of these questions are relevant for a cultural theory of democratisation.

No one has ever surveyed enough actors at sufficiently frequent intervals to test such a complete theory. However, a simulation can reveal the kinds of patterns that we should be looking for. Suppose that we have four elite actors – the executive, the legislature, the courts, and the military. Suppose further that each one has an orientation toward the regime that ranges from 1 (pro-democracy) to 0 (anti-democracy). Let us also assume that there is a mass public that has a variety of attitudes, also ranging from 0 to 1. Some are political support attitudes, from the very general and abstract to the very specific. These include support for democracy as an abstract principle, for the actual democratic regime, for the government, for government leaders, and for government policies (which could be further broken down, if necessary). The mass public also has other attitudes that may be related to democracy, such as trust, tolerance, and moderation.

Finally, the simulation lumps together all the non-attitudinal factors as a single variable that we will call "performance." It stands for economic performance, maintenance of public order, war, corruption scandals, and every other event that might influence elite or mass attitudes. Again, this variable could be broken up into a variety of variables to make the simulation more realistic, but this is not necessary in order to identify the fundamental patterns that interest us here.

The patterns of convergence reveal which actors, and which attitudes, are most important in each scenario. If one specifies purely top-down influence (elite positions shape mass attitudes, but elites are not constrained by mass attitudes) and if performance is neutral, then mass attitudes eventually converge on the average position of the elite actors. If one specifies purely bottom-up influence (the mass public constrains elites, who exercise no leadership over the mass public), then elite positions converge on the average mass position. If influence flows in both directions, then the simulation reveals vicious or virtuous circles that spiral toward the positions of the most influential actors. Such scenarios are completely endogenous: every element is both a cause and an effect.

If elites have more influence over the mass public than the mass public has over elites, then positions converge toward elite positions faster than they do toward the mass public's positions. If the patterns of influence are more bottom-up than top-down, then convergence is faster toward the mass public's positions. However, if any element is exogenous – a cause but not an effect – then all the endogenous elements converge toward its position. For example, if performance has a prolonged and consistently positive impact (without being influenced itself by mass attitudes or elite positions) and is the only exogenous element, then eventually the elite and the mass public converge toward pro-democratic attitudes. In the same way, negative performance leads to anti-democratic attitudes.

In practice, performance (or whatever the relevant exogenous forces are) is rarely so consistently and uniformly positive or negative in the long term; it is variable, so attitudes may never converge. Nevertheless, this simulation suggests an agenda for research on political culture and democratisation. First, the most important question is whether any elements in the system are exogenous, because they will drive the whole process in the long run. Second, we must specify which elements are endogenous, because they will tend to vary together. Third, it would be very interesting to know whether the patterns of influence are more bottom-up or more top-down. The answer has obvious implications for democratic theory, as well as for understanding democratic breakdown and consolidation.Cross-national survey research has been growing explosively, but it is still not adequate for answering these questions. This framework would require surveying not only the mass public, but also any elite groups whose behaviour may be relevant for regime change or consolidation. Furthermore, all these surveys would have to be repeated frequently, at intervals of weeks or months, to be able to detect patterns of convergence. It may be impossible to carry out such research, especially in non-democratic regimes where elites refuse to grant interviews.

Political Culture and Mass-Led Regime Change

The best place to begin taking stock of the literature is with the pathways to regime change or survival in which the mass public takes the leading role. These are only a minority of the pathways because usually elite involvement is necessary and the mass public plays only the indirect role of pushing or constraining elite attitudes and actions.

Many scholars reject the notion of democratic "consolidation" because it presupposes a situation in which it is no longer possible for a democratic regime to break down. However, "consolidation" can be interpreted in a less categorical way, to mean that a breakdown is very unlikely in the near future, while recognising that in the distant future all bets are off. In this sense, democratic consolidation is not a regime attribute that can be observed; rather, it is a prediction that can be made if one has a sound understanding of the warning signs of imminent regime breakdown.

Linz and Stepan propose a conception of democratic consolidation based on this kind of understanding. They propose that there are three dimensions of consolidation – behavioural, attitudinal, and constitutional – and that consolidation is achieved when civil society, political society, economic society, the state, and the rule of law all reinforce one another.

Violent mass disturbances such as rioting and civil war can initiate a transition *from* either democracy or non-democracy. Although such disturbances cannot complete a transition *to* a new regime without elites taking a leading role, they can be sufficient first steps and they should be examined here because mass attitudes presumably help cause them. Peaceful demonstrations can similarly start but not finish a transition, although they involve different attitudes and actions.

One would expect that if any attitude is closely associated with democracy, it would be support for democracy as the best form of government. This is not the case, however: an index of four democracy-support variables is correlated at only .351 with Freedom House scores for 1995 and at .506 with average Freedom House scores for 1981-2000.

Clearly, there are many countries that are not democratic despite strong popular support for it, and many countries that are democratic despite weaker support. Democracy does not come about simply because many people want it, or fail whenever they become disillusioned with it. There are several reasons for the weak correlation. First, there is surprisingly little variation in support for "democracy" in principle.

Questions that ask whether respondents support something called "democracy" tend to find high and stable support almost everywhere. In the World Values Surveys in 38 countries in the mid-1990s, for example, the percentages of people who agreed relatively strongly with the statements, "Democracy may have many problems but it's better than any other form of government" and "Having a democratic system" is very good or fairly good "way of governing this country" averaged 90 percent in Western Europe and 81 to 86 percent in the six other regions, falling below 71 percent in no country except Russia, where it was 51 percent. Using a different question, the regional Barometers found lower, but still majority, support: an average of 80 percent in Western Europe, 70 percent in twelve relatively democratic African countries, 59. Furthermore, there does not seem to be a trend in any direction since the 1970s, when systematic cross-national survey research began. A second reason for the weak correlations is that simply asking people whether they support democracy probably does not tell us what we want to know about culture and democratisation. For one thing, it is important to gauge the levels of *relative* support for democracy compared to alternative regimes. Rose, Mishler, and Haerpfer argue that the "Churchillian" hypothesis applies well to Eastern Europe and Russia: we should expect democracy to survive despite low support when citizens believe it is the worst form of government except for all the rest.

Mattes and Bratton confirm this argument in Africa. It is also reasonable to suppose that high support for democracy could coexist with non-democracy if the non-democratic regime had even higher support. For another thing, correlations between support for democracy and indicators of democracy such as the Freedom House index or Polity may underestimate the association because the democracy indicators were not designed to capture differences in the quality of democracy. If we had more sensitive indicators at the high end of democracy, we might find that societies with a very high level of support for democracy are in fact more democratic than societies with only a moderately high level of support. Many of the new democracies are not very democratic, and there is some evidence that their citizens tend to be less supportive of democracy. As long as we use indicators that make all democracies appear equally democratic, the observed relationship appears weak.

But the most important reason for the weak correlation is that "democracy" means different things to different people. For example, summarising survey research in three Latin American countries in 1999, Roderic Camp reports that "First, among Latin Americans there is no consensus on what democracy means. Second, only Costa Ricans see democracy in largely political terms, very similar in content to the view professed by North Americans. Third, the Mexicans and Chileans... view democracy in social and economic, not political, terms."

Because of these divergent interpretations, asking people whether they support "democracy" is, in effect, asking them whether they support whatever democracy means to them. Because democracy has become practically synonymous with "good government," it is not surprising that support is so high virtually everywhere. The best example of this is Venezuela. The 2005 Latin Barometer reported that support for democracy was higher in Venezuela than in any other Latin American country except Uruguay, at a time when Freedom House and many international observers were lamenting the rise of the illiberal, less democratic, regime of Hugo Chives. In reality, Venezuelans were bitterly divided about their regime. Chives's supporters believed that their leader had replaced a corrupt, elitist regime with the country's first true democracy, while his opponents believed that Chives was destroying a fairly successful liberal political democracy. They all agreed that "democracy" was good, but they had entirely incompatible understanding of the word. For this reason, Mitchell Seligson has said that "if you want to measure support for democracy, the one thing you should never do is use the word "democracy" in the question."

There is some debate about whether this is good advice, as there has long been a divide between idealists. for whom "meaning for the analyst has taken priority over meaning for the participants" and a phenomenology approach, which respects subjective meaning more Several research projects have sought to describe what "democracy" means to the citizens themselves. This can be fascinating work that furthers the goal of thick understanding. However, it must not tempt political scientists into concept stretching.

Because respondents cannot help but interpret the word "democracy" in their own ways, it is more useful to examine survey questions that refer to institutions and practices that we mean by democracy rather than to some undefined version of democracy. Some surveys ask whether it would be preferable to let the army rule or to have "a strong leader who does not have to bother with parliament and elections." The most common questions of this sort ask how much confidence or trust respondents have in various institutions, some of which are inseparable from liberal democracy, such as elections, political parties, and the legislature. Although confidence tends to be high in the political community and the principle of democracy, confidence in specific democratic institutions tended to decline from the 1960s to the 1990s in older democracies and was very low in most of the newer democracies

Engagement with parties declined in 17 out of 19 wealthy democracies, confidence in parliament declined in 11 out of 14 countries, and in 12 out of 13 countries, growing numbers of citizens agreed that "politicians are only interested in votes," "MPs are out of touch," politicians and government "don't care about people like me," "politicians are untrustworthy," and "there are many dishonest politicians". In Latin America by 2005, confidence had sunk to an average of 31 percent in the courts, 28 percent in congress, and 19 percent in political parties.

The fear that this trend presaged the breakdown of even established democracies was not fulfilled by the first decade of the 21st Century, and some came to believe that it is healthy for citizens to distrust their representatives. This optimistic view makes sense in the wealthy, older democracies, at least in the medium term. Individuals who distrust democratic institutions tend to be if anything more, not less, supportive of democratic principles. But it is hard to discount the possibility that distrust of institutions will eventually metastasis into a rejection of democracy in principle. As Putnam, Phoria, and Dalton note, "If the decline in public confidence is justified (because of growing corruption, for example), then we might applaud citizens' ire but not its cause, just as we would be glad to have discovered a child's fever without being glad that her temperature was high".

Other Mass Attitudes

But it may be that attitudes that are not explicitly about democracy or democratic institutions may have a greater impact on the birth and survival of democracy. The related attitude that has been most studied is generalised interpersonal trust, sometimes called simply "social trust," to distinguish it from "political trust" in politicians and political institutions. Interpersonal trust was one of the components (along with political efficacy and pride in institutions) of Almond and Verba's civic culture, which they believed to favour stable democracy in the U.S. And Britain, compared to West Germany, Italy, and Mexico . Other scholars flashed out the reasons for this hypothetical connection. Inglehart was best known for emphasising the cultural shift to post-materialism, but he also argued that interpersonal trust lowers the stakes in politics, which favours democratic legitimacy and stability. Putnam et al. added that social trust—a natural by-product of face-to-face participation in secondary associations—is self-reinforcing, because if society is generally trusting, it becomes rational for individuals to be trusting as well, and unwise to be distrustful. This virtuous circle encourages public officials to be responsive, which improves the quality of democracy, and presumably high-quality democracies tend to be more stable.

Generalised trust has declined in some democracies, but not in others. The evidence for a causal relationship has been mixed. For example, one study using World Values Survey data for 17 countries reports that there is an association between social trust and trust in the police, civil service, and parliament at the aggregate, cross-national level, but not at the individual level. This is probably because there tends to be much less cultural variation within countries than between them, which may make it impossible to detect this kind of weak relationship except in cross-national samples, where the variation on both variables is wider. This interpretation is consistent with a study of three Latin American countries in which social trust at the individual level is weakly related to support for democracy only when the model includes no country dummies, which capture more general cross-national differences. When actual democracy, rather than support for democracy, is the dependent variable, the most extensive and rigorous study finds that interpersonal trust explains only 15 percent of effective democracy and has no significant impact on formal democracy, even in a simple cross-sectional model with only one control variable. As Inglehart and Welzel conclude, the cultural variable that has the most direct and important impact on democracy is probably not interpersonal trust.

Over the years, various scholars have pointed to tolerance, moderation or consensus, and subjective well-being. But again, the most extensive and rigorous study – Inglehart and Welzel's – concludes that all other attitudes take a back seat to self-expression values. In a comparison of approximately 60 countries, the level of self-expression in the early 1990s explains 32 percent of formal democracy and 55 percent of effective democracy, averaged for 2000-2002. Political trust, overt preference for democracy, obedience, and other values are significantly related to democracy only to the extent that they are correlated with self-expression, for their coefficients fail to reach conventional significance levels when models control for self-expression.

There are many reasons to reserve some skepticism about their finding: the available samples limit the analysis of change to just the impact of values in the early 1990s on average levels of democracy in 2000-2002, their models fail to control for anything except prior democratic experience, the causal pathways and relevant actors are undefined, and there is still some doubt about how to interpret "self-expression values" which in the section in question are confusingly re-dubbed "liberty aspirations". But the best evidence available at this point suggests that the aspect of culture that is most closely associated with democracy cross-nationally and over time is self-expression.

Culture and Behaviour

Inglehart and Welzel spin an elaborate and plausible theory about the causal pathway that links self-expression values to democratic transitions. They argue that transitions happen when and where self-expression values increase the numbers of civil rights activists and dissidents. As these changes swell the ranks of civil rights movements and back them up with greater mass support, it becomes more likely that liberal elites will endorse regime change. When pro-democracy activists eventually take the initiative, these elites are less likely to attempt to repress them.

These are excellent hypotheses that suggest possible causal connections in several stages, and Inglehart and Welzel produce empirical evidence in support of two links in their chain. They demonstrate that elites (those with education) almost always value self-expression more than society in general does They also show that self-expression in the early 1990s is strongly associated with Anheier et al.'s Civil Society Index for 2000 in 31 countries. They also refer to several confirming case studies. Unfortunately, this evidence tells us nothing about several of the other links in the hypothesised chain. Are the individuals who value self-expression the same individuals who are politically active? Do societies that value self-expression more also consider civil rights and other movements more legitimate? Does the growth of self-expression increase the probability that elites will support democracy and refrain from repressing pro-democracy activists? Is this true for the elites who can actually make a difference? We must look elsewhere to find out whether all the elements of this plausible theory are empirically true.

Thorough testing is essential because there are compelling competing arguments suggesting that mass culture does *not* have an important impact on transitions to democracy. One strain of theorising holds that attitudes and behaviours that we usually think of as antithetical to democracy may actually help spur transitions, or at least not harm them. Nancy Bermeo argues that moderation is not required for transitions to democracy. She points out that Portuguese democracy emerged from a Socialist revolution and Spanish democracy has coexisted with Basque terrorism. She also calls attention to successful transitions in Brazil, Chile, Ecuador, South Korea, Peru, and the Philippines despite high strike rates. Echoing Barrington Moore, who argued that violence was necessary to break the power of conservative anti-democratic classes, Elizabeth Wood makes the case that armed insurgencies in South Africa and El Salvador brought authoritarian elites to the bargaining table. In these cases, the economic costs of violence were necessary to persuade business, political, and military leaders that it was time to share power.

These arguments do not contradict Inglehart and Welzel's finding of an association between culture and transitions to democracy as much as it might appear at first glance, for two reasons. First, Bermeo's brief is with moderation, which is not one of Inglehart and Welzel's self-expression values. In fact, extremism and perhaps even violence may have more in common with the qualities that Inglehart and Welzel emphasise: challenging elite authority and being critical rather than passive citizens. Second, extremism and violence are usually characteristics of a minority, not the majority culture. It is perfectly possible for the majority to be moderate and peaceful even where there is an extreme or violent minority, and the existence of such a minority may in fact make authoritarians more eager to transfer power to moderates. Such a situation would resemble formal theories that focus on pacts or alliances between soft liners and moderates: in effect, a "good cop, bad cop" routine acted out on an immense stage. A synthesis of these two theories would suggest that a good combination for transitions to democracy may be two subcultures: one radical, violent, but minority; the other moderate, peaceful, and the majority. But at this point this is mostly speculation, tested in only a handful of cases studies.

It is also possible that mass culture has *no* impact on transitions. One of the most prominent students of culture and democracy, Larry Diamond, has stated that "democratic culture is certainly not a precondition for the initiation of democracy. . ." because elites and activists usually have decisive influence at this stage, as opposed to during consolidation. It could also be that a democratic mass culture has only indirect influence. Mass support for democracy (or moderation, tolerance, or trust) may percolate up through society, either inducing elites to change their minds or replacing authoritarian elites with new leaders who are more in sync with attitudes of the majority culture.

There are opposing points of view about the impact of political culture on the *survival* of democracy. On the one hand, Linz and Stepan argue that belief in democracy as "the only game in town," the only legitimate means for resolving conflict, is one of the defining aspects of democratic consolidation; and democratic consolidation, in turn, means a low probability of breakdown.

To complete the syllogism, the more people believe in democracy, the less likely democracy is to break down and the more likely it is to survive. In Linz and Stepan's definition of "consolidation," supportive mass attitudes and behaviour are absolutely required: citizens who want political change must shun violent means in favour of peaceful, constitutional activity. They accept fundamental democratic rules and comply with the law; if they protest, they do so peacefully. Ideally, they vote, and they do not vote for anti-system parties or leaders. Inglehart and Welzel argue that the rise of self-expression values similarly helps existing democracies survive. The more citizens value self-expression, the more social movement activists there are, the more legitimate non-activists consider them to be, and the more likely elites are to be responsive to mass demands. Such democracies are more effective and therefore more likely to survive.

On the other hand, there are many reasons to question any tight linkage of democratic survival and mass culture. First, now that public opinion surveys have become common in new democracies, we know that democratic regimes can often survive for years even when the public has little confidence in political parties, legislatures, courts, elections, and other democratic institutions. Rose, Mishler, and Haerpfer have pointed out that we should not expect disillusionment to turn citizens against democracy unless they believe that some alternative regime is preferable. In the absence of a more legitimate alternative, democratic regimes can hobble on without enthusiastic support for a long time. Second, Putnam's thesis has come in for heavy criticism. It is not clear that participation in voluntary associations promotes trust and cooperation; at the very least, such effects depend on the type of association. One would not expect salutary consequences unless citizens have face-to-face contact, the group is more horizontal than hierarchical, and it reaches out into the community rather than bonding members into a united front against outsiders. Weimar Germany was full of associations, which did not stop, and may have aided, the rise of Nazism. Third, it is anything but clear how participation in clubs, social movements, and other secondary associations affects major outcomes such as regime change. There has been considerable research on social movements, but it has mostly focused on their causes rather than their consequences. It seems clear, for example, that democracy favours the formation of social movements, but whether social movements favour democracy remains an open question.

Fourth, much of what we do know suggests that elite opinion matters much more than mass culture. Democracies can fail despite a broad popular preference for democracy. In *Ordinary People in Extraordinary Times*, Nancy Bermeo advances the provocative argument that mass public opinion almost never favours authoritarianism.

Rather, elites—the executive, party leaders, parts of the armed forces—mistakenly interpret the demands of anti-democratic minorities as representative of the majority, and overreact. Sometimes elites install a right- or left-wing non-democratic regime in the mistaken belief that the majority wants it, and sometimes they lead a coup to prevent what they falsely perceive as a revolution from taking place. Bermeo's thesis may contradict the naive assumption of political culture theorists that regimes express mass preferences, but it is quite plausible from a lay person's understanding of politics: the squeaky wheel gets the grease and silent majorities tend to be ignored. Her brief cases studies of the failed democracies of interwar Europe lack the public opinion evidence necessary to make her case convincingly; it is always possible that elites judged, and responded to, mass *opinion* correctly, even if it was not fully expressed by votes, membership, or the other available indicators of *behaviour*. However, her more detailed analysis of four more recent South American cases—Brazil 1964, Uruguay 1973, Chile 1973, and Argentina 1976— have the benefit of public opinion data, which does establish that these right-wing military authoritarian regimes were not a fulfilment of the wishes of the majority.

In Brazil, although there was majority support for land reform, which conservatives and the military considered threatening, the majority never wavered in its preference for democracy. In Uruguay, majorities wanted the military to remove President Bordaberry but only in order to restore democracy; the military assumed power in spite of massive popular opposition and resistance. In Chile there was polarisation that was dangerous for democracy, but only among party elites, not among the mass of voters. Most Argentine in 1976 may have been exhausted by violence and strikes and grateful for the military removal of Isabel Person, but there is little evidence that they preferred prolonged military rule. Bermeo's argument is convincing for these cases in the narrow sense that popular majorities appear not to have turned against democracy *per se* or to have been polarised to the point of having more people at the extremes than in the centre.

However, while making her case, Bermeo also demonstrates that there is sometimes majority support for military coups and does not exclude the possibility that non-majority levels of polarisation may sometimes lead to disruptions of political order that make it difficult for democracy to survive, even if relatively few desire that outcome. Her evidence is therefore compatible with the possibility that mass, though not necessarily majority, attitudes make an indirect contribution to the breakdown of democracy. Overall, however, her analysis reinforces the conclusion that the search for cultural explanations of regime change should not focus on the mean or modal attitudes of the undifferentiated mass of ordinary people, but on the attitudes of groups in society who are in a position to effect change, whether they are extremist social movements, political party leaders, or military officers.

A fifth counter argument is that elite leadership shapes culture rather than culture constraining elite attitudes and actions . Most of the research on this question has examined the relationship between US members of Congress and their constituents, regarding policy, not regime choice, so the implications of this relationship for regime change are virtually unexplored, although they remain worth exploring rigorously. The one exception to this is the attention paid to ethnic violence. In this line of research, few scholars believe that violence (which obviously can undermine democracy) is an automatic expression of deep, primordial hatreds. Rather, contemporary emphasis is on "political entrepreneurs" (leaders), who reinforce latent religious, ethnic, racial, linguistic, and national identities and exploit them to maximise their own political power. It has also been shown that leaders sometimes have the ability to prevent violence where it otherwise would be expected to break out.

Sixth, it has often been argued that culture is epiphenomenal: it has little direct, independent impact once one controls for the forces and events that shape both culture and the outcomes that it supposedly causes. Welch cause this the phenomenon of the "retreating cause": the closer one comes to understanding when, where, and why culture matters, the more it appears that "culture" is only a mask for the forces that really matter.

There two other ways that it is commonly thought that mass culture might affect the survival of democracy. First, democracy may die not with a bang, but a whimper: apathy, withdrawal from participation, abstention, delegitimation of institutions and leaders. Perhaps democracy dies not because citizens care too much, but because they care too. This seems to be the motivating assumption behind the large literature on political culture and turnout, party membership, group membership, and voting behaviour.

5

Modern Democracies and Governance

At the most basic level, it can be argued that modern liberal democracies suffer from a number of structural characteristics that prevent them from tackling global collective action problems in general. These are:

— *Short-termism.* The electoral cycle tends to focus policy debate on short-term political gains and satisfying the median voter. The short duration of electoral cycles ensures that politicians are concerned with their own re-election, which may compromise hard policy decisions that require a great deal of political capital. It is extremely difficult for governments to impose large-scale changes on an electorate whose votes they depend on, in order to tackle a problem whose impact will only be felt by future generations.

— *Self-referring Decision-making.* Democratic theory and politics builds on a notion of accountability linked to home based constituencies. It assumes a symmetry and congruence between decision-makers and decision-takers within the boundaries of the nation-state. Any breakdown of equivalence between these parties, i.e. between decision-makers and stockholders, or between the inputs and outputs of the decision-making process, tends not to be heavily weighed. Democratic "princes" and "princesses" owe their support to that most virtuous source of power: their people. The externalities or border spill-over effects of decisions they take are not their primary concern.

— *Interest group concentration.* In democracies, greater interest group pluralism reduces the provision of public goods because politicians are forced to adopt polices that cater to the narrow interests of small groups. The democratic process rewards small, well organised interest groups and results in their proliferation. Also, strong competition among such groups leads to gridlock in public decision-making, delaying both the implementation and effectiveness of public goods provision.

— *Weak multilateralism.* Governments accountable to democratic publics often seek to avoid compliance with binding multilateral decisions if this weakens their relationship to their electorate. There is a notable exception; it occurs when strong democratic governments can control the multilateral game. Concerns such as these have generated scepticism about the compatibility of democratic forms of governance with the need for the drastic and urgent changes in policy required to combat climate change. The implication is that they are unable to meet the scale of the challenge posed by climate change, and that more coercive forms of government may be necessary. Such thinking finds its historical precedent in the work of the "eco-authoritarians" of the 1970s, who argued that it might be difficult in democracies to constrain economic activity and population growth that results in pressures on the environment. They suggested that some aspects of democratic rule would have to be sacrificed to achieve sustainable future outcomes, since authoritarian regimes are not required to pay as much attention to citizens' rights in order to establish effective policy in key areas.

Democracy Versus Autocracy

This type of argument has, however, been undermined by a body of theory arguing that there are a number of reasons why democracies are more likely than authoritarian regimes to protect environmental quality. Democracies have better access to information, with fewer restrictions on media and sources of information, and greater transparency in decision-making procedures. They encourage the advance of science, which is responsible for our awareness about climate change and other forms of environmental threat in the first place. Scientists and other experts are free to engage in research, exchange new evidence and travel to and obtain information from other countries. These factors make it more likely that environmental issues will be identified and placed on the political agenda, and tackled according to appropriate measures of risk. Moreover, concerned citizens can influences political outcomes not only through the ballot box, but through pressure groups, social movements and the free media – channels that are closed in autocracies. The presence of civil society also serves to inform the public, act as a watchdog on public agencies, and directly lobby government. There are many examples of cases where environmental interest groups have been able to overwhelm business interests pursuing environmentally damaging practices and of cases where they have changed the public agenda.

At the same time, authoritarian regimes have fewer incentives to adopt or stick to sustainable policies. Environmental concerns are often trumped by economic development plans and external security, as was the case with the Soviet regime. Leaders are unaccountable to the public, and have less ground to enact long-term policy . And in authoritarian regimes, those in power control a substantial fraction of society's resources, encouraging pay-offs to a relatively small elite, resulting in less public goods provision.

It does not seem unreasonable, then, to expect a strong correlation between democracy and environmental quality. Indeed, among the 40 highest carbon emitters internationally (cumulatively responsible for 91% of total world emissions), the countries that have the best records are all democracies. However, upon closer examination, the record is less compelling, and detailed empirical evidence is inconclusive. Environmental quality is not just measured by a broad based commitment to addressing emissions of carbon and other greenhouse gases (GHGs). While some studies have shown that authoritarian regimes have worse records than democracies on environmental protection, others find no evidence to suggest that this is the case. Indeed across a range of measures and geographical areas numerous studies prove that outcomes are varied.

On balance, while evidence on the link between political institutions and environmental sustainability does seem to suggest that democracies are preferable to authoritarian regimes, we might expect the effect to be far greater than it actually is. Why is this the case? Part of the reason might be attributed to the different types of transmission mechanisms that translate policy commitment into policy outcomes. Battig & Bernauer, for example, find that while the effect of democracy on political commitment to climate change is positive, the effect on policy outcomes, measured in terms of emissions and trends, is ambiguous. They observe that the causal chain from environmental risks to public perceptions of such risks, to public demand for risk mitigation, and to policy output is shorter than the one leading from risk via policy output to policy outcome. Because of that, outcomes are infuenced by a range of other factors, such as the properties of the resource in question, mitigation costs, and the efficiency of implementing agencies. Politicians might easily declare a set of public policy commitments to climate change mitigation, but the outcome of such efforts is affected by factors that are often outside of their control. The result is that policymakers respond quite well to public demands for more environmental protection, but tend to discount implementation problems, hoping that voters will not be able to identify these within a short enough time period to use their votes as a punishment for any failure to deliver.

Commitment Deliberative Democracy Approach

An additional concern is that political commitment to tackling climate change is critical, yet may require political leaders to adhere to a particular course of action that is potentially unpopular, and hence contrary to structural democratic pressures. The actual implementation of policies that reduce global warming may infringe on the democratic preferences of citizens. In such a context, political leaders can be caught between a desire for recognition and esteem in the international community—recognition that comes from peer admiration for leadership—and the need to ensure accountability to domestic electorates. However, good democratic leadership is not confined to policymaking alone—it also involves educating constituents about pressing issues that may not be obvious to them. In this sense, the fact that democratic publics do not always have fully formed preferences is an advantage as well as a risk. Citizens can significant shift their preferences, faced with new information and evidence about pressing issues. The democratic citizen that is capable of being "fact-regarding, future-regarding and other-regarding," is not simply a myth.

Such an approach to democratic "will formation" can be found within the tradition of what is known as deliberative democracy, broadly defned as "any one of a family of views according to which the public deliberation of free and equal citizens is the core of legitimate political decision-making and self-governance"

Deliberative democrats advocate that democracy moves away from any notion of fixed and given preferences, to be replaced with a view that democracy should become a learning process in and through which people come to terms with the range of issues they need to understand in order to hold defensible positions. They argue that no set of values or particular perspectives can lay claim to being correct and valid by themselves, but rather are valid only in so far as they are capable of public justification. Individual points of view need to be tested in and through social encounters which take into account the point of view of others. Ultimately, the key objective is the transformation of private preferences via a process of deliberation into positions that can withstand public scrutiny and test. Empirical findings show that citizens can and do alter their preferences when they engage with new information, fresh evidence and debate. These can lead to new and innovative ideas about public policy and about how democracy might function and work.

Deliberative democracy can, in principle, increase the quality, legitimacy and therefore the sustainability of environmental policy decisions. This is partly due to the uncertainty associated with environmental issues, which demands a wide range of experience, expertise and consultation. The complexity of climate change problems also require integrated solutions that have been vetted by multiple actors and that cut across the narrow confines of expert knowledge and the responsibilities of established institutions and organisations. And the concerns of environmental justice require the political process to be as inclusive as possible, giving voice to the under represented, including future generations. Effective and just action on climate change depends upon the continuing involvement of citizens in the making and delivery of policy; conventional representative democracy is a poor way to achieve this alone. To remodel environmental politics around deliberative democracy is thus to create an opening for a change in the way democracies address environmental management in general, and climate change in particular.

In shifting from policy commitments to real and binding action, democracies have all too often been unable to override the problems of short-termism, collective action and other factors that cut against emission reductions efforts. This is not to say that democracies are incapable of tackling climate change. Rather, certain aspects of them typically fall short. The question now is whether democratic systems can be evolved to handle the problem better, and how this may be achieved.

In shifting from policy commitments to real and binding action, democracies have all too often been unable to override the problems of short-termism, collective action and other factors that cut against emission reductions efforts. This is not to say that democracies are

Democracy, Governance and Climate Change

Complex global processes, from the ecological to the financial, connect the fate of communities to each other across the world, yet the problem solving capacity of the global system is in many areas not effective, accountable, or fast enough to resolve current global challenges. What has been called the paradox of our times refers to the fact that the collective issues we must grapple with are of growing cross-border extensive and intensity, but the means for addressing these are state-based, weak and incomplete. While there are a variety of reasons for the existence of these problems, at the most basic level the persistence of the paradox remains a problem of governance. The abilities of states to address critical issues at the regional and global level are handicapped by a number of structural difficulties, domestic and international, which compound the problems of generating and implementing urgent policies with respect to global goods and bads.

One significant problem is that a growing number of issues span both the domestic and the international domains. The institutional fragmentation and competition between states can lead to these issues being addressed in an ad hoc and dissonant manner. A second problem is that even when the global dimension of a problem is acknowledged, there is often no clear division of labour among the myriad of international institutions that seek to address it: their functions frequently overlap, their mandates conflict and their objectives often become blurred. A third problem is that the existing system of global governance suffers from significant deficits of accountability and inclusion, which can result in less economically powerful states and, hence, their entire population being marginalised or excluded from decision making.

Today, there is a new found recognition that global problems cannot be solved by any one nation-state acting alone, nor by states just fighting their corner in regional blocs. What is required is collective and collaborative action – something that the nations of the world have not been good at, and which they need to be much better at if the most pressing issues are to be adequately tackled. The failure to generate a sound and effective framework for managing global climate change is one of the most serious indications of the challenges facing the multilateral order. The former British chief scientist Sir David King has warned that the threat posed by climate change is more serious than that of terrorism, and Sir Nicholas Stern has referred to it as "the greatest market failure the world has ever seen" In the broad view of the scientific community climate change has the capacity to wreak havoc on the world's diverse species, bio-systems and socioeconomic fabric, and the process has clearly begun.

Anarchic Inefficiency

The number of actors and variety of organisations involved in both agenda setting and policymaking at the level of global environmental governance has increased substantially over the past decade. In addition to private, public and civil society actors, new types of actors have emerged such as Trans-national activist networks, private rule-making organisations, government agencies and public-private partnerships. Moreover, established organisations have adopted new roles and responsibilities. For example, many intergovernmental organisations have acquired a higher degree of autonomy from the governments that have established them, and many NGOs now engage in agenda setting, policy formulation and the establishment of rules and regulations. However, the increased engagement of diverse actors does not necessarily guarantee either effectiveness or equal access of diverse voice. In fact, it often leads to double representation of the west and north through both powerful states and NGOs.

At the institutional level, while many international environmental agreements exist, and possess some admirable characteristics, they are often both poorly coordinated and weakly enforced. Furthermore, they are supported by a plethora of different international organisations fulfilling various functions. The current constellation of over 200 international environmental agreements suffers from a problem of what might be called "anarchic inefficiency," featuring a diverse set of players whose roles are largely uncoordinated among each other. The most prominent

The UN system, including the United Nations Framework Convention on Climate Change (UNFCCC), the Environmental Management Group (EMG) and the Centre for Sustainable Development (CSD)

While international action on climate change relies overwhelmingly on the evidence presented by the UNFCCC (including the Kyoto Protocol), the UN system overall has so far been ineffective in reducing GHG emissions, and is hampered by major divisions between north and south. The internal UN system is also still arguably uncoordinated on climate change, although there are plans to change this. The EMG, chaired by United Nations Environmental Program (UNEP), is a key vehicle for this cooperation, but it remains too early to judge its progress. The CSD has engaged with NGOs in a constructive manner, and has an important agenda-setting role, but is also relatively ineffective.

Global Environment Facility (GEF)

The GEF has a climate change remit, including serving as the main financial mechanism for UNFCCC. However, it has suffered legitimacy problems: developing countries have opposed GEF control of the Kyoto Adaptation Fund, perceiving a voting bias in favour of richer countries and the control of the World Bank. The current governance structure of the Adaptation Fund is regarded as an interim solution until this can be resolved. Elsewhere, the GEF has delivered important grants for climate change mitigation and adaptation, but has a tendency to support smaller technical or pilot projects that are not mainstream in countries or economic sectors.

The OECD Environmental Directorate

While this division of the OECD is technically proficient (having conducted agenda-setting work, for example, on environmental indicators and economic modelling of carbon markets) it is globally unrepresentative. It also regards climate change as amenable to technical, pro-growth economic solutions, contrary to the views held by many of the key actors in the debate.

The World Trade Organisation (WTO) Committee on Trade and Environment

Collaboration between the UNEP and the WTO was proposed in 2006, yet the Committee has not even been able to agree to a limited environmental package within the Doha Round. There is little appetite to recognise climate change damage as grounds for unilateral member state exceptions (GATT/WTO Article XX) to world trade rules. Collaboration is, therefore, largely symbolic—the WTO is seeking more environmental legitimacy, while the UNEP wants access to WTO deliberations.

Environmental Chamber of the International Court for Justice (ICJ)

The ICJ has thus far played an insignificant role, with no cases since its formation in 1993. It has been hampered by limited rules of standing and divided opinion over the need for a separate International Court for the Environment.

Representation and the Responsibility of the Wealthy

Problems with representation at the level of global governance are high on the list of obstacles to addressing climate change. Multilateral bodies need to be inclusive; unless both developed and less developed states come on board, the net reduction of GHG emissions becomes a much harder task, if it can be achieved at all. Ensuring effective representation is not a question of just providing a seat at the negotiating table in a major IGO or at a major conference. For even if there is parity of formal representation (a condition typically lacking), it is generally the case that developed countries have large delegations equipped with extensive negotiating and technical expertise, while poorer developing countries frequently depend on one person delegations, or have even to rely on the sharing of a delegate, and lack the negotiating strength to participate fully in discussions. This is indicative not only of the problem of unequal access to decision-making, but of inequality of all types of resource. Many developing countries do not readily command the public funds, capacity or technology to come into compliance with agreed regulations designed to reduce emissions. As a result any future agreement cannot simply build on the traditional burden sharing approach of dealing with a problem inherent in the global commons; given the scale of transformation that is required for a sustainable future, wealthy industrialised states will have to bear a signifcant part of the cost of the transformation in developing countries.

Policy Debate

The greatest differences in the debate about the politics of climate change tend be revealed in issues of how to square the circle of participation, effectiveness and compliance. Or, to put the point more broadly—is it possible to combine coherently democracy, markets and universal standards?The answer is far from straightforward; if international rules become stricter, we can expect reluctant states to become even more reluctant to be bound by them, while if participation increases, agreement may only become possible via lax rules.

A critical component of a global deal will be the way in which market incentives are structured. In terms of targeting GHG emissions, two principal market-based instruments exist: cap and trade and taxation. Supporters of the former include Stern who points out a number of disadvantages with taxes. They do not allow certainty over how big future GHG reductions will be, since estimates are imprecise and there is a long flag time between policy output and actual outcomes. They are hard to coordinate internationally, and developing countries are unlikely to agree such arrangements, which impose economic burdens on industries without offering the of setting gain of being able to sell emissions permits. Moreover, electorates in general are mistrustful of governments' use of tax resources, potentially opposing them in the belief they provide an excuse for "stealth taxation". A better approach is to set targets, and then seek out the cheapest method (via the price mechanism) of reaching those.

Cap and Trade System

According to its supporters, cap and trade makes the most sense of the options available, because it allows for greater certainty about eventual emissions levels and produces better incentives for producers. At this point, it also appears to be the approach most likely to be adopted at the global level, with a European Union Emission Trading System (EU ETS) already in place, and a successful precedent in the form of markets for sulphur in the United States. However, global markets in carbon and other GHGs are likely to be far larger and more complex than any previous emissions trading schemes, with a commensurate increase in levels of risk, opportunity for leakage and distributional consequences. Negotiating a comprehensive global accord and meshing national systems so that they operate coherently will be a highly fraught and difficult process, if it can be achieved at all.

Indeed, while cap-and-trade seems to be an ideal solution on the surface, it is in fact an odd way to do business. Politicians like it because it is market-based, does not require the imposition of unpopular taxes, and can be worked out with special interest groups in back room negotiations. Indeed, with regular auctions to sell of emitting rights, and the lack of a long term or stable price, cap and trade is a lobbyist and trader's dream. Yet, putting the dangers of rent seeking aside, it is not even clear that cap and trade will lead to required emissions reductions. As Sachs observes, "a cap-and-trade system can be more easily manipulated to allow additional emissions; if the permits become too pricey, regulators would likely sell or distribute more permits to keep the price 'reasonable.' Since the long-term signals from cap-and-trade are less powerful than a multi-year carbon tax, the behavioural changes (e.g. choice of the type of power plant) brought about by cap-and-trade could well turn out to be far fewer, as well." Such concerns are borne out by the existing record on carbon emissions trading. The global market grew to £126 billion last year, up from £63 billion in 2007 and nearly 12 times the value in 2005. This represented the value of a total of 4.8 billion tonnes of carbon dioxide, up 61% from the 3 billion tonnes traded in 2007. However, the actual emissions cuts made and sold by United Nations-registered clean energy projects in developing countries fell by 30 % in 2008 to 389 million tonnes.

Tax on Carbon

Contrary to the claims of cap and trade advocates, it can thus be countered that taxes are less likely to result in policy failure. Economic efficiency demands that those who create emissions should pay the costs, and taxes are the simplest way of forcing them to do so. Their advantages are many. They offer a broader scope for emissions reductions, as opposed to trading systems which can only be implemented among private firms or countries, and not among households and individual consumers. In this sense, they are the more democratic option, since they create greater coverage and are less susceptible to strategic lobbying for exceptions by firms or non-governmental organisations. Their universal guiding principle is distributive, since they simultaneously discriminate against polluters while allocating priority to the most vital cases of environmental need. They involve less administrative costs, are less complicated and more familiar to policymakers, and provide new avenues of generating revenue to tackle climate change for governments that are increasingly unwilling to incur political costs by expanding general taxation. Finally, they place a clear price on emissions for many years ahead, allowing for better long term policy planning. Of course, there remains the substantial challenge of shifting taxation structures away from their primary focus on work and production toward a greater emphasis on pollution, externalities and consumption. It goes without saying that this will require a great effort, marked by short-term and long term objectives, which could be weakened by new election results, changing coalitions and so on.

New Policy Mix

In reality, the policy mix is likely to contain multiple policy instruments. The prospect of large revenues from permit auctions has established signifcant political and economic interests in the creation and maintenance of markets for GHGs. Cap and trade also offers the potential for far greater levels of private sector funding than is the case for government financed funds and schemes, and will create signifcant private sector flows from developed to developing countries, an absolute necessity for reaching a global deal. However, if policymakers are serious about putting a true price on carbon and other GHGs – essential if markets are to sort out efficient supply and demand side responses – then taxation will have to form a key element of policy as well, in order to ensure predictability of outcome, and the generation of new resources for the provision of urgent environmental goods.

Unfortunately, putting a price on all GHG emissions (whether through tradable permits or taxes) is not enough on its own to deliver the needed reductions. Existing market-based schemes, such as the EU ETS, or carbon taxation by individual European countries and US states, have so far failed to generate large scale research into the development of breakthrough technologies. Such schemes might eventually result in a levelling of or even a slight reduction of emissions, but will only stimulate a marginal diversification into alternative forms of energy such as solar and wind power. This is because private sector firms under invest in research and development if they fear they will not be able to earn a decent profit on resulting product development. What is ultimately required is a fundamental overhaul of energy systems through transformation technologies that require a combination of factors to succeed – not only market incentives, but also applied scientific research, early high-cost investments, regulatory changes (e.g. building codes and practices), infrastructure development, information instruments (e.g. eco-labelling of energy appliances) and public acceptance.

To ensure flexibility and encourage innovation, regulations should be based on achieving particular results, rather than simply specifying the methods or technologies to be used to achieve those outcomes. Care needs to be taken in choosing instruments in a policy mix to ensure that they are complementary and avoid unnecessary overlap, and that they are cost-effective. By setting too high a price or too tight a cap, policy will result in excess costs, while choosing policies that are too lenient will forego the potential benefits of added, cost-effective mitigation measures and risk the failure of meeting required targets.

Elements of a Democratic Global Deal

Climate change is a problem with global causes and

consequences. A coordinated international effort is therefore required to achieve cost effective and successful mitigation policies. However, the nature of the problem also means that international agreements will be difficult to reach. Countries and regions have very different interests in achieving a solution, implying a highly contested distribution of costs and benefits. In addition, developing countries, given their relatively small contribution to historical emissions, object to having their development impeded by restrictions. Finally, the challenges associated with enforcing a global solution may make some nations reluctant to participate, adding a source of uncertainty about how cost-effective the policies will be. However, despite the vigorous debate surrounding the type of policies required to combat climate change and how they should or should not be implemented, there is considerable overlap on what the political elements of a global deal might look like. At the most general level, most commentators agree that it should be broadly inclusive, multifaceted, state-centric and sustainable.

Participation

The key requirement is participation from all countries, and most importantly, participation by the most powerful democracy in the world. The world has been waiting for the United States to join the collective effort against climate change; there is now reason to believe that it is ready to act. The integration of less developed states is also crucial, as already noted. Even if the developed states of the world were to cut their emissions to zero by 2050, without signifcant cuts in the rest of the world the overall goal of keeping a global rise in temperatures to under 20C would be missed. Developing countries need to be convinced that they can simultaneously reduce their emissions and increase their growth rate by increasing their energy efficiency. They need, for instance, to eliminate distortions in their energy markets, such as large oil subsidies. But for most developing countries, the cheapest form of energy is coal (or other high-emission energy sources), and in those cases, there is a real trade-of. Money spent to reduce GHG emissions is money that could be spent to provide education, better health and clean water, or to grow faster. In such cases, developed countries, it can be argued, should pay for the incremental costs. However, as Victor et. Al. have pointed out, this is unlikely to happen – it is simply unrealistic to expect industrialised nations to contribute the tens or hundreds of billions of dollars needed for such a compensation scheme when official development assistance (including for wars in Iraq and Afghanistan) currently stands at around $100 billion for all purposes. Moreover, the countries that would get the most compensation, such as China, are now west's most potent economic competitors.

Offset Schemes and Financial Incentives

The alternative is some form of offset scheme that allows industrialised nations to fund emissions reductions in developing nations, and counting those reductions towards their own legal commitments. The idea is that this would require industrialised nations to pay a majority of the costs while also laying a foundation for the creation of a global emissions trading market. This was the aim behind the creation of the Clean Development Mechanism (CDM). However, although the CDM has, after a difficult start, been successful in creating a global market for GHGs, its design is fundamentally fawed, and it has done very little to actually cut emissions or to assist host countries in achieving sustainable development.

Another important requirement will be the prevention of deforestation, which contributes 17% of current carbon emissions, almost twice as much as transport. Developing countries' tropical forests are an important source of carbon sequestration, yet they are not provided with any compensation for these environmental services. Providing them with financial incentives will help to reduce emissions from frosted lands and invest in low-carbon paths to sustainable development. In this regard, encouraging steps have been made in the implementation of the United Nations Fund for Reducing Emissions from Deforestation and Forest Degradation. However, the establishment of a final framework for the transfer of funds is still some years away, with a final agreement only likely to come into effect after 2012. Moreover, there are serious concerns about the appropriate geographical scale of accounting and incentive mechanisms, monitoring, land tenure, elite capture of funds and the potential for fraud

Participation and deliberation on a global scale are necessary, yet in their current forms, existing instruments of global environmental governance are ill-equipped to achieve results. What is needed are representative institutions armed with the capacity and legitimacy required to translate policy commitments into real world outcomes. If a global deal is going to work it must have an answer to the problem of governance, and embody an institutional structure that shapes and determines decisions which reflect the whole world in an evenhanded way. Recourse to inclusive and broadly representative global decision-making channels is the most appropriate and effective way of doing this, and strengthening mechanisms of global governance will be key to constructing a global democratic response to the issue.

Democracy and the Policy Menu

The challenge of tackling climate change will require the development of considerable additional institutional capacity and policy innovation. The goal of achieving this capacity, and the means to get there, will be undermined if countries of all stages of development are not directly involved in the shaping of solutions. Current policy development demonstrates this concern. The short term path to effective environmental governance is to integrate a broader set of interests into existing multilateral governance capacity. The existing mandate of the GEF could be broadened in order to help coordinate and fund international environmental agreements and reflect developing country priorities. Complementary to this, the UNEP could increase its status and responsibilities by becoming a specialised UN agency, with all the compulsory UN funding that this entails. The central challenge in the years ahead of compliance monitoring and enforcement could be facilitated through a formal international mechanism for settling environmental disputes through mediation and arbitration, potentially similar to the World Bank's investment dispute body. Enhancing the capacities and responsibilities of the GEF and the UNEP in this way would be a step toward the more consolidated and formal institutional capacity of a World Environmental Organisation as a longer term goal, driven perhaps by the G2 + 1, but accountable to the G195.

Key Role of the State

In all of these challenges, states remain the key actors, as they hold the key to both domestic and international policymaking. The implementation of international agreements will be up to individual states, emissions trading and carbon pricing will require domestic legislation, and technological advance will need state support to get of the ground. However, state strategies at the domestic level should involve the creation of incentives, not overly tight regulation. Governments have an important role in "editing" choice, but not in a way that precludes it altogether. This approach is represented in the form of what Giddens calls "the ensuring state," whose primary role is help energise a diversity of groups to reach solutions to collective action problems. The state, so conceived, acts as a facilitator and an enabler, rather than as a top-down agency. An ensuring state is one that has the capacity to produce definite outcomes. The principle goes even further; it also means a state that is responsible for monitoring public goals and for trying to make sure they are realised in a visible and legitimate fashion.

This will require a return to planning – not in the old sense of top down hierarchies of control, but in a new sense of flexible regulation. This will require finding ways to introduce regulation without undermining the entre-preneurialism and innovation upon which successful responses will depend. It will not be a straightforward process, because planning must be reconciled with democratic freedom. There will be push and pull between the political centre, regions and localities, which can only be resolved through deliberation and consultation. Most importantly, states will require a long term vision that transcends the normal push and pull of partisan politics. This will not be easy to achieve.

All this takes place in the context of a changing world order. The power structure on which the 1945 multilateral settlement was based is no longer intact, and the relative decline of the west and the rise of Asia raises fundamental questions about the premises of the 1945 multilateral order. Democracy and the international community now face a critical test. However, addressing the issue of climate change successfully holds out the prospect of reverting a rule-based politics, from the nation-state to the global level.

Civic Learning in Changing Democracies

The times, they are a changing in long established European and North American democracies. Alarming numbers of young citizens seem to have turned their backs on government and conventional politics. It appears that contemporary politics in most societies increasingly fail to capture the interest and attention of young citizens, who are generally skeptical of politicians and party affiliation, and increasingly unlikely to vote. A study of voting turnout by age in 15 European democracies conducted by the Institute for Democracy and Electoral Assistance in Sweden concluded that youth voting decline is a serious and widespread problem for contemporary democracies looking to the new generation of citizens for participation, legitimacy and support.

To many observers, the civic deficit problem appears to run far deeper than voting. For example, Rahn finds a strong correlation between national integration in the global economy and diminished citizen identification with a range of civic activities and indicators of national citizenship. Some scholars have concluded that there is a distinctive Millennial Generation (roughly composed of those turning 21 around the turn of the century), and that this cohort is profoundly apolitical, as highlighted by a rejection of traditional citizen roles centred around civic duties such as voting. For example, 71 percent of British *Millennials* believe that voting makes no difference. The numbers of British youth who aspire to enter public service are dwarfed by nearly a fifty-to-one preference for entrepreneurial business careers. A follow-up survey in Britain in 1999 compared the *Millennials* to the general population and found that 40 percent of 18-24 year old in Britain were not even registered to vote, compared with just 8 percent of the general population. O'Toole observes that a media stereotype of the youth engagement crisis in Britain has evolved around the factoid that more young people voted on the reality TV show *Big Brother* than in the 2001 general election. (In a personal communication, Stephen Coleman avers that the possibility of multiple voting on Big Brother may cloud this claim).

Young Citizens and Politics

A general survey on the status of young people in Europe revealed a remarkable convergence of trends reported by researchers in 15 European Union member states and three nations outside the EU. A bulletin on the report posted by one of the participating research institutes sounded this alarm: "Young people's and young adults' limited political participation—voting, membership in political parties, youth organisations, and representation in decision-making bodies—is considered a major problem in most Western European countries. Young people's declining political engagement and participation in society are perceived as a challenge for the future of representative democracy.

A survey of the "civic and political health of the nation" in the United States concluded that the American Millennials might be better termed the "Dot Nets," both out of their strong self identification as a generation and their preferences for communicating through various digital interactive media, factors that seem important for thinking about civic education initiatives. Like their European counterparts, the American Dot Nets are turned off to conventional politics and government, but highly involved in issue activism, political consumerism, and protest activities.

Some observers contextually such trends in less alarmist terms based on theories of social change, arguing that recent generations have entered a time of more personalised, less institutionally (e.g., party, union, church) organised politics in which citizens participate by other means through "self actualising" or "self reflexive" involvement in personally meaningful causes guided by their own lifestyles and shifting social networks.

If we apply such perspectives on social change and political identity to the question of what defines the Millennials as a generation with similar cross-national political tendencies, we might consider first that they entered society at the height of the current wave of economic globalisation. Among other things, this period has been defined by high levels of labour market dislocation (more frequent career changes, less employment security, periods of unemployment and underemployment) and an overriding sense of generalised risk. Unlike earlier periods of modern era change, the contemporary experiences of risk and dislocation are negotiated by individuals largely through independent identity management strategies. The Millennials are less guided by encompassing ideologies, mass movements, party and governmental support structures, and other factors that might help individuals focus on government and politics in times of strain.

Living in these disrupted social contexts, young citizens find greater satisfaction in defining their own political paths, including: local volunteerism, consumer activism, support for issues and causes (environment, human rights), participation in various Trans-national protest activities, and efforts to form a global civil society by organising world and regional social forums. Bang has called this a generation of "everyday makers" who define their own sense of politics according to networks of personal relationships aimed at adding value to their lived experiences. Observers like O'Toole and Bang argue that new generations of citizens are simply redefining what they mean by politics, and that social scientists should embrace this shift. Others counter that citizens greatly diminish their political capacity when they replace familiar public action repertoires centred on government and collective identities with narrower discourses fashioned from highly personalised and localised concerns.

When politics becomes so personal, public policies that try to embrace the Millennials may fail because governments tend to deliver collective solutions, and collective solutions do not fit personalised problems. Consider, for example, the reaction of a 19 year old black woman (one of O'Toole's respondents) to an effort by the British Labour Party to address economic and social dislocation among young people:

> ......this New Deal thing that Tony Blair has come up with, it's not for everybody, it does not suit everybody's needs. It basically puts everybody in a little box and expects them to go either this way or that way. It doesn't work for everybody... You have to treat people as individuals, not just a little group so that everybody does have the opportunity to do something.

Some observers contend that changing definitions of citizenship are a natural feature of democratic life. This is surely true. However, the compelling issue remains that the turn away from such defining democratic activities as voting may also represent a serious threat to the core of democratic civic culture. In addition, the redefinition of politics in highly personal and localised terms raises questions about whether procrustean governments can appeal to their new generation citizens on the terms those governments were primarily designed for: delivering collective solutions to broadly defined social problems. These concerns present clear challenges for thinking about and designing effective civic education programs that may appeal to the young citizens who go through them, and at the same time serve the interests of democracy in changing societies. Since there appear to be very different brands of citizenship in play within the same societies, how can civic education address and reconcile these differences without forcing unappealing, one-size-fits-all models of political consciousness and behaviour on entire cohorts of young citizens?

Challenge for Civic Education

The challenges to civic education in this picture are obvious. Most policy makers define and fund civic education programs (which are run primarily in the schools) based on highly conventional citizen models which centre around the idea of the "Dutiful Citizen" (DC). At a minimum, the DC is expected to learn about the basic workings of government and related political institutions, to understand the values of the national civic culture, to become informed about issues and make responsible voting choices. The challenge for civic education, simply put, is how to integrate and adapt these conventional DC virtues to the changing civic orientation of the new "self- Actualising Citizen" (AC) who may see her political activities and commitments in highly personal terms that contribute more to enhancing the quality of personal life, social recognition, self esteem, or friendship relations, than to understanding, support, and involvement in government.

Civic identifications and practices, if they are to be adopted, must have some anchors and inducements in the lived experiences of individuals both inside and outside of the education and socialisation settings in which they are introduced. The Dutiful Citizen continues to have obvious appeal, particularly to educational policy makers, based on the reasonable perception that citizen activities centered on voting and informed opinion are necessary to instill in new generations in order to ensure the viability of democratic polities. At the same time, recognising that young citizens today may have substantially different social and political experiences than their elders did at comparable stages of life also seems important to incorporate into models of civic education. In short, effective civic education models need to address substantive changes in citizen roles, while finding ways to motivate young people to find ways to engage meaningfully and effectively in civic life.

Case Study of Australia

Australia offers an interesting national case both because of the awareness in the policy community of generation changes among young citizens, and because of the difficulty of incorporating this awareness into the classroom curriculum. Part of the policy innovation and implementation problem no doubt stems from the fact that there are so many sites of civics curriculum coordination and breakdown—as is the case in many nations. For example, the Civics Education Research Group at Canberra University lists 45 distinct sites of input and coordination—from international organisations such as the International Association for the Evaluation of Educational Achievement (IEA), to national governmental policy agencies involved with citizenship, education and immigration, to numerous state education boards and private councils. At the same time, the issues confronting the Australian civics project have been fairly well defined by The Australian Council of Education Research (ACER) following participation in the landmark IEA study of 90,000 fourteen year old in 28 nations.

Australian students scored around the middle of the international distribution in terms of overall civics skills scores. The authors of the ACER report conclude that despite this passing performance on the skills and knowledge tests, the data revealed a deeper problem. The adequate performance of Australian students on basic civic knowledge and skills measures did not translate into a desire to engage in the corresponding activities of civic life defined by the IEA study as "conventional citizenship". This is a form of what Rahn describes as the disconnection between identification and engagement, or the "being and doing" aspects of citizenship. Among the disturbing findings: 83% felt that joining a political party was not important in order to be considered a good citizen; only 55% felt that knowing about the nation's history was important; only 50% regarded following issues in the media important; and 66% regarded engaging in political discussion as unimportant. The relatively strong commitment to voting was down played in the report as merely echoing the compulsory status of voting in Australia. Yet what seemed equally clear in the IEA study is that the AC side of civic life is far more attractive to young Australians: 80% said it was important to engage in activities that benefit others, 74% wanted to protect the political environment, and 68% were concerned about human rights. The authors conclude that Australian students were inclined to look outside government for solutions to political problems.

What were the implications of this increasingly familiar young citizen profile for Australian civic education? The results of the IEA study became the basis of a report from the Australian Council of Educational Research on the goals for civic education in Australia. The recommendations of the ACER report included a sensible blend of the AC and DC sides of contemporary citizenship. Their recommendations below, taking the liberty of noting what seem to be the DC goals above the dotted line and the AC goals below it.

1. Knowledge of Australian political institutions and structures
2. Values concerning democracy, the rule of law, social justice, equity and fairness
3. Commitment to including all Australians in the political process
4. An obligation to see citizenship in an international perspective
5. Understanding the everyday lived experiences of young people and their apparent alienation
6. Recognising schools and classrooms as democratic institutions
7. Accepting that citizens are constructed by multiple identities rather than a single identity.

Where is Australia in crossing the AC/DC divide? The Ministerial Council on Education, Employment, Training and Youth of Australia surveyed national civic education policy, and analysed all available documents from agencies promoting or conducting civics education programs. The first conclusion was that civics is not even among the 8 key learning areas established for all schools in Australia. Indeed, there is concern that civics has slipped from the required curriculum in many nations, reflecting the educational turn toward basic academic skills and, perhaps, reflecting underlying struggles to de-politicise the schools. The second conclusion of this national survey was that only three content areas were widespread throughout Australian civics curriculum documents: 1) Australian democratic heritage and operation of government and law; 2) Australian national identity and cultural diversity; and 3) the set of skills and values necessary for informed and active participation in civic life. These goals are very similar to the three DC goals identified in the recommendations from the IEA study. Still missing from the general civics learning picture in Australia were the goals that might engage the AC citizen.

Communication-Based Model of Civics Education

The case of Australia suggests that even when the challenges of addressing complex citizenship are recognised, the solutions are elusive. In part, this may be due to generation differences in the perceptions of citizenship that favour policies and curriculum designed by older citizens who do not experience public life from the standpoint of younger generations. This may be compounded by the false, but commonly heard, impression that approaches to civic education that include AC perspectives necessarily sacrifice DC virtues. The overriding problem may be the absence of a model for integrating both AC and DC elements of citizenship in a coherent curriculum.

Using Standpoint Issues to Communicate Identity

A starting point for engaging AC learners who experience a distant and often disagreeable DC world is to allow them to define their own political standpoints—and avoid immediately requiring them to locate those standpoints in terms of conventional politics. This may be easier than it initially appears. Political standpoints for the AC emerge fairly easily around issues that matter in their daily lives. Moreover, exploring shared experiences with those issues enables shifting the framing of those experiences from private to common concerns.

There is evidence that the Dot Nets are concerned about issues and problem-solving, and even more inclined toward collective identification with their peers than predecessor generations. For example, the U.S. Civic health of the nation survey found higher levels of generation identification (69%) among the Dot Nets (those born between 1977 and 1987) than among GenX (42%), the Baby Boomers (50%), or the Matures (51%). However, in keeping with their AC citizenship bias, the Dot Nets were by far the least likely (38%, 48%, 60%, 59%) to say that good citizenship entails responsibility. At the same time, the Dot Nets are as likely as any generation to have engaged directly in political consumerism in support of environmental and other causes, and they are nearly twice as likely as other citizens to have participated in protest politics. What can be done to channel these clear indications of political interest and potential for common identification in more conventional political directions?

A simple proposition about civic learning consistent with these trends is that conventional skills such as engagement and information-seeking begin with motivation—generally powered by interest in specific issues or problems. A promising beginning to any civic learning experience is to empower the learners to find issues in their immediate communities that seem important to the people with whom they live and associate. One model for this is the Student Voices project, a national civic learning program developed by the Annenberg Public Policy Centre in the United States. Student Voices begins by training students to take simple surveys of their communities and bring the results (community concerns) back into the learning environment (usually a classroom) to explore through deliberations under the guidance of the learning facilitator (usually a teacher). The Student Voices model is interesting because learners introduce issues with which they identify personally, and they contribute through group deliberations to the development of a class issue agenda that results in a collectively constructed issue or problem that becomes the focus for subsequent civic learning. A similar model is offered by the Project Citizen curriculum developed by the Centre for Civic Education in the U.S.

Once learners have identified with a personal issue and participated in constructing a collective framing for a common issue (which may or not end up resembling their initial issue), they have taken the first step in understanding how to construct a public discourse and negotiate interests in common with others with whom they identify. These elements of the civic learning process can be enhanced through a combination of conventional and technology-driven communication processes. For example, the results of deliberations can be posted on discussion boards for follow-up reactions from those involved in the deliberations, and for sharing with others engaged in similar experiences in the same school, across the city, or around the world.

The mixture of face-to-face deliberation and subsequent individual-level input through online messages and chats can create a sense of personal ownership in the issue adopted by the learning community. The issues may cover a wide variety of topics, from crime, drugs, education, and teen recreation issues, to local or global environmental concerns. The actual issue is less important than its origins in individual and collective definition and mutual recognition processes, aided by the willingness of the facilitator not to impose too much definition from on high.

Navigating the Political Information Environment

Young citizens are immersed in what may be the richest, yet most fragmented information environment in human history. The channels that young citizens use to gather information and to communicate about their political issues are important considerations in creating engaged citizens. Tuning out is surely as useful a skill as knowing what and when to tune in. Media literacy training can create awareness of the dilemmas of incorporating DC information skills into the often discouraging real world media experiences of young citizens. This entails lessons aimed at more critical de-construction and use of available information channels, and at finding channels that address the issue at the centre of the learning experience. These aims can be advanced by introducing civic learners to several different slices of the media environment in which they live. Some obvious candidates for attention include: *election communication*, *conventional news and entertainment*, and *the digital information sphere*.

Electoral communication is important to highlight in order to demystify the process through which campaigns seek votes, a process that often excludes substantial voter blocs such as young people. Painting today's democratic process with a broad brush finds parties and politicians scrambling for electoral support by placing their appeals in the hands of professional communication consultants who target narrow voter blocs to gain tactical electoral advantage. The near universal consensus among these consultants is that spending precious campaign budgets on messages aimed at young voters is a waste of time and money. Young people are deemed hard to reach through conventional media strategies, and even harder to convince that politicians are not all alike. The idea that campaign messages and candidate images are marketed to voters much the same way that commercial products are sold may help young citizens to see that, in communication terms, they represent demographic market segments—highly prized for selling fashion and entertainment products, but less valued in electoral marketing strategies. A simple proposition about youth disengagement is that since they are not asked in meaningful terms to participate in the electoral process, they don't.

This introduction to political communication offers learners an honest appraisal of their place in the political scheme of things in most countries, and may help them see why many of their peers reject a political system that implicitly ignores them. At the same time, it is important to show that electoral results do have consequences for various social groups, including young people. It is also important at this point to introduce citizen engagement options—both electoral and non-electoral that provide both information and pathways to effective action concerning the issue defined in the last learning module. The general goal here is to begin moving away from the idea of the citizen as a passive spectator in the electoral arena, or more generally, in relation to government, and toward a model of active citizenship.

Understanding the political influence of news and entertainment media offers a next step for helping young citizen's think about their political views. A major obstacle to active citizenship is the relationship that many young citizens establish with the mass (particularly commercial) media. The absence of citizens —particularly young citizens—playing central roles in conventional news and public affairs programming reinforces impressions that issues are too confusing or that there is nothing that ordinary people can do about them. In addition, the portrayal of scandal and unpleasant images of politics may further reinforce negativity toward politics, politicians and government. Whether these media trends actively produce or merely echo a late modern culture of anti-politics, the evidence is clear that most mass media content, particularly on commercial television, ranges from apolitical, at best, to overtly negative toward politics. And, what may be just as civically isolating, most youth programming aims at full immersion in a commercialised environment selling fashion, entertainment, and other consumer products as the core elements of social identities anchored in lifestyles. Examining that media environment seems an appropriate next step in understanding the broad rejection of politics and the common experience of being lost when thinking about the problems and issues that do matter.

Case materials suitable for a politically focused media literacy curriculum abound in nearly every national context. Consider, for example, the market research materials produced by the Gérman public service broadcaster ARD. The monthly reports called *Media Perspectives* often publicise the network's market research with a focus on audience demographics and content comparisons between public service and commercial television outlets. These studies demonstrate common, cross national audience trends such as the greying of the public service news audience, and the disproportionate appeal of infotainment news on commercial channels to younger viewers. The implications of these trends for politics and citizenship are dramatic. For example, people who exclusively watch news on German public service channels consistently demonstrate two to three times the levels of interest in political affairs, depending on what is happening during the periods when polls are taken.

The explanation for this political interest gap is most likely a combination of what these audiences are offered by different media sources, and what interests they bring to their viewing in the first place. For example, an analysis of news content on the public and private channels shows that political content fills 66% and 63% of news programming on the two leading German public channels, ARD and ZDF, compared to just 29% and 28% on the leading private channels RTL and Sat. Audience political tastes are considerably at odds as well, with public service audiences preferring information about national politics, state politics, social issues and international affairs, and private channel audiences ranking natural disasters, crime, and accidents as their favourite news fare.

The moral of this media literacy story is that media choices matter. While it may be difficult to convince young learners to tune in public service news, there are other high quality and personalised news sources that may appeal to them. In learning environments with school or home access to the internet, the most obvious direction for Dot Nets who have issues that they want to understand is the rich sphere of discourse and information on the Web.

The digital information sphere offers a rich menu of interactive information options for individuals seeking information about issues that motivate learning and action. For example, the BBC has launched a prototype experiment called *can*, which enables citizens to define and post their own issues, link to broad networks of similarly concerned individuals, find information about public actions and government responses, and, ultimately, push for BBC coverage of their concerns. There are also many dubious sites that merit another round of communication literacy training in the digital sphere. In general, however, the information habits of *netizens* suggest two promising trends (based on research in the U.S.): 1) young people increasingly prefer their information in online, interactive environments, and 2) veteran internet users are among the most informed citizens.

A policy problem facing the incorporation of information technologies in civic education is that nations vary greatly in the development and distribution of internet access. For example, the United States leads in the category of computer-based online access, while Germany and France have been slower to introduce the levels of service competition and infrastructure necessary to democratise this important communication medium. However, increasing numbers of schools are wired, and next generation mobile phones will have search and information features that may enable young people to do more than down load the latest hit songs as ring tones.

Where access is available, young people follow. In the United States, the internet now rivals regular news programming and comedy shows as the leading sources of information about politics for young people. More importantly, those who use the internet are far better informed than those who rely on other sources of information, and these *netizens* are far more interested in politics. The universal attraction of young people to digital communication technologies can be important for motivating engagement with their chosen issues, and, as outlined in the next set of recommendations, for helping to establish collective identifications with those issues as well.

Citizenship as Communication Practice

Personalising the information process in the ways that many ICTs make possible may risk fragmenting publics and isolating individual citizens. Developing a highly individualised sense of politics may not be regarded as a problem in the AC world, but it is often seen as antithetical to the DC view of the democratic polity. In order to counter the perils of isolation through overly personalised digital media experiences, the learning environment for next generation citizens must be designed to appeal to the affinity for networks and communities of interest. Interactive communication technologies should be aimed at creating echoing online environments that enable others to engage with and contribute to emerging understanding of the public issues at the centre of the learning experience. This sense of common engagement with one's own and with others' issues introduces the experience of being part of a public as a core element of the learning process.

Research on the learning environments preferred by Dot Nets suggests that there are a number of fundamental changes that can be introduced productively into the traditional learning environment. As part of a Microsoft effort to design educational technology, Peden has summarised an effort in the United States to create national classroom technology standards for teachers. According to this perspective, the key to the successful introduction of technology in the learning environment is not just delivering hardware or software applications, but reorganising the social and psychological contexts in which they are used. Peden contrasts the new learning preferences with the traditional classroom learning environment as outlined below:

merging Learning Preferences that May Be Enabled by ICTs

New Learning Preferences	*Traditional learning Environment*
Student/group Centered	Teacher centered
Multimedia	Single media
Collaborative work	Isolated work
Critical thinking/informed decision-making	Fact/knowledge-based learning

These norms for introducing technology into the learning environment are also happily aligned with a more democratic experience for the AC learners. Current DC approaches to civic education often seem lamentably at odds with the ideal AC experience of peer-to-peer, non-hierarchical, network participation. For example, conventional civics education often treats the subject matter as: a) another academic subject, b) with right and wrong responses arbitrated by the teacher as central authority, and c) students competing in isolation for academic favour. For example, the results of the IEA survey of high school students in the U.S. Suggests that the dominant learning experience in civics classrooms was the traditional learning model of isolated learners, receiving fact-based material from teachers. For example 89 percent of 9th graders reported reading from textbooks, and 88 percent reported filling out work sheets, compared to only 45 percent reporting debating and discussing ideas, 40 percent engaging in role play or mock trials, 31 percent receiving visits from leaders, and 27 percent writing letters to express their opinions.

Further analysis of the U.S. IEA data by Campbell indicates that favourable attitudes toward a whole range of political activities were associated with the degree to which classrooms were more open, interactive, and focused on participation. However, the dilemma in his findings is that these open participation conditions seemed less likely to occur in mixed race classrooms, suggesting that young people are less likely to engage with each other across racial lines. The potential for ICTs to promote less racially cued communication might is worth exploring in this context.

In general, research indicates that not only do students prefer interactive learning environments, but that these environments matter for the translation of civics skills into civic practice. For example the U.S. "Civic health of the nation" study found that those who participated in high school debate were far more active politically after they entered public life than those who had no debate experience. The debaters were nearly twice as likely to attend community meetings and sign petitions, and three times as likely as those who did not debate to participate in boycotts. Joining groups in high school also significantly boosted a range of adult civic activities including regular voting.

The lesson seems clear: learning environments that emphasise old style, fact based, teacher-centered pedagogy may succeed in imparting abstract facts and skills of the sort that can be tested, but, to return to the findings from the Australian case, they do not help young citizens translate that knowledge into later civic practice. Perhaps the message here is that providing learners with tools to experience actual civic practice in the learning environment makes more sense. Communication environments that offer collective experiences and provide public displays of group projects may create a first semblance of public life. The Student Voices projects described earlier illustrate these principles, as learners are introduced to an interactive digital web environment that enables them to tailor information and communication to their group issue projects. In addition to having access to external media input for information purposes, this interactive web environment also enables learners to communicate among themselves about emerging understanding of issues, and about the ways in which government and larger publics might become engaged with their causes.

Translating Communication Skills into Participation

It is important for this issue-driven civic learning process to link ultimately to the entry points of public life such as press, government, issue organisations and community networks. For nearly every problem or issue identified by young citizens-in-training, there is abundant public information available about it, and much of that information shows how citizen interest and advocacy networks are trying to win the attention of government. In addition, citizens in nations that have embraced e-government initiatives have increasing access to relevant government activities through online record archives, and through televised coverage of government proceedings that are often archived digitally and streamed on demand. Perhaps most importantly, civic activists and public officials are often available to address the concerns of young citizens, whether through personal visits or participation in computer chats. Using these and other channels, the interactive learning situation can ultimately connect citizen-learners to sources of information about their political concerns, and to networks of citizens and officials involved in making policy about them.

One model that illustrates this linkage to the larger political world is Student Voices in the United States. The website for the project introduces a set of information resources, along with linkages to government and civic organisations. Once there is an active connection between a group's issue project and relevant spheres of politics and government, it is important to facilitate real contact with the various actors those spheres. It turns out that representatives of civic groups and public institutions are generally willing to meet with young people, and to have remarkably open exchanges about their political concerns. Various formats can be developed for bridging the learning environment and the policy arena. For example, Student Voices links into local elections by inviting candidates to talk with students in schools and preparing students to interrogate candidates in a press-debate format held in an open public forum that is televised on local public access television. In addition, class issue projects are often presented as public policy recommendations, and judged in a civics fair by community leaders. Students have even produced series of public affairs programs from their own perspectives that were aired on local public television and then archived and streamed on demand over the web. Linking the classroom and the surrounding political environment is also a major goal of Project Citizen.

Building bridges between the citizenship learning environment, the public sphere, and the policy process not only results in learning a set of civic skills, but, more generally, developing a higher regard for participating in the political world of civic activism, government and elections. In some cases, students have become actively involved in the policy process they developed as part of their issue projects. The overall result of this integration of the civics learning environment with the real political world is a bridge between the AC and DC models of citizenship that offers next generation citizens a broader repertoire of civic action than they might acquire in conventional approaches that, no matter how well-intentioned, risk reproducing the same aversion to the DC model of citizenship that many young citizens bring to the learning situation in the first place.

6

Sociological Issues in Indian Democracy

Democracies fall into two basic categories, direct and representative. In a direct democracy, all citizens, without the intermediary of elected or appointed officials, can participate in making public decisions. Such a system is clearly only practical with relatively small numbers of people – in a community organisation or tribal council, for example, or the local unit of a trade union, where members can meet in a single room to discuss issues and arrive at decisions by consensus or majority vote.

Modern society, with its size and complexity, offers few opportunities for direct democracy. Today, the most common form of democracy, whether for a town of 50,000 or nations of 1 billion, is representative democracy, in which citizens elect officials to make political decisions, formulate laws, and administer programmes for the public good. Ours is a representative democracy. Every citizen has the important right to vote her/his representative. People elect their representatives to all levels from Panchayats, Municipal Boards, State Assemblies and Parliament. There has increasingly been a feeling that democracy ought to involve people more regularly and should not just mean casting a vote every five years. Both the concepts of *participatory democracy* and *decentralised governance* have thus become popular. Participatory democracy is a system of democracy in which the members of a group or community participate collectively in the taking of major decisions.

Values of Indian Democracy

Like so many other features of modern India we need to begin the story about modern Indian democracy from the colonial period. You have just read about the many structural and cultural changes that British colonialism brought about deliberately. Some of the changes that came about happened in an unintended fashion. The British did not intend to introduce them. For instance, they sought to introduce western education to create a western educated Indian middle class that would help the colonial rulers to continue their rule. A western educated section of Indians did emerge. But, instead of aiding British rule, they used western liberal ideas of democracy, social justice and nationalism to challenge colonial rule.

Social change in modern India is not just about Indian or western ideas. It is a combination as well as reinterpretation of western and Indian ideas. We saw that in the case of the social reformers. We saw the use of both modern ideas of equality and traditional ideas of justice. Democracy is no exception. In colonial India the undemocratic and discriminatory administrative practice of British colonialism contrasted sharply with the vision of freedom which western theories of democracy espoused and which the western educated Indians read about. The scale of poverty and intensity of social discrimination within India also led to deeper *questioning of the meaning of democracy.* Is democracy just about political freedom? Or is it also about economic freedom and social justice? Is it also about equal rights to all irrespective of caste, creed, race and gender? And if that is so how can such equality be realised in an unequal society?

Many of these issues were thought of much before India became free. Even as India fought for its independence from British colonialism a vision of what Indian democracy ought to look like emerged. As far back as in 1928, Motilal Nehru and eight other Congress leaders drafted a constitution for India. In 1931, the resolution at the Karachi session of the Indian National Congress dwelt on how independent India's constitution should look like. The Karachi Resolution reflects a vision of democracy that meant not just formal holding of elections but a substantive reworking of the Indian social structure in order to have a genuine democratic society.

The Karachi Resolution clearly spells out the vision of democracy that the nationalist movement in India had. It articulates the values that were further given full expression in the Indian Constitution. You will notice how the Preamble of the Indian Constitution seeks to ensure not just political justice but also social and economic justice. You will likewise notice that equality is not just about equal political rights but also of status and opportunity.

Constituent Assembly Debates

In 1939, Gandhiji wrote an article in the 'Harijan' called 'The Only Way' in which he said "... the Constituent Assembly alone can produce a constitution indigenous to the country and truly and fully representing the will of the people" one based on "unadulterated adult franchise for both men and women". The popular demand in 1939 for a Constituent Assembly was, after several ups and downs conceded by Imperialist Britain in 1945. In July 1946, the elections were held. In August 1946, The Indian National Congress' Expert Committee moved a resolution in the Constituent Assembly. This contained the declaration that India shall be a Republic where the declared social, economic and political justice will be guaranteed to all the people of India. On matters of social justice, there were lively debates on whether government functions should be prescribed and the state should be bound down to them. Issues debated ranged from right to employment, to social security, land reforms to property rights, to the organisation of panchayats. Here are some snippets from the debates:

CONSTITUTION AND SOCIAL CHANGE

India exists at so many levels. The multi-religious and multi-cultural composition of the population with distinct streams of tribal culture is one aspect of the plurality. Many divides classify the Indian people. The impact that culture, religion, and caste have on the urban–rural divide, rich-poor divide and the literate-illiterate divide is varied. Deeply stratified by caste and poverty, there are groupings and sub-groupings among the rural poor. The urban working class comprises a very wide range. Then, there is the well-organised domestic business class as also the professional and commercial class. The urban professional class is highly vocal. Competing interests operate on the Indian social scene and clamour for control of the State's resources.

However, there are some basic objectives laid down in the Constitution and which are generally agreed in the Indian political world as being obviously just. These would be empowerment of the poor and marginalised, poverty alleviation, ending of caste and positive steps to treat all groups equally.

Competing interests do not always reflect a clear class divide. Take the issue of the close down of a factory because it emits toxic waste and affects the health of those around. This is a matter of life, which the Constitution protects. The flip-side is that the closure will render people jobless. Livelihood again, is a matter of life that the Constitution protects. It is interesting that at the time of drawing up the Constitution, the Constituent Assembly was fully aware of this complexity and plurality but was intent on securing social justice as a guarantee.

Constitutional Norms and Social Justice

It is useful to understand that there is a difference between law and justice. The essence of law is its force. Law is law because it carries the means to coerce or force obedience. The power of the state is behind it. The essence of justice is fairness. Any system of laws functions through a hierarchy of authorities. The basic norm from which all other rules and authorities flow is called the Constitution. It is the document that constitutes a nation's tenets. The Indian Constitution is India's basic norm. All other laws are made as per the procedures the Constitution prescribes. These laws are made and implemented by the authorities specified by the Constitution. A hierarchy of courts (which too are authorities created by the Constitution) interpret the laws when there is a dispute. The Supreme Court is the highest court and the ultimate interpreter of the Constitution.

The Supreme Court has enhanced the substance of Fundamental Rights in the Constitution in many important ways. The Constitution is not just a ready reference of do's and don'ts for social justice. It has the potential for the meaning of social justice to be extended. Social movements have also aided the Courts and authorities to interpret the contents of rights and principles in keeping with the contemporary understanding on social justice. Law and Courts are sites where competing views are debated. The Constitution remains a means to channels and civilise political power towards social welfare.

Rural Social Transformation

Panchayati Raj translates literally to 'Governance by five individuals'. The idea is to ensure at the village or grass root level a functioning and vibrant democracy. While the idea of grassroots democracy is not an alien import to our country, in a society where there are sharp inequalities democratic participation is hindered on grounds of gender, caste and class. Furthermore, traditionally there have been caste panchayats in villages. But they have usually represented dominant groups. Furthermore, they often held conservative views and often have, and continue to take decisions that go against both democratic norms and procedures.

When the constitution was being drafted panchayats did not find a mention in it. At this juncture, a number of members expressed their sorrow, anger and disappointment over this issue. At the same time, drawing on his own rural experience Dr. Ambedkar argued that local elites and upper castes were so well entrenched in society that local self-government only meant a continuing exploitation of the downtrodden masses of Indian society. The upper castes would no doubt silence this segment of the population further. The concept of local government was dear to Gandhiji too. He envisaged each village as a self-sufficient unit conducting its own affairs and saw *gram-swarajya* to be an ideal model to be continued after independence.

It was, however, only in 1992 that grassroots democracy or decentralised governance was ushered in by the 73rd Constitutional Amendment. This act provided constitutional status to the Panchayati Raj Institutions (PRIs). It is compulsory now for local self-government bodies in rural and municipal areas to be elected every five years. More importantly, control of local resources is given to the elected local bodies.

The 73rd and 74th amendments to the Constitution ensured the reservation of one third of the total seats for women in all elected offices of local bodies in both the rural and urban areas. Out of this, 17 per cent seats are reserved for women belonging to the scheduled castes and tribes.

This amendment is significant as for the first time it brought women into elected bodies which also bestowed on them decision making powers. One third of the seats in local bodies, gram panchayats, village panchayats, municipalities, city corporations and district boards are reserved for women. The 1993-94 elections, soon after the 73rd amendment brought in 800,000 women into the political processes in a single election. That was a big step indeed in enfranchising women. A constitutional amendment prescribed a three-tier system of local self-governance for the entire country, effective since 1992-93.

Powers and Responsibilities of Panchayats

According to the Constitution, Panchayats should be given powers and authority to function as institutions of self-government. It, thus, requires all state governments to revitalise local representative institutions.

The following powers and responsibility were delegated to the Panchayats:

1. To prepare plans and schemes for economic development
2. To promote schemes that will enhance social justice
3. To levy, collect and appropriate taxes, duties, tolls and fees
4. Help in the devolution of governmental responsibilities, especially that of finances to local authorities

Social welfare responsibilities of the Panchayats include the maintenance of burning and burial grounds, recording statistics of births and deaths, establishment of child welfare and maternity centres, control of cattle pounds, propagation of family planning and promotion of agricultural activities. The development activities include the construction of roads, public buildings, wells, tanks and schools. They also promote small cottage industries and take care of minor irrigation works. Many government schemes like the Integrated Rural Development Programme (IRDP) and Integrated Child Development Scheme (ICDS) are monitored by members of the panchayat.

The main income of the Panchayats is from tax levied on property, profession, animals, vehicles, cess on land revenue and rental. The resources are further increased by the grants received through the Zilla Panchayat. It is also considered compulsory for Panchayat offices to put up boards outside their offices, listing the break up of funds received, and utilisation of the financial aid received. This exercise was taken up to ensure that people at the grassroots level should have the 'right to information' – opening all functioning to the public eye. People had the right to scrutinise allocation of money. And ask reasons for decisions that were taken for the welfare and development activities of the village.

Nyaya Panchayats have been constituted in some states. They possess the authority to hear some petty, civil and criminal cases. They can impose fines but cannot award a sentence. These village courts have often been successful in bringing about an agreement amongst contending parties. They have been particularly effective in punishing men who harass women for dowry and perpetrate violence against them.

Panchayati Raj in Tribal Areas

Many tribal areas have had a rich tradition of grassroots democratic functioning. We give an illustrative example from Meghalaya. All the three major ethnic tribal groups, namely, the Khasis, Jaintias and the Garos have their own traditional political institutions that have existed for hundreds of years. These political institutions were fairly well-developed and functioned at various tiers, such as the **village level, clan** level and state level. For instance, in the traditional political system of the Khasis each clan had its own council known as the 'Durbar Kur' which was presided over by the clan headman. Though there is a long tradition of grassroots political institutions in Meghalaya, a large chunk of tribal areas lie outside the provisions of the 73rd Amendment. This may be because the concerned policy makers did not wish to interfere with the traditional tribal institutions.

However, as sociologist Tiplut Nongbri remarks that tribal institutions in themselves need not necessarily be democratic in its structure and functioning. Commenting on the Bhuria Committee Report that went into this issue Nongbri remarks that while the Committee's concern for the traditional tribal institutions is appreciable, it fails to take stock of the complexity of the situation. For notwithstanding the strong egalitarian ethos that characterised tribal societies the element of stratification is not altogether absent. Tribal political institutions are not only marked by open intolerance to women but the process of social change has also introduced sharp distortions in the system, making it difficult to identify which is traditional and which is not.

Political Parties, Pressure Groups and Democratic Politics

In a democratic form of government political parties are key actors. A political party may be defined as an organisation oriented towards achieving legitimate control of government through an electoral process. Political Party is an organisation established with the aim of achieving governmental power and using that power to pursue a specific programme. Political parties are based on certain understanding of society and how it ought to be. In a democratic system the interests of different groups are also represented by political parties, who take up their case. Different interest groups will work towards influencing political parties. When certain groups feel that their interests are not being taken up, they may move to form an alternative party. Or they form pressure groups who lobby with the government. Interest Groups are organised to pursue specific interests in the political arena, operating primarily by lobbying the members of legislative bodies. In some situations, there may be political organisations which seek to achieve power but are denied the opportunity to do so through standard means. These organisations are best regarded as movements until they achieve recognition.

It is obvious that all groups will not have the same access or the same ability to pressurise the government. Some, therefore, argue that the concept of pressure groups underestimate the power that dominant social groups such as class or caste or gender have in society. They feel that it would be more accurate to suggest that dominant class or classes control the state. This does not negate the fact that social movements and pressure groups also continue to play a very important role in a democracy.

Caste Politics

'Region' as a factor has only assumed significance in the nineties. Since after the disintegration of the 'Congress framework' of politics, observers have noted the 'regionalisation' of politics. Rise of regional and State-based parties to prominence is an expression of this regionalisation. But apart from the dramatic proliferation and rise of regional parties, less noticed and more interesting aspect of regionalisation has been related to 'all-India' parties. The Congress, Bharatiya Janata Party (BJP), Communist Party of India (Marxist) (CPI-M), have themselves become regionalised in terms of their strategies and practices.

Regionalisation refers to five factors. (i) *Issues* are/have become region specific. Although the press may continue to project issues in 'all-India' terms, these make sense only when translated into regional contexts. This applies equally to 'secular-communal' divide or to 'globalisation.' (ii) Secondly, *leadership* is structured regional and ratified regional. Parties may still project towering 'national' leaders but State level leadership is more relevant and only through this kind of leadership people relate to 'national' politics. (iii) Regionalisation further means that *social forces* are constituted at the regional level. Therefore, the support base of parties can be identified only at State level. Whether one can describe the base of parties at the all-India level by adding up its base at state level is somewhat doubtful. (iv) Fourthly, in electoral and mobilisation context, the *set of choices* exists at the State level. People, as voters and as groups, have to choose from among the State level choices only. (v) Following from the above factors, political *competition* takes place at the level of region. Consequently, the outcome makes sense only at the regional level. It is in this sense that the 'theatre' of politics has shifted to States — away from the 'all India' theatre.

Before turning to the question how does this regionalisation link up with caste, let us briefly explore the elements conveyed by the term 'region.' Territoriality is the most obviously conveyed element. However, the territoriality expressed by the term 'region' often has a flexibility and indeterminacy with regards to its physical boundary. In this sense, region refers to a wide range of territorial configurations: locality, sub region, State, supra-State region etc.We shall be invoking these various territorial units. Secondly, 'region' can bypass territoriality and convey a broader and perhaps more fluid element of 'space'. Thus understood, region would refer to a non-territorial, non-physical 'sphere' just as it would refer to a physical territory. We bring this element of 'region' into the discussion because caste can be seen both as interacting with territory and as providing space for following certain kind of politics. It needs to be seen how caste as social space interacts with region as territorial space.

One more point may be raised at this introductory stage. How does 'region' as territory become politically sustainable? It is possible to think of many factors, which prop up region as a relevant factor in politics. But the point is that territoriality needs to be translated as a political factor. Language, culture, economy, etc. provide a base to territoriality in order to sustain in politics. It may be argued that caste is not only yet another base, but one, which potentially combines other factors—particularly economy—in providing a base to region to operate as a factor in politics. Thus, we can imagine a complex relationship between caste and region—a relationship of interdependence: caste expresses through region (as territoriality), region becomes politically sustainable on the basis of caste; is bound up by territoriality and in constituting the social space, caste takes the form of a region.

We hope to understand the politics in post-congress phase by exploring the tension and relation between caste and region. The post-congress politics is often characterised by coalitions. However, an alliance of regional parties does not seem to be a possibility. On the other hand, caste emerged in the 1990s as a possible framework within which politics would be organised. However, it now appears that politics of backward castes—or OBC politics as it is popularly known—seems to be stagnating. Thirdly, expressions of regionalism are vocal in some part but muted in others. Fourthly, apart from region and caste, another contending framework of politics has emerged—that of Hindutva.

Cast as a system of vertical division, sustains on the basis of localisation. Caste hierarchy may invoke the ideologies of *chaturvarnya* and of purity-pollution. But the hierarchy makes sense operationally, only when it is concretes in a local situation. Studies concentrating on *Jati* by sociologists and social anthropologists, have always pointed out how hierarchical ranking of *Jati* makes sense in the context of village or small localities. Similarly, cultural, ritual life of members of *Jati* is organised around village or locality. It is only in comparison to some other caste within a locality that the higher or lower status of caste can be experienced. Anthropological studies, thus, look at the extent of intermixing among castes and the finer ethic followed in the course of such intermixing within a locality to assess the extent of separation and communalist among castes. A statement that 'carpenters dine with iron smiths' does not carry any meaning unless it is specified as to where this interdining took place. In other words, *Jati* as a unit of social relations, ritual status and cultural universe is firmly based within the framework of well-defined territorial boundaries. As much as vertical, horizontal separateness of a caste, too, has a locality as a point of reference.

Often, we find distinct 'pockets' of various castes. Most castes are not only specific to a certain State but also specific to a particular area. This means that a caste, which has a concentrated existence in one area, may also constitute numerically large or significant group in that area. In a study of north India, Schwartzeberg has shown how caste concentration takes place at village and district level. He shows that more than fifty percent of Ludhiana's population is Jat, and Chamars and Majahabis have separate pockets in Punjab. The same applies to UP, Bihar, Orissa, etc. He argues that both in the case of peasant castes and Dalits, exclusivity seems to be the rule. This means that if in one village, Jats are the largest group; other peasant castes would almost be non-existent. Similarly, in districts where Majahabis are numerous (e.g. Amritsar), other Dalit castes are rarely seen.

This section gives an indication of the strong link between caste and localities or sub-regions. In the case of peasant castes, the regional base is considerably expansive while non-peasant castes are often confined to smaller pockets. This pattern is evident in State after State: In Tamil Nadu (TN), Vanniyars belong to North and South Arcot, Salem and Chingleput Thevars in Ramnad; Nadars earlier belonged to Tirunelveli. Similarly, Izhava sub castes belonged to different parts of Kerala – Tiyyars to North, Izhavas to central parts and Tandans to south. The Vokkaligas of Karnataka are concentrated in the Mysore region, Constituting around 29 percent of the population of Mysore State). In Maharashtra Agris are concentrated in one district of Konkan-Raigad, Levy Patils in Jalgaon district of North Maharashtra, Vanjaris in Nasik, Ahmednagar and Bead district. Iravati Carve and Dandekar have given a detailed sketch of the residential pockets of different castes of Maharashtra. The Malis of Rajasthan belong to Jodhpur region, and most smaller castes are concentrated in specific areas. The case of Jats of Western UP is too famous to require a mention. In Bihar, Bhumihars have a concentrated strength in the south while Rajputs have in the western parts. Kammas belong to Andhra region and Reddis to Royalism. One can keep multiplying this list of examples. M.N. Srinivas observed in 1957 "this kind of relationship between a caste and a region is widespread in India...". More specifically, as Wash brook observes in the context of TN, most endogamous Jatis extended over no more than a few adjacent villages.

This association of many castes with specific territorial 'pockets' has produced two political results. One is the rise of 'locally dominant' castes. Srinivas' early use of the term 'dominant caste' was specifically with reference to a small locality or village or group of villages: In his 1955 essay 'The social system of a Mysore Village' Srinivas mentions that "The concept of the dominant caste is important for understanding inter-caste relations in any local area.". Elaborating on the concept in 1957, he uses the phrase 'locally' dominant and then adds, "Occasionally a caste is dominant in a group of neighbouring villages if not over a district or two, and in such cases, local dominance is linked with regional dominance.". As far as 'local dominance'' is concerned, there seems to be a direct link between domination and numerical preponderance. Large size of population, though, has one other implication. Often, a caste has numerical advantage when it also has a high degree of control over resources - at the village level, land. Thus, economic power and size combine to produce patterns of local domination. If one carefully follows Srinivas' account of locally dominant caste in Mysore, two things can be drawn from it: a) this political effect of caste-region interface is an outcome of local hierarchy based on caste and b) Just as dominance of one caste the subordination of other castes is a result of 'localisation'. Castes, which are 'trapped' by circumstances into that locality, face subordination. For some castes, localisation produced opportunities and experience of domination whereas, for others, localisation portends the fate of subordination.

The other, more commonly noted political result of caste pockets relates to electoral politics. Localised pockets of castes have come to mean that candidates of a particular caste will always get elected from certain areas. Our study of Maharashtra gives ample evidence of this: The Maratha-Kunbi caste cluster, which is spread almost over the State, manages to send largest number of MLAs to State legislature irrespective of political upheavals. In 51 constituencies, the elected candidate has always been a Maratha, consecutively for six elections since 1978. In other 19 constituencies also, a candidate of the same caste has been elected since 1978 (these exclude SC constituencies).

Thus, in one-fourth constituencies, the caste of the MLA has been the same since 1978. More specifically, Agris always get elected from Raigad district, Leva Patils from Jalgaon district, Telis from Wardha and Bhandara districts, Lingayats from Solapur and Kolhapur districts, Malis from Amravati district, etc. It is clear that there exists a tendency among parties to match caste by caste in selection of candidates. But the case of Maharashtra suggests that local pockets of castes have an important implication for the phenomenon of regional dominant castes. It is only through such localised pockets that smaller and non-dominant castes get an opportunity to stake their claims to power. If smaller, non-dominant castes are not concentrated in one area, they are not likely to get any representation on their own strength. In other words, localised concentration facilitates a space for contesting the domination of State-level dominant caste. In Uttar Pradesh (UP), the Kurmis and Binds have formed their separate parties, Apna Dal and Pragati-sheel Manavsamaj Party respectively and it has been observed that in 1999 Apna Dal did get large number of votes in five Lok Sabha (LS) constituencies although no candidate of the party was elected. The Binds, one of the more backward castes, rallied behind their caste candidates and made their presence felt in seven LS constituencies. This clearly shows that the Kurmis and Binds can draw upon their localised demographic 'resource' to at least protest against the domination of Yadavs; just as Maratha domination in Maharashtra can be contested through localised pockets of other non-Maratha castes.

Construction of Regional Dominant Castes

Localised concentration leads to localised domination and possibilities of some representation. One the other hand, throughout the twentieth century, certain Jatis evolved into castes spread over a large territory. This gave rise to the regional dominant castes. From mid-fifties onwards, politics in most states centred around one (or two) regional dominant caste(s). In most cases, middle level (often peasant) castes sought to contest the ritual superiority, material ascendance and political domination of 'upper' castes - mostly Brahmans, and in the north, Kayasthas and Thakurs. In the first half of twentieth century, the middle-caste protests took the form of non-Brahman movements in Maharashtra and in the south. In the second half of twentieth century, the middle castes extended their claims to state power at the regional level. In both these phases, the middle castes sought to transcend the localised nature and assume a 'regional' identity.

The non-Brahman movements in Maharashtra and south were concerned with creating 'regional' non-Brahman identities. In Maharashtra, the invocation of Shivaji and Maratha rule by the non-Brahman movement was crucial in bringing various peasant castes together. The movement also facilitated the emergence of Maratha politics on a larger scale geographically. In Tamil Nadu, the non-Brahman movement was built upon the collapse of caste and region. The Brahmans were excluded from Dravid identity. In Karnataka, the Vokkaliga 'Caste' came into being by the fusion of various peasant Jatis such as Morasui, Hallikar, Halu, Nonboard, and so on. In Gujarat, Kanabis of different areas came together in 1931 to constitute themselves as 'Patidars', although, Saurashtra Kanabis are still looked down upon by Gujarat Patidars. Also, the Leva and Kadvi divisions of Patidars are supposed to refer to sub-regional differences. Yet, from 1931 onwards, the 'Patidar' identity has evolved as a regional or State level identity. Similarly, despite internal tensions, Kshatriyas of Gujarat have been organising themselves as one group. Rajputs, who are in the forefront of the Kshatriya mobilisation, are regional differentiated. Gujarat Rajputs being mostly tenants or landless, sought to align with Kolis and Bariyas as Kshatriyas. Saurashtra Rajputs being landowners resisted the claims of non-Rajputs to Kshatriya status. However, over the years, the Kshatriya group of castes in Gujarat as a whole has provided a counterpoint to Patidar politics. The Kshatriya Sabha took an initiative in bringing together Rajputs and Kolis and shaping their politics. The Jats are probably the most regional structured caste. Various Khaps of Jats span specified villages and a meeting of all Khaps, the Sarvakhap meets to discuss common matters. But alongside Khaps, Jats of western UP as well as adjoining Haryana are also organised through the all India Jat Mahasabha, which always extended support to Charan Singh.

It can be argued that both the rise of non-Brahman movement and rise of middle caste as dominant caste in many States follow a similar pattern. A protest against castes ranking high in the hierarchy gives an impetus to these processes. But these processes gain momentum when small, localised, endogamous Jatis overcome their localisation by seeking either in mythology or history a link with a larger territorial unit. They ignore or under play the details about ritual separation and instead amalgamate large groups into their new boundaries, often expanding traditional identities. This development is accompanied by formation of territorial or even 'all-India' associations -Mahasabhas or Mahasanghas-of the newly evolved caste group. A moderately reformist posture follows vis-a-vis intra-caste practices, particularly marriage practices. Since the process is ideologically rooted in opposition to upper castes, the claims of such 'castes' relate to share in power, opportunities for material uplift and amelioration of tradition-inflicted disabilities. Central to this whole process is the journey from locality to region (mostly State). Once a caste crosses the threshold of locality, the possibilities of realising political claims become very real. A geographical expanse allows the concerned caste to make claims on representational basis besides the basis of caste injustice. Besides, association with a larger region allows access to other strategies like regional ideology, cultural-historical claims, etc. In fact, most dominant castes, as also proponents of non-Brahman movement, claim that the heritage of that region belongs to them; they are the true and authentic bearers of symbols associated with the particular region; they represent the culture of that region; the non-Brahmans are true Dravids, the Marathas are bearers of the symbol of Shivaji, Patidars exemplify the essence of Gujarati culture or Jats represent the true Kisans.

Linguistic States

If a caste claims that it represents the regional culture better than others, if follows that there will be a strong connection between such dominant castes and regionalist movements. Today we can talk about dominant castes in the context of States because in most cases, States have been linguistic States. These States constitute a region not only in just a geographical-administrative sense, but in sociocultural and political sense also. Hence the link between dominant castes and States.

One can come across many examples of different patterns of relations between caste and regional identity. These include assertions by upper castes, convenient collaboration between upper and middle castes, the rise of contending middle castes, exclusion of upper castes, etc. Probably the latest example would be Uttaranchal where caste played an indirect role. When the union government decided to implement the policy of reservations for OBCs, stiff opposition came from upper castes of Uttaranchal. It was argued that this region did not have OBCs–at least not in large numbers. From the point of anti-reservation movement, the issues of separate identity of hill people distinct from plains people, came to the forefront. Without much exaggeration, it could be said that formation of Uttaranchal is an instance of upper caste assertion where 'regional' distinctiveness was indirectly claimed on the basis of different caste composition of the population. Historically, such upper caste assertion may be detected in the regional nationalism of Orissa. When the Oriya speaking territory was part of Bengal, Brahmans and Karans came together to shape Oriya opposition to Bengali domination. In 1912, this same social force invoked Oriya nationalism to protest against Orissa's annexation to Bihar. Since the creation of Orissa State, the upper castes have generally retained their hold over the State's politics, culture and economy.

As far as collaboration between upper and middle castes is concerned, Maharashtra can serve as a very good example. Although the non-Brahman movement had considerably villainised Brahmans, the Samyukta Maharashtra Movement (SMM, Movement for united Maharashtra State) saw the Brahmans and sections of Marathas collaborating and mobilising the masses on the basis of regionalist sentiments. This collaboration had a major long-term effect. While formation of Maharashtra State ushered the Marathas into position of power, the sharpness of non-Brahmanism was almost lost. The Brahmans, of course, were not in a position to make a comeback to politics, but nor were they hounded out of politics in particular or the public domain in general. On the contrary, Brahmans continued to dominate culture, education, media, under the benign auspices of 'Maharashtra Dharma. More tangentially, the regional assertion led by Brahmans and Marathas displaced the main focus of non-Brahman movement, considerably weakening anti-caste discourse. Instead, Maratha domination became legitimised in the name of non-Maratha lower castes, identified in the sixties as Bahujan Samaj (majority of masses)–the contemporary OBCs. Caste-Region nexus in Maharashtra, thus, exemplifies the process of one caste legitimating its claims by usurping the claims of other smaller castes of that linguistic region.

Just as the Gujarati-Marwari baniya was the cause of Marathi Brahmans and Marathas coming together, the prominence of Tamil Brahmans resulted into the unity of Telugu Brahmans and non-Brahman castes of Andhra. Although initially the non-Brahman Telugus joined Justice Party, they were not enamoured by the anti-Brahman rhetoric. Instead, their anti-Brahman sentiment got directed against Tamil Brahmans, allowing cooperation among Telugu speaking people on regional-linguistic basis. This weakened the non-Brahman movement in Andhra. It has also been argued that co-option of elite Reddys into the congress facilitated a less acrimonious relationship between Brahmans and Reddys. The examples of Maharashtra and Andhra show that regionalism can intervene in the competition between upper castes and middle castes. Secondly, these examples suggest that regionalism can help a smooth transfer of State level political apparatus to middle castes. Often, in this 'smooth' transfer, radicalism as a basis of political claims is lost and claims of lower castes get a short shrift through symbolic gestures and tokenism.

Starting off from limited collaboration between upper and middle castes, Maharashtra and Andhra Pradesh witnessed the rise and assertion of middle castes. A similar assertion was witnessed in UP once the Jats of western UP became politically organised.The Jat assertion took the form of a demand for 'backward' status. From this, Charan Singh also attempted to project himself as representative of backwards. However, following Jats' association with land, their leaders, Charan Singh earlier and Tikait later, harped on a farmer identity as the identity of Jats in particular but of Gujjars as well. Interestingly, during Takait's farmers' agitation, at one stage, activists of Bharatiya Kisan Union proposed that they should ask• for a separate state for western UP. Thus, the caste of Jats is an example of middle caste assertion at the regional level. Politics of Haryana is another instance of Jat assertion at State level while in Rajasthan; the Jat assertion took the form of a concerted effort to claim backward status. The Jats of Rajasthan deviated from pro-congress politics to vote for BJP in 1999 for the sole purpose of getting their backward status recognised. The Jat Mahasabha decided to vole for BJP once Vajpayee promised to concede their demand.

Many States have witnessed keen competition between two castes or caste clusters. In instances of such competition, the contending castes usually belong to a middle status. In Rajasthan, the competition between the Jats and Rajputs has been rather neatly transformed into a bipolar party situation. Gujarat and Karnataka are the other two examples of contending middle castes but politics there is not organised so neatly. The Patidars of Gujarat rose to prominence in the course of nationalist movement. The Patidar caste also gained control over resources and sought to displace the Brahmans and baniyas from political power. However, Gujarat politics is characterised by congress efforts to attract Kshatriyas, Swatantra Party's efforts to forge an alliance of Patidars and kshatriyas, Patidar alliance with Brahmans and Banias in opposition to reservation and growing affection among Kshatriyas towards the congress. These developments have led to the emergence of BJP as a Patidar force in the nineties. Karnataka witnessed a tussle between Vokkaligas and Lingayats right from the time of creation of a Kannada speaking State. Vokkaligas dominated Mysore area but they felt that if the other Kannada speaking areas were brought together, Lingayats would get an upper edge. Therefore, two Kannada speaking States were demanded. This has been recorded by the State Reorganisation commission Thus, here is an example of a large caste cluster opposing a unified linguistic State for fear of loosing its numerical advantage. Vokkaligas dominated Mysore politics between 1947 and 1956 (when one Kannada speaking State come into being). Since 1956, although Lingayats did get an upper hand, political dominance was shared by these two contending caste clusters till 1972. It was noted by Ambedkar that linguistic States would only lead to consolidation of the 'upper' castes, jeopardising the interests of scheduled castes. In Punjab, for instance, the scheduled castes were not very supportive of the demand for a separate State of Punjab by reorganising the State on linguistic communal lines. Even Sikh untouchable kept away from that demand fearing that a reorganised Punjab would facilitate domination of Jat Sikhs.

Tamil Nadu manifests a pattern of caste region relationship, which is distinct from other States in many respects. It did not throw up any single dominant caste although Vellalas and Nadars benefited the most from the Dravid non-Brahman movement. Secondly, the non-Brahman movement dealt with the issue of regional identity right from the beginning in the second decade of twentieth century. Non-Brahmanism was identified with Dravidianism. While attempting to unite all non-Brahman castes on the Dravid platform, the Dravid movement refused to recognise Brahmans as part of Dravid society. Just as this movement sought to effect a fusion of many non-Brahman castes, it also aspired to build a 'Southern' identity opposed to 'north'. In 1937 the movement led by Periyar waged an anti-Hindi agitation. The logical culmination of anti-Hindi, anti-north Dravidian non-Brahmanism was reached in 1939 when Justice Party demanded 'independent' Dravidsthan. Thus, caste-region interaction in Tamil Nadu strengthened an exclusionary regional nationalism. Further, it also sought to delegitimise Brahmans not only from their superior caste position but also from the scope of regional identity. However, this exclusion did not last long. Once the regional claims were realised through formation of Madras State and non-Brahman claims were translated into an extensive policy of reservations, Brahmans were incorporated as members into the Tamil society. Brahmans are accommodated as ideologies and legitimises of the regional legacy of Dravid movement. It is indeed ironical that a strong non-Brahman movement, through its regionalism allowed a re-entry of the Brahman caste both into the elite and into the political arena in general.

In the nineties, the political assertion of the Vanniyars marked the political scene in Tamil Nadu. However, Vanniyars have a long history of separate political organisation. In spite of the efforts of non-Brahman movement to bring together all non-Brahman castes, Vanniyars were organised through Tamilnad Toilers' Party and Common-weal party. Although DMK supported the latter in 1952 with a view to defeating Congress, Kamraj was successful in bringing both Vanniyar parties into congress fold. Another backward caste, the Thevars, backed the forward bloc for a long time. These details suggest that in spite of very vocal non-Brahman movement, Tamil politics did not throw up any single middle caste around which State politics could be organised. Even the large and dominant castes in a given district, do not account for more than one fourth of the population of that district. Probably, this peculiar situation led to sustained recourse to militant regional nationalism, particularly by the Dravid parties. However, as Wash brook observes, this Dravidianism 'neutralised many of the caste based issues of conflict that dominated Tamil Nadu politics in the first half of the twentieth century'. Perhaps, those contradictions, which Dravidianism sought to push under the carpet of regionalism, have resurfaced in Tamil Nadu with Dalit – OBC conflicts and Hinduisation of some backward castes. In the absence of any particular caste group as central to politics, Tamil politics took on an exclusionary character: exclusion of Brahmans, Aryans, North Indians and less explicitly, exclusion of even Adi Dravids.

Ruptures

Demography, agrarian relations, political economy of post-independence period combined to produce the strong linkages between region and caste. In particular, the different patterns of caste relations gave substance to region as a political category in States like Andhra Pradesh, Tamil Nadu and Karnataka. These developments established the feature of region specific dominant castes in most parts of India. This feature came under stress at two stages when certain types of caste politics attempted to cross the regional boundaries. Both these ruptures in the established pattern of caste-region equation came as opposition to upper as well as newly dominant castes in various regions. In the interplay of caste and region, Dalits and OBCs were/are often excluded or marginalised. Therefore these sections attempted to breach the happy coincidence of caste and region by pursuing the project of all-India 'Dalit politics' and all India 'OBC politics'.

At the intellectual level, Ambedkar was the first to grasp the implications of 'linguistic States' in terms of the consequent marginalisation of Dalits. But even before the issue of linguistic States came up, Ambedkar had realised the need to mobilise Dalits at an all-India level if they were to stake claims to political power. Thus, in the 1940s, abandoning the Independent labour party, he formed the Scheduled Castes Federation (SCF). On the one hand, through SCF, he sought to intervene in the negotiations for India's freedom and wrest minimum share in power. On the other hand, the SCF was also visualised as a major opposition (of SCs) to the upper caste dominated Congress in the period immediately after independence. The failure of the SCF notwithstanding, it is important to note that Ambedkar saw the unfolding of a process of conflict between SCs and upper castes and also believed that a united all-India instrument of SCs can alone take on the task of contesting upper caste claims. Although he once again veered to a more broad based party in the form of Republican party of India (RPI), this party came to be identified as Dalit party and could not sustain the all-India claims which Ambedkar had always insisted upon. In the mid-eighties, Kanshi Ram formed the Bahujan Samaj Party. This party is seen primarily as the party of Dalits. The BSP has made its presence felt outside of UP, in Punjab, Rajasthan, Madhya Pradesh, etc. And hopes to spread to Maharashtra and Karnataka also. In this sense, BSP manifests an all-India ambition and an awareness that upper caste domination has to be fought at the all-India level. Thus, initial lead by Ambedkar and more contemporarily the formation of BSP, challenge the caste-region nexus. They seek to problematic the caste question at the national level and force a solution through intervention in national politics. The approach of BSP is more instrumentalist than Ambedkar's approach. The former believes that only in a period of instability can Dalits force their entry into the network that controls national state apparatus. Therefore, unity of Dalits at all-India level and unity between Dalits and other disadvantaged castes are seen as strategies for shifting power away from Brahmanical (Manuvadi) sections of society towards the Bahujan Samaj (the masses).

In the mid-sixties, Lohia argued that 'backward castes' constitute a majority and they should be given a fair share in power. This was reminiscent of the arguments of non-Brahman movement in the south and in Maharashtra.

Although backward caste politics gradually emerged in UP and Bihar, it was only in the nineties that it became an issue at an all-India level. After the agitation against reservations in Gujarat and Bihar in the late seventies and early eighties, the agitation in many north Indian States on the issue of reservations for backward castes underlined the simmering conflict between what Lohia had described as forwards and backwards. Since the controversy over recommendations of the Mandal commission, sections of backward castes showed awareness about reservations and share in power. This resulted into large-scale mobilisation of backward castes dramatically catapulting protagonists of backward castes into positions of power.

These developments had two effects. Firstly, the political discourse in the country as a whole, changed considerably. 'Social justice' became the central term around which this discourse was constructed. Such a construction facilitated the entry of caste question onto the all-India political scene rather than remaining State-specific. Backwardness of certain castes and consequent political disadvantage was no more seen in State-specific contexts; instead it was conceived as a phenomenon following from Brahmanical Hindutva and domination of national politics by upper castes. As such, taking over power at Delhi was seen as the remedy. Secondly, 'OBC' (as the backward castes came to be known) claims were quickly recognised by the various political parties. In particular, the BJP exhibited remarkable adaptability by introducing changes in the social composition of its key workers in Maharashtra, Madhya Pradesh and UP. Most other parties, too, underwent the process of 'Mandalisation', the Congress probably being the slowest and most reluctant, However, even the Congress manifested awareness of this factor in Rajasthan, Gujarat, Madhya Pradesh, etc. In other words, OBC politics did not throw up any all-India instrument—any party claiming to be representative of OBC interests - instead; it forced certain changes in political parties and in politics in general. Social composition of many legislatures changed during the decade of 1990 to 2000. Reservations for OBCs became less controversial and also became part of the policies adopted by various parties. At least at the formal level, parties conceded the claims of OBCs in terms of share in power. Politics of backward castes became an all-India phenomenon.

In the case of Dalit politics, one can witness a steady fragmentation in the post-Ambedkar period. This fragmentation takes place at three levels: party factionalism, State-specific distinction and intra-Dalit fragmentation. The RPI could never project itself as a united party of Dalits. Various rival RPI parties emerged competing with each other. The absence of a single effective political instrument resulted into the fragmentation of Dalit votes also. On the other hand, concrete political issues faced by Dalits took a State specific turn. In Maharashtra, for instance, the issue of 'renaming' a university after Dr. Ambedkar remained an emotive issue for Dalits for over a decade.

In States like Bihar, atrocities by various middle castes became the main concern of Dalits. In Tamil Nadu, frustration with Dravid politics, non-accommodation in the regional identity and conflicts with lower OBC (Thevars and Vanniyars) has been shaping Dalit politics at State level. The long history of Marxist-Leninism agrarian struggles in Andhra Pradesh has produced Dalit radicalism in that State. Such State-specific situations are inevitable because of differences of levels of Dalit consciousness and differences in the political economy at State level. This means that the arena of conflict and the response by Dalits varies from State to State. The main adversaries of Dalits are also not necessarily common across States. The voting preferences of Dalits are also likewise shaped at State level. Dalits of

Rajasthan, Gujarat, MP, Maharashtra tend to vote in favour of Congress Dalits of W. Bengal and Kerala prefer the left fronts in those States. In UP, the BSP has established itself as the main party of Dalits. In Bihar the BJP led alliance gets more Dalit votes than RJD of Laloo Yadav, probably because of the JD faction led by Ramvilas Paswan who allied with BJP. Similarly, in Karnataka also, the BJP alliance gets more Dalit votes than the Congress.

A further complication regarding the Dalit situation needs to be noted. While ideologise of Dalit politics prefer to project 'Dalit' as one social force, even at State level, Dalits do not constitute a unified social force. For various reasons, the State-specific reasons not the least, internal stratification among Dalits of different States in a reality. In Maharashtra, the (ex) Mahar Dalits are seen as politically advanced, the Matang and Chamar Dalits resist the 'Mahar domination'. The Mala-Madiga dispute in Andhra Pradesh reached such a proportion that the State government decided to divide reservation between these two communities.

The Dalits of Bihar other than the Paswans do not look upon Ramvilas Paswan as their leader. In Karnataka, the large group of Madigas demand that the reservations for Dalits should be split; giving a fixed quota to Holey as and other Dalits which will allow Madigas to enjoy 90 percent of the reservations. In UP, Jatavs are seen as politically powerful and getting all advantages. The Balmikis and Passes feel deprived, In West Bengal, the Namsudras and Rajbanshis have their 'pockets' in Faridpur, Khulna, Jessore and in north Bengal districts of Cooch Behar, Jalpaiguri, Dinajpur, respectively. These two communities are seen as taking advantage of the reservations. All these details suggest the difficulty in organising an all India Dalit politics, Only by intervening in the State level political process; Dalits stand any chance of affecting politics.

The case of OBCs is not very different. To begin with, the 'OBC' category, though a convenient short hand for a large mass, is not very definitive. It includes, formally, castes included by governments in the State lists of other backward classes. As such, the question, 'Who are the OBCs?' Is itself a controversial one. Inclusion or exclusion in the OBC list is often a matter of politics for those castes who have attained enough political skills. It is a common experience that castes would press for inclusion in the list of OBCs–Jats in Rajasthan, Vokkaligas and Lingayats in Karnataka are two famous examples. This gives the mass called OBCs an amorphous character but moreover, produces tensions within the OBCs between more backward and less backward sections. Needless to say, all these factors develop in the backdrop of State specific situations. Except on general issue of reservations, all OBCs cannot be mobilised on an all-India level. Therefore, in the nineties, on the heels of Mandal controversy, many OBC organisations rallied round the issues of reservations. However, when it came to organising the nuts and bolts of OBC politics, the State specific situations asserted themselves. Thus, Janata Dal, which sought to bask in the glory of its pro-Mandal stand, witnessed internal bickering: the Orissa unit under Biju Patnaik distanced itself from the Mandal platform while the Karnataka unit under Hegde made its displeasure about 'Mandalisation' known to national leadership. Both State units felt it unnecessary to have V.P. Singh as a campaigner.

Much mobilisation on the Mandal platform took place in UP and Bihar. The politics of backward castes did not articulate in a substantial manner in Orissa and Andhra Pradesh. It did not have much relevance to Tamil Nadu since that State has had a long history of non-Brahman politics. In Karnataka, Congress under Devraj Urs had earlier mobilised the OBCs. Therefore, in the nineties, the Mandal platform did not evoke much enthusiasm there. In

Maharashtra, the small OBC castes cannot match the strength of the Maratha-Kunbi caste cluster. This leaves the States of Uttar Pradesh and Bihar as the main theatre of OBC politics. In a sense, the so-called all-India claims on behalf of OBC politics are based on politics in north India where the caste issue has emerged onto the political scene rather late. Thus the phenomenon of OBC politics is much more relevant to UP and Bihar than to other States.

The internal stratification among 'OBCs' is another matter where State specific issues come to the forefront. As noted above, identification of certain castes as OBCs, is itself State specific. This is borne out by the case of Jats and more effectively, by the case of Lingayats of Karnataka. The State government went on appointing commission after commission in order to resolve the issue of whether Lingayats are backward or not. Even when the issue of identification is resolved, the question of share of different castes/caste groups continues to pose a challenge. In the field of reservations, most States seem to be veering to the strategy of classifying OBCs into two or three groups and assuring them separate 'quotas' of reserved seats. This classification, again, takes place in the context of State politics as has been exemplified by the decision of BJP-led UP government.

Besides reservations, the question of 'share' involves claims over power. Various backward castes not only want to be 'included' in the apparatus of power, they hope to use power to their advantage and if possible, gain controlling share in power. Negatively put, backward castes push for exclusion of the upper castes so that complexion and content of power would change substantively. These claims bring a double conflict into focus. On the one hand there is a conflict between the already established dominant caste and the aspiring caste/caste group. The constellations of these conflicts are again State specific because the ideological battle line of upper vs. Backward translates differently in each state. In Maharashtra, for example, when Maratha domination is sought to be challenged, Kunbis, who are included in the list of OBCs, would pose a problem. The 'Maratha' caste cluster includes Kunbis. Thus, the battle is between the dominant caste and a section of OBCs vs. Other OBCs. In Karnataka, the OBCs compete with Lingayats who themselves have been claiming inclusion in the list of OBCs. Political economy of each State produces patterns of dominance in accordance to which these battle lines get defined. The other conflict involves the aspiring castes themselves. When the Brahmanical castes were displaced, on the whole, only one caste (or mega-caste bloc) sought to replace them at the State level. With democratisation penetrating larger sections in the contemporary period, a peculiar development has taken place. Just as the established dominant caste is about to be displaced, more than one claimants emerge to stake claims over power. This does not allow any single caste to stabilise in power. The recent history of UP and Bihar shows that among the OBCs, when one caste surges ahead 'on behalf' of OBCs, its representational claims are delegitimised by competitors from within the OBC fold. The Yadavs of UP and Bihar, who claimed in the nineties that they were leading the OBC revolution, have been challenged by non-Yadavs in both the States. Both these conflicts are reflected in the party preferences of OBCs. Backward castes in different States vote differently and within a State, they are often divided among different parties.

These claims and counterclaims have, in fact, further regionalised politics during the nineties. The unprecedented rise of regional parties in the nineties has been singularly unassociated with 'regionalism.' Caste occupied the centre stage of political discourse and regional parties became the vehicle of this often incoherent and fractured discourse.

The discussion so far suggests that the two 'ruptures' have been in fact, ideological formulations, which seek to challenge upper and middle caste domination by unifying all lower castes. This formulation has not been able to assert itself as a concrete principle around which politics is organised. The objective caste situation varies from the presupposition that all 'lower' castes have same experience of political exclusion/marginalisation. Also, the subjective identification of various castes with politics of 'lower' castes varies both caste wise and State wise. As a result, instead of being able to rupture caste-region nexus, both Dalit politics and OBC politics have themselves yielded to this nexus and become regionalised.

State as a sociolinguistic region is a very convenient unit for caste to operate. Although many instances can be shown where small castes intervene in local political process, effective role of caste can be detected at the State level only. At the same time, castes cannot assume all-India identities and caste alliances cannot be easily forged at the all-India level. The political salience of caste increased only after castes transcended the 'local' identities and by forging new 'mega' caste identities became significant players at 'regional' level. However, this process probably stops at the regional level. Efforts of Kurmis to forge an alliance with Kanbis and Kunbis did not succeed. The Yadavs of UP and Bihar follow separate politics from each other. Even in the case of Jats, though the Jat Mahasabha exists, Jat politics in Punjab, Rajasthan, Haryana and western UP cannot be clubbed together. Thus, patterns of caste politics cannot be replicated in different regions nor can they become all-India in their reach or spread. In this sense, caste as a factor in modern politics, has become well entrenched or rooted at the regional/State level. It retains its existence and relevance at local level while as the preceding section argued, existence of caste at all-India level or across States is more ideological than concrete.

The relevance of caste at the regional level flows from the following four factors: a) Social relations of hierarchy are identifiable at the regional level, some times even sub-regional level. The fact that somebody is a Brahman simply places that person in an ambiguous position of superiority outside the region where that person belongs; but in the region where S/he belongs, a fine tuning will be made depending upon whether that person is a Chitpavan or not. To take a concrete example, being a 'Maratha' carries meaning only in the context of Maharashtrian society. The Marathas will be simultaneously seen as farmers, warriors, ex-land lords, etc. Rather than their ritual status either as Kshatriyas or shudras, the historically constructed and materially experienced identity as 'powerful' will be quickly brought into focus. Regional associations also allow myths and prejudices / stereotypes operate as markers of ranking. These do not make sense outside of that region. Therefore for most castes, a hierarchical ranking is relevant only in specific region. Social relations based on these assumptions of hierarchy shape social attitudes about claims of power by different castes, giving way to competition or caste conflict. Thus, when non-Brahmans of Maharashtra were claiming separate representation in early twentieth century, the Brahmans derided them by asking what business ordinary agriculturists had in the legislature. All the same, Brahmans accepted -though unwillingly - Maratha entry into the political arena. In contrast, the claims of Dalits are not so silently accepted. Conflicts at the village level take place when Dalits in a village try to capture the village panchayat.

Historically, many middle castes and some times even lower castes seek upward mobility in their ritual / social status. Studies of caste point out that this happens when a caste achieves material strength. It must be noted that the process of gaining upward mobility is strictly region-based. It is not so merely because one particular caste in one region attains material strength. It is also because, the claims are made regional and accepted / legitimised regional. Such 'mobile' castes even change their caste names and this is accepted in the given region. Transformations from Kunbi to Maratha or Kanabi to Patidar are of course famous. Similarly, the mobility of Nadars (erstwhile shanars) of Tamil Nadu has been well documented (Hardgrave, 1969). Other examples include the awadhias, mahatos, jhanuks taking up Kurmi identity, gwalas, gopes, becoming Yadavs, Padayachis of Tamil Nadu becoming Vanniyar Kshatriyas, etc. Such mobility facilitates horizontal unity among castes. These developments are 'internal' matter of the concerned regions and often indicate the emergence of regional powerful caste groups. Thus, changing 'definitions' of caste status give rise to patterns of competition in each region.

In the course of competition among castes, regionalism or sub-regionalism can be very easily invoked. Regionalism servers either of the two purposes. It can project one caste/ group as inheritor, protector or representative of regional identity and pride. This way, an assault on that caste or caste group is easily seen / shown as assault on regional pride and self-respect. Implicitly, this also means that advancement of the interests of that caste constitutes regional advancement and therefore, the demands of the caste group can be transformed into demands for regional development. To be sure, regionalist politics is shaped by many factors. Once caste and region are identified, the interests of caste can be projected as regional interests. Alternately, regionalism can be invoked to construct a broad social alliance of different castes. In this second formulation, distinct caste identities are supersede by the ideology of regionalism. This often helps the already dominant castes.

Apart from the ideology of Regionalism, region can provide yet another advantage to the 'dominant' castes. Every dominant caste seeks to legitimise its dominant position on the basis of some ideological argument. Region as the social unit having a common cultural-linguistic context automatically forms a basis from which justification of domination can be adduced. Alternatively, arguments by the dominant caste make sense within the region. Thus, Jats' claim of being Kisans or Haryana Jats' claims for a martial tradition appeal the people in those respective regions rather than outside the regions. Similarly, Lingayats' claims of reformisms in the orthodox Brahmanical Hinduism become relevant only in the Kannada speaking region. The ideology of 'Maharashtra Dharma' justifying the Brahman-Maratha leadership or the Bhadralok ideology of elite domination also has similar region-specific appeals. Thus, region is the unit at which caste domination is sought to be legitimated. In the 'dominant caste thesis', the emphasis on numerical strength has deflected attention from both the contents of domination and the ways of attaining domination. Mere numerical strength would not lead to domination; claims of 'high' status usually accompany numerical strength. But a high ritual status is not the only 'ideological' component. 'Dominant' castes employ a more complex set of ideological arguments in order to win the 'dominant' position and we argue that region provides a helpful playground for working out these arguments.

It follows from this that any counter hegemonic assaults on the dominant caste would emanate from a similarly regional situated arguments. In Tamil Nadu, the non-Brahman movement sought to delegitimise the Brahmans by suggesting that Brahmans are not true Dravids. In Maharashtra, too, Phuley's argument turns to this point when he argues that Brahmans-Aryabhats-came from outside-Iran. But more forcefully, Phuley brings in the imagery of non-Brahmans as 'natives' by virtue of their association with agricultural activity. If both, the claims of domination and challenges to them, are regional situated, region becomes a theatre of caste conflicts and configuration caste with political and economic dimensions.

Given the mutually reinforcing relationship of caste and region in contemporary Indian politics, it is argued here that challenges to concrete instances of caste domination (as distinct from notions of caste superiority) can meaningfully rise at the regional level. This would further strengthen the links between caste and region. These links produce region/State-specific configurations of caste, which fit the region's political economy. In the light of this argument certain trends may be noticed. These trends indicate the possible ways in which caste is likely to be constructed in Indian politics. In a way the following discussion engages caste itself as a 'region' or sphere.

In many parts of the country, instead of neat polarisation, 'more complicated and fragmented constellations of power' emerged. Thus, in the arena of caste politics, on the one hand new 'dominant castes' have emerged on the scene; at least many new 'ascendant' castes have come to the forefront. On the other hand new equations have emerged. The most noted one is the BJP led equation of upper castes and lower OBCs in Uttar Pradesh. In Maharashtra, the Charmakars and Matangs have been veering away from Congress and RPI, preferring the Shiv Sena and BJP. The Bahujan Mahasangh in Maharashtra has been trying to forge an alliance of Dalits and OBCs. These new equations do not necessarily follow a similar pattern across the States. But one common factor needs to be noted. In the emerging alliances traditional boundaries of ritual status are seldom followed. Alliances would be formed depending upon the perceptions about which caste/caste group monopolises resources (including reservations). Beside, the choice of allies is often ad hoc, contingent upon who are perceived as adversaries. Underneath this contingent nature of alliances, there seems to be a consideration of two factors. One is consideration of material factors. Castes/caste groups tend to ally when their material interests do not clash —or in fact compliment—each other. The other consideration is share in power. When an alliance is likely to obtain some power for the caste, such an alliance becomes acceptable. Both these considerations go beyond simple alliances based on ritual status—alliances are not made simply because castes occupy a common status as Shudras or Dalits.

Secondly, and partly following from the above, there is a disintegration of caste 'blocs' of Dalits and OBCs. The trend seems to be moving in the direction of 'ethnicisation' of caste. One factor contributing to this process seems to be the pressure of modern reformist discourse delegitimising vertical structure of caste hierarchy. In this background, caste survives, if not as upper-lower then, as 'different' groups having different culture, ritual, 'histories', etc. Thus, caste becomes a 'community'. But ethnicisation of caste has other reasons as well. One is that small castes still find no place in calculations for electoral purposes. They may be relevant in constructing caste 'blocs' but do not receive the benefits either politically or materially. In such situation, organising a single caste as one community becomes useful for gaining some access to power and resources. It is not necessary for us here to accept this logic but that seems to be a factor influencing the process of formation of single caste organisations.

Such organisations function simultaneously as sociocultural associations, pressure groups pursuing immediate material concerns of the caste and vehicles of caste elites for riding into the power structure. Although it is tempting to look at such caste organisations as a political resource, they imply localisation of caste. Such localised ethnicisation is bound to entrap castes both into local boundaries and issues of culture, identity, history rather than of material advance

Thirdly, after reaching a high point through 'Mandlisation', caste appears to be reaching a dead end in terms of its mobilisation potential. At one stage (in the fifties) caste interests were advanced through regional mobilisation. In the next phase, (late seventies onwards) mobilisation took place on the issues of reservations for OBCs (in Bihar, Gujarat) followed up by the Mandal issues and claims of the leaders of OBCs for power sharing. The nineties have witnessed acceptance of OBC reservations as State policy. During the same period, various parties incorporated OBCs resulting in the changed composition of representatives. These developments have meant that the space to be occupied by caste issue is bound to shrink except for further competition among OBCs for greater share in power. At the local level, provision enabling reservations to SCs, STs and OBCs in local government bodies, has ensured that no effective mobilisation can take place and no party will take interest in such mobilisation. This does not imply that caste has lost relevance but that as an organising principle of politics, caste may have reached its limits. Like region earlier, caste may have to search for catalysts that will revitalise the emotive and mobilisation capacity of caste as a sphere of politics. In other words, the capacity of caste to construct new social forces and make politics revolve around them has become rather suspect.This obviously raises doubt about the democratising potential of caste as a sphere. The caste-region nexus meant that just as domination of a caste or caste group would get established, it will be challenged by rival groups or by newly emerging lower sections. However, if our assessment that caste alliances are ad hoc and less mobilisation is correct, then the arena of caste politics is likely to lose the potential to democratise Indian polity.

7

Political Sociology of Poverty

Any attempt to comprehend the Indian experience of poverty eradication through construction of welfare state and political mobilisation in the last five decades needs to recognise that India is a post-colonial society where a) the colonial heritage in the statecraft, and b) the legacy of anti-imperialist national movement in the political community and political culture, play critical roles. This relationship between the 'colonial past' and the 'democratic present' is very significant for understanding the changing nature and orientation of the state and society in the context of poverty in India since independence in 1947.

It is also necessary to remember the differences between the rise of democratic polity in Europe and the emergence of welfare state in India. To quote Jawaharlal Nehru, a pioneer of democratic socialism during the anti-colonial movement between 1920s and 1940s and the first Prime Minister of free India from 1947 to 1964, "In Western countries, full blooded democracy with adult suffrage came to the people very late, in the Twentieth Century". They had in the meantime profited from the Industrial Revolution. They got the resources before they gained democracy so that when the demands came for better living conditions they had the resources to fulfil them.

The results of the Indian endeavour of poverty eradication are not satisfactory in international terms. But the specific and comparative aspects of India help us in contextualising the Indian project of nation building through planning for a poverty free welfare state and a socialistic society between 1950 and the end of the millennium. They also provide insights about the international standing of India in the community of nation-states, where the largest democracy of the world is found to be lagging behind Sri Lanka, China and Indonesia. The Indian political process is being shaped by continuous interaction between the imperatives of interest group dynamics, democratisation, decolonisation and nation-building. These four factors provide the basis for legitimacy of the post-colonial state. They also give content to the concepts of 'public welfare' and 'national interest'.

As a consequence, there were several changes in the state and society relationship in India during this period, which have caused i) decline of politics and rise of economics, ii) rise of dominant caste coalitions and decline of upper caste hegemony, iii) erosion of national constitutional consensus and rise of centrifugal movements, iv) stress on decentralisation along with weakening of the process of centre-formation including planning, v) rise of movements of erstwhile marginalised categories of people e.g. women, depressed classes like Dalits and Scheduled Tribes, ethnic groups, etc., vi) rise of 'region' instead of 'nation' as the operational category of the party system, vii) weakening of the middle class political culture as well as rise of crime-politics nexus with patronage from the neo-rich classes, and viii) rolling back of the welfare state under the pressure of global forces of liberalisation.

The relationship between poverty, politics and state has continued to play a significant role in the political sociology of independent India as it did during the colonial era. The issue of poverty came onto the State's Agenda through different processes after the end of colonial period. First there was a constitutional process which was a consequence of the nationalist discourse where "Community Development" and decolonisation were presented as two sides of the same coin. It created an appropriate focus in the making of the constitution of independent India.

Secondly, there came a developmentalist phase which gained importance during the drive for promoting capacity building among the rural cultivators through "Land Reform" in the 1950s. The idea of 'poor peasant' became unacceptable in the discourse of development under the Congress Raj. Of course, it failed to include the landless labourers in its conceptualisation of recasting the rural power structure through 'land reforms'.

Then came the phase of nation wide rural agitations in the 1960s. The newly created propertied peasants started asking for increase in state's patronage and, the popularised peasants urged for radical transformations to ensure jobs, wages, dignity and justice. The states' responses were crystallised as the "Green Revolution".

Finally, India became market oriented in the 1980s as state-centric initiatives became counter productive at worst and ineffective at best. There was a new faith in market mediated system management among the propertied sections of Indian peasantry as well as the urban propertied classes. It was termed "the era of liberalisation". Rolling back of the state did show some results in the first few years. But the bifurcation of the propertied and the popularised was reinforced by the end of the 1990's. Thus there are new indications of pressures about continuity of chronic poverty and creation of 'new poor' in the context of liberalisation. In fact, it may be appropriate to suggest that after the 'first generation reforms' or 'structural adjustments' and the consequential rolling back of the state, there is resurfacing of poverty in rural and urban sectors resulting in unrest and conflicts. This rediscovery of poverty is accompanied by re-focusing of the political agenda of the India political sectors including political parties, trade unions, peasant bodies and other major components of the power pyramid in India.

In short, the link between active political mobilisation (of varying intensity) and rural transformation has played a vital role in shaping the destiny of the poor. The state and its legislative and bureaucratic apparatus have been a secondary factor. Hence the change in the national economic scenario with reference to peasants in general, and poor rural masses in particular has been primarily a political phenomenon.

Constitutional Content

The conceptualisation of poverty free welfare state in India has been accomplished in two phases: i) the period of national movement for freedom from foreign rule, and ii) the making of Indian Constitution through a constituent assembly. The Indian national movement was able to focus the attention of the masses on growing poverty and the recurrence of famine which was due to defective policies of the colonial government. It was the view of leading public men like Dadabhai Naoroji (1825-1917), M. G. Ranade (1842-1901) and R. C. Dutt (1848-1909) that the solution to the social and economic backwardness of India could not be found through the British Government's policy of laissez-faire, but that only a national government which actively promoted development by direct government action could bring about improvement in living standards. The resolutions of the Indian National Congress from 1929 onwards emphasised the need "to make revolutionary changes in the present economic structure of the society and to remove grave inequalities in order to remove poverty and ameliorate the condition of the masses". The resolution of 1931 underlined that "political freedom must include real economic freedom of the starving millions" and elaborated the fundamental rights which should be included in the Constitution of free India to provide a basis for it. It was followed by the formation of a National Planning Committee with Jawaharlal Nehru as Chairman in 1937 on the initiative of Subhash Chandra Bose as the President of Indian National Congress.

A complementary process of conceptualisation was contributed by the constant debate about the nature and priorities of the state in post-colonial India among the Gandhians, socialists, communists, radical humanists and other ideological groups in the national movement. The charter of demands and agitations by various class organisations of peasants and industrial workers provided the guidelines for the approach of the national movement to poverty and its eradication from villages and towns of India. In fact the decisive push to the colonial rule came with large scale peasant mobilisation in the last decades of the freedom movement.

The concept of welfare state became the lodestar of the Constituent Assembly of India. It made its impact on the thinking of the leading lights of the Assembly who wanted to secure 'justice – social, economic and political' for all citizens of the Republic. They were clear that without social and economic democracy, political democracy had no meaning in a poor country like India. The Preamble, Fundamental Rights (Articles 12 to 35), Directive Principles of State Policy (Articles 36 to 51), and the special provisions for Scheduled Castes and Tribes and Backward Classes (Articles 330 to 342) are significant dimensions of the Indian constitution from this perspective. They have created the imperatives for progress from political democracy to social and economic democracy which means "working for a certain measure of well-being for all".

The Preamble of the Constitution commits the state to the development of a free society based on the dignity of the individual in which there would be equality of status, opportunity and justice. The state has to endeavour towards harmonisation of interests between individuals, groups, and between individuals and groups on one hand and interests of the community on the other. The Preamble places justice above the other principles of liberty, equality and fraternity.

The values embedded in the Preamble are elaborated in the Fundamental Rights and the Directive Principles. The Fundamental Rights have covered all the traditional civil and political rights included in the Universal Declaration of Human Rights. There are six broad categories of the fundamental rights:

1. The right to equality (Articles 1, 15,16,17, and 18)
2. The right to freedom (Articles 19 and 21)
3. The right against exploitation (Articles 23 and 24);
4. The right to freedom of conscience and free profession, practice and propagation of religion (Articles 25 to 28);
5. The right to minorities to conserve their culture, (Articles 29 and 30); and
6. The right to constitutional remedies for the enforcement of all these Fundamental Rights (Article 32).

The Directive Principles of State Policy are basically inspired by the concept of a welfare state. Article 37 declares that the Directive Principles are "fundamental in the governance of the country" and that "it shall be the duty of the State to apply these principles in making laws". However these are non-justiciable. Article 38 defined the aim as follows; "The State shall strive to promote the welfare of the people by securing and protecting as effectively as it may a social order in which justice – social, economic and political, shall inform all the institutions of the national life". In Article 39, stress was laid on the right to adequate means of livelihood, equally for men and women; equal pay for equal work for both men and women; conditions of work ensuring health and strength, protection of children and youth against exploitation and against moral and material abandonment. It is also laid down that the state should ensure that 'the ownership and control of the material resources of the community are so distributed as best to subserve the common good'; and that the 'operation of the economic system does not result in the concentration of wealth and means of production to the common detriment'.

Furthermore, the duty is enjoined on the State that 'it should, within the limits of its economic capacity and development, make effective provision for securing the right to work, to education and to public assistance in cases of unemployment, old age, sickness and disablement, and in other cases of undeserved want' (Article 41). The state should also provide for 'securing just and human conditions of work and for maternity relief '; and 'security to all workers - agricultural, industrial and otherwise - a living wage, conditions of work ensuring a decent standard of life and full enjoyment of leisure and social and cultural opportunities' (Articles 42 and 43).

Particular stress is laid on special assistance to the weaker sections of the people, including the Scheduled Castes and the Scheduled Tribes and the other weaker sections with a view to promoting their educational and economic interests and to protecting them from social injustice and exploitation. With regard to rural economy, Articles 40 and 48 enjoin the application of modern scientific methods to agriculture and animal husbandry and the implementation of programmes and improvements through self-governing Panchayats. Promotion of cottage industries on an individual and cooperative basis is mentioned in Article 43.

Article 45 fixed a definite time limit during which the State would endeavour to provide free and compulsory education for all children until the age of fourteen years from the commencement of this Constitution.

The above principles were given a more precise direction when Parliament accepted the socialist pattern of society as the objective of social and economic policy in December 1954. In 1976, the 42nd Amendment Act added certain new directives to the Constitution of India:

a) that children are given opportunities and facilities to develop in a healthy manner and in conditions of freedom and dignity;

b) that the operation of the legal system promoted justice on a basis of equal opportunity, and in particular the State provided free legal aid in cases of economic and other disabilities;

c) that the participation of workers in management of industries is secured; and

d) that the environment is protected and improved and the forests and wild life are safeguarded.

Anti–Poverty Mobilisations

The direction of post-colonial polity in India was evolved during the three Five Year Plans between 1951 and 1965 in the context of peasant mobilisation and other protest movements. Self-reliance was the basic goal of the Nehruvian agenda under the hegemony of the Congress Party. It is important to recognise that the response to the peasant movements in the Fifties by the nascent post-colonial state and the hegemonic ruling party, Congress, was:

a) to eliminate intermediaries for creating a broad based proprietary class in the village who took interest in promoting agricultural production;

b) to facilitate infrastructure facilities through a variety of inputs and concessions;

c) to ensure minimum price support through purchase of agricultural products by public sector corporations.

The impact of these reforms created two opposite results .

1. It promoted the expansion of owner-cultivator class which came from upper and upper-middle strata of the caste system; and

2. It created insecurity among tenants, agrarian workers, and semi-bonded tillers due to increased pressure of market forces upon the agricultural sector.

Agriculture was changing into a 'market oriented, cash based, and profit claiming occupation, causing deterioration of the situation of the poorer strata in rural India. In short, there was emergence of commercialisation, pneumatisation and market/profit oriented production due to the state's plans and programmes between 1950 and 1965. The number of agricultural proletariat grew at an exponential rate. But the strategy of "incremental democratic modernisation" encountered a series of problems from 1963 onwards, which made the Nehruvian approach obsolete in many spheres of State policies. A new set of national issues regarding food scarcity, increase in prices, national defence, foreign dependence, economic stagnation, and regional inequalities generated a cumulative stress between 1963 and 1967. As a consequence a new agenda called Ten Point Programme came into being.

The dilemma of dependent accumulation and declining dominance of the Congress Party created a shift in India's direction of development. The slogan of "Jai Jawan - Jai Kisan" (victory to the soldiers - victory to the peasants) symbolised the new thrusts of the State. The 'sixties saw a wave of disenchantment with the entire planning process'. There was visible growth of discontent in the late sixties.

Between anti-Congressism and Naxalism, there was a great range of activism and mobilisation all over rural and urban India. This coincided with the 4th Five Year Plan and the 5th Lok Sabha elections. Despite the intelligence and experience, Indian planning had gotten into a rut. The results were disappointing. It was time, therefore, for the planners to ask themselves whether the things they had been trying to do were really correct. Thus the period of the 4th Five Year Plan was marked by political weakness and economic anxieties. The poorer sections of the society and the pro-poor political formations were making impressive moves for collective action. It was the era of second wave of land conflicts after the late nineteen forties and early fifties.

The second wave of rural mobilisation in the sixties contained two distinct groups of rural masses. There was a movement launched by the newly emerged proprietary classes constituted by rich farmers and middle peasant proprietors. The communists called them 'Kulaks' which was an exaggeration of their economic capacity. They were also named 'Bullock Capitalists'. Their mobilisation was aimed at securing increased patronage from the state. They did not come into conflict with the interests of the industrial and commercial urban proprietary classes. It was led by peasant based regional political formations which came into existence in 1960s in several provinces of India. Many of them got amalgamated into a national political party, Bharatiya Lok Dal, led by Charan Singh in 1974.

Another movement was launched by the agrarian poor with increasing prominence of the agricultural workers. The movements of the rural poor in the 1960s and 70s were centred around a combination of economic, social and political issues. Economically, they were in need of security of employment, minimum wages, rights over a certain share of the produce, distribution of surplus lands, and reduction and liquidation of debts. Socially, they were agitated about violation of legally acquired rights, gender discrimination, violence and humiliation by upper caste/class men and public officials. Politically, they were attempting to resist repression and terror of the upper and middle castes who had recently turned into land owning classes in rural India. They found a nexus of the newly emerging proprietors and the nascent post-colonial state. They also felt that the state was paying more attention to the proprietary classes as it considered them as the agents of development. They were led by the left wing parties like Communist Party, Communist Party (Marxist), Socialist Party and Communist Party (Marxist-Leninist).

The rural poor in the 1960s comprised o a) popularised peasants, b) agrarian workers belonging mostly to the depressed castes and tribes and other marginal groups, and c) a large section of women. Their struggles gave rise to uncomfortable questions regarding the usefulness of the socioeconomic framework of developmental planning adopted after independence. They exposed the limits of the development policies as they had failed to improve the condition of the poor even after three Five Year Plans, and a generation long political stability in the form of Congress rule. They brought the nation 'face to face' with the continuity of unimaginable forms of exploitation and oppression of the rural poor. It was an indictment of the post-colonial state and its patronage to newly propertied castes and communities in the name of development and nation building since 1950s.

Politics of Poverty Eradication

The issue of poverty became a central question during 1964-71. It was triggered by the Lohia-Nehru-Nanda debates in

Lok Sabha in 1964 about the nature of poverty and its extent. It became recognised as a political imperative of democratic governance as a large number of people were still trapped in economic settings which forced them to live below the levels of subsistence. It was legitimised by the slogan of Garibi Hatao (eliminate poverty) by the Congress Party under the leadership of Indira Gandhi who routed most of the anti-Congress political parties in the general elections of 1971-72. It appeared that after a long wait, the moment had arrived for fulfilling the dreams of Swaraj by creating an egalitarian social order based upon economic self-reliance and democratic social transformations.

It is another matter that the electoral mandate was not translated into effective socioeconomic steps due to a variety of reasons – domestic as well as international. Low savings, limited investment, sluggish industry, a steep rise in the money supply and a sharp decline in agricultural production were the prominent features of economic administration. The problems were further complicated by international 'price revolution' and a phase of 'stagflation' in the world economy. In 1973-74, inflation had turned everything topsy-turvy. It was coupled with the crisis of leadership within the Congress Party at the Central and the provincial levels. The situation gave rise to multiple political pressures, student-youth movements and working class protests which culminated in a national movement against the failures of the government in terms of checking corruption, controlling price rise, creating employment, and providing relief to the poor. It was led by Jayaprakash Narayan, one of the founders of democratic socialism in India and was supported by socialists and others. After a phase of indifference and tolerance, the ruling party declared the State of Emergency due to the intensity of internal protests. At the same time, it had to adopt a 20-Point programme of welfare measures to show that even in a situation of crisis, the government is committed to continue the process of relief and welfare.

Inspite of these adversities, the change in the orientation of the political community and the policy makers in the early 1970s, was remarkable. According to C.T. Kurien (1979), "When a small group in the Planning Commission proposed in 1962 that the central concern of our planning has to be the removal of poverty as early as possible, it was a novel and consequently very suspicious idea. But within a decade it had become not only the accepted economic dogma, but also a highly articulated political programme". The new mood was reflected in the Fifth Five Year Plan. For example, Towards An Approach to the Fifth Plan (1974-79) proclaimed "there would seem to be a conspicuous element of historic inevitability in a direct approach to reducing poverty becoming the main thrust of the Fifth Five Year Plan. The Plan is being formulated by a government that has massive mandate from the people, both in the Parliamentary elections of 1971 and the state elections of 1972, on the basis of a programme whose centre piece is Garibi Hatao. The homogeneity of the Governments at the Centre and most of the states during the formulation and early years of the Fifth Plan is guaranteed. This should enable bold and imaginative proposals being put through on the basis of an enlightened national consensus."

Thus, the Fifth Five Year Plan was a landmark due to its special thrust on creating the maximum possible dent on the low end poverty while ensuring that the country moves one more step in the direction of economic independence. It was also remarkable due to its recognition that the Indian economy had reached a stage where larger availability of resources makes it possible to launch a direct attack on – a) unemployment, b) underemployment, and c) poverty. It clearly admitted that the twin causes of poverty are i) underdevelopment, and ii) inequality and it is inadmissible to ignore or underplay either factor. Therefore, it pointed out that the problem of poverty couldn't be overcome within the foreseeable future by efforts in one direction only.

India entered the phase of liberalisation in 1980s under Prime Minister Rajiv Gandhi and the process continued inspite of change in leadership at the level of the Prime Minister. The year 1991 was the beginning of an explicit phase of rolling back of the state due to the imperatives of liberalisation. Relatively higher growth was recorded during 1980-2000 and particularly during 1990s which was a decade of structural economic reforms. It also showed decline in poverty and improvement in health and literacy levels of the people of India. But India continues to suffer from high levels of illiteracy, high rate of infant mortality, high incidence of disease, disability, and malnutrition even after half a century of freedom and democracy. Allocations for health and education have been only 4.1 per cent of the GDP (1996-97) which was lower than several developing post-colonial countries like Malaysia and Sri Lanka.

The sociological consequences of the liberalisation-globalisation drive have been summarised by Yogendra Singh (2002) as state versus market dilemma. He argues that the extent to which the power of market increases and expands, the significance of the state as a supreme political institution, undergoes major alterations. Idealistically, some protagonists of the market even anticipate the end of the notion of sovereignty. For societies such as India, where nation-building has still not reached the level of integrative maturity, such fears of the end of sovereignty or a threat to it due to unhindered play of the global market force cause not only acute anxiety but also pose a challenge.

Poverty and Conflict Lines

Analysis of poverty-politics relationship needs understanding of power dynamics and conflict patterns because inequality of access to resources generates processes of conflict in the context of interests between the included, the marginal and the excluded sections of any society. The conflicts make reform and strategies and processes of poverty elimination imperative. This requires a multi-dimensional understanding of the interconnections of the spheres of state, market and community and the interrelatedness of the local, regional/ national, and global domains. All these need special attention in exploring the challenges of chronic poverty.

Poverty and the poor are always associated with (a) resourcelessness, (b) choicelessness, (c) insecurity and (d) deprivation which creates incapacities in the pursuit of dignified life in a given society for a person, household, group or community. Furthermore, those suffering chronic poverty also suffer several simultaneous disadvantages including gender, age, caste, ethnicity, location, etc. According to A.R. Desai a new class configuration has emerged as a direct consequence of the conjunction of peasant mobilisation and government measures over the last few decades. It contains the following categories of rural population:

a) *Rich Farmers and Land lords* owning 15 acres and more, possessing 50 per cent of the total land and constituting 7 per cent of the population,

b) *Middle Farmers* with 5 to 15 acres of land, possessing 30 per cent of the total land and constituting 19 per cent of the population,

c) *Poor Farmers* owning between 1 and 5 acres, possessing 17 per cent of the total land and constituting 30 per cent of rural population, and

d) *Agricultural Labour* without land or owning less than 1 acre of land, possessing about 2 per cent of the total land and constituting 44 per cent of the population. The national picture also suggested presence of five categories on the basis of household income with 10, 19, 12, 192 and 420 million persons in them

The population below poverty line (1993-94) has two major features: i) Overwhelming presence of the Scheduled Castes and Scheduled Tribes population, ii) Assam, Bihar, Madhya Pradesh, Maharashtra, Orissa and Uttar Pradesh were found to be above the national figures of population below poverty line where as West Bengal, Tamil Nadu and Karnataka were within the proximity of national figure.

The relation between the resourcelessness of the chronic poor and settings of conflict is rooted in the quest for security and dignity through ending of choicelessness of the chronic poor in a variety of ways. Such households, loaded with a complex set of disadvantages and assetlessness, are usually involved in subsistence type of activities which get them poor returns. Since their earnings are meager, they survive on small amounts of borrowed money or they are forced to suffer from hunger. They are mostly unable to change the power relationships and there are no mechanisms of grievance redressal. The powerful local forces, in conjunction with the corruptible sections of the state apparatus, manipulate and misappropriate the common resources and pubic funds which create further helplessness and frustration. It has been termed as 'web of poverty' with centrality of continuous alienation of the people trapped in it and occasional confrontation in the society. This could lead to social tension, despair or a combination of both.

The increasing visibility of a "fault line of deprivation and conflict" is a consequence of such a setting in India today. It is visible in a number of districts of Uttar Pradesh, Bihar, Orissa, Jharkhand, Chattisgarh, Madhya Pradesh, Andhra Pradesh, Assam, Tripura and Arunachal Pradesh . In the terminology of bureaucracy and media, these states have a number of districts which are conflict prone due to the effective presence of "Naxalites", "Senas" (private armies), externally aided "extremists", and separatists. Despite the variation of labels, all of them indicate presence of deepening social conflicts around issues of deprivation and poverty. It is another matter that the pattern, form and objectives of mobilisation of discontent are defined by: a) social cleavages, and b) the political conditions of the states.

At the same time, the growth of economic, social and cultural disequilibria, rooted in chronic poverty and resourcelessness is a cause of national concern. It affects governability as well as social and economic development. It also promotes increasing togetherness between poverty and political violence, which causes legitimisation of crises and invites use of police force to control its proliferation. If the state gets tough, it creates "martyrs" and myths. If the state remains tolerant and mild it faces escalation of violence and disruption of law and order. The feeling of political and economic exclusion invites entrepreneurs of violence. Therefore, the advocates of violence enjoy such settings where a large number of persons are found to be living on the margins of the economy and society.

The issue of chronic poverty and conflict is associated with the persistence of insecurity in the life setting of a person, household, group, or community. Human security suggests that people can exercise their choices in pursuit of secure and dignified existence in society safely and freely. It has two main aspects; a) safety from chronic threats such as hunger, disease and repression, and b) protection from sudden and hurtful disruptions in the patterns of daily life whether in homes, in jobs or in communities. According to the United Nations approach, the many threats to human security, differing for individuals at different times, fall into seven categories:

1. Economic insecurity,
2. Food insecurity,
3. Health insecurity,

4. Personal insecurity,
5. Environmental insecurity,
6. Community and cultural insecurity,
7. Political insecurity

These insecurities and threats can affect people everywhere. Famines, ethnic conflicts, social disintegration, terrorism, pollution and drug and human trafficking can no longer be confined within national borders. Some global challenges to human security arise because threats within countries rapidly spill beyond national frontiers, such as greenhouse gases and trade in drugs. Other threats take on a global character because of the disparities between countries -disparities that encourage millions of people to leave their homes in search of a better life, whether the receiving country wants them or not. And frustrations over inequalities in incomes and political power often build up into serious civil conflicts between groups, whether ethnic, religious or social.

Those suffering chronic poverty are caught in the midst of a set of basic conflicts which perpetuate their insecurity through 'capability poverty', resourcelessness and choicelessness. Some of these conflicts are silent and invisible e.g. the crisis due to ecological factors. Several others are visible as demonstrated by the sufferers of class, caste, ethnic gender, religious (communal) and racial discrimination. Together they contribute towards the continuity of chronic poverty in a cumulative manner by sustaining the logic of power relations and marginality of the chronic poor in the discourse of power. They envelop the institutions and processes of state, market and community.

The most visible and loud conflicts in the context of chronic poverty are found to exist around a) class, b) caste, and c) tribes (ethno-regional issues).

Class-based Conflicts

The class based conflicts have industrial and rural spheres. Both kinds of conflicts are sinking into marginality in terms of their impact. In the industrial arena, economic liberalism has led to flexible labour market policies like subcontracting, outsourcing and the engagement of temporary and part-time workers in core activities of the labour process. India's integration into the global economy and far reaching structural adjustment for it in the 1990s has weakened the strategic position of the trade unions. According to the Labour Bureau figures of the Government of India, there has been a decline in the number of man-days lost due to strikes and lockouts in 2000 compared to the figures for 1992. Furthermore, more man-days are lost due to lockouts than strikes.

In the rural arena, 298 million persons constitute the labour force engaged in agricultural and allied activities which is 79 per cent of the total work force. A majority of the work force engaged in agriculture consists of small and marginal farmers and agricultural labourers. About 80 per cent of total rural labour households (over 30 per cent of total rural households) are agricultural labour households. Of them, the Scheduled Castes and the Scheduled Tribes constitute nearly 50 per cent. In general agricultural labourers suffer from seasonal unemployment, job insecurity, poverty, indebtedness, and lack of access to productive assets. They suffer from lack of social security and inability to form their own organisations. The economic reform measures have worsened their condition due to recent hike in the prices of food grains. There is also decline in their position in comparison to their counterparts in other activities in both rural and urban areas inspite of absolute rise in their wages. The hope of 'land to the tillers' generated before independence has receded beyond the realm of realisation.

Situations of direct and indirect conflict between the poor in rural and urban spheres of the economy and the propertied sections and the state are spreading in various parts of the country. A cycle of conflicts, control and suppression and re-emergence with added strength appears to occur in significant number of rural areas in most of the poor states. The issues causing conflict in rural areas are security of employment, minimum wages, share in the produce, securing of surplus lands, reduction and liquidation of debts and violence by the land owning classes. There are also tensions and clashes in the context of sexual and cultural oppression and political denial. In fact the year 2000-01 has been a difficult one for rural economy. Income has declined. Agricultural production has been sluggish; food production has declined by almost 5 per cent. Suicides persist. The rural development programmes have recorded declining growth. A combined view of the situation of the rural labourers, marginal farmers, and the rural sector's contribution to the national economy gives a depressing picture. It is marked by limited growth of high and upper middle-income households, increased regional disparity, and the general tenor of the National Agricultural Policy which ignores the agricultural labour and marginal farmers and may accentuate the preexisting inequities with possibilities of social strife and disenchantment .

Table 1. Suicides of Farmers in Karnataka (from 1-4-2003 to 8-09-2003)

Districts	*No. Of Suicides*	*Districts*	*No. Of Suicides*
Bagalkot	7	Belgaum	13
Bangalore (Rural)	8	Davangere	30
Bangalore (Urban)	1	Bellary	9
Bidar	4	Chitradurga	6
Hassan	15	Gulbarga	3
Chamarajnagar	3	Bijapur	1
Haveri	14	Dakshina Kannada	–
Uttara Kannada	–	Gadag	6

Dharwad	8	Koppal	7
Mandya	22	Chickmagalur	6
Raichur	2	Tumkur	9
Shimoga	18	Kolar	6
Mysore	8	Kodagu	2
		Udupi	--
		Total	208

The situation in the urban settings is diffused. But there is growing discontent due to the increasing belief that the current development policies do not have the capability to create the framework within which the conditions of the poor might improve. In urban India slums are growing at the rate of 5 per cent. 24 per cent to 28 per cent of the urban population in Karnataka, Maharashtra and Delhi lives in slums as a fall out of poverty and deprivation. This provides a setting of recurring conflict between the urban poor and the Government Machinery as they are created out of 'illegal encroachment of government land'. There is high frequency of inter-community strife and conflicts. In fact violence is forced upon them as a way of living. The slum dwellers work mostly in the unorganised sector (in jobs requiring less skill and training). Their incomes are quite insufficient to enable them to lead a dignified life and enjoy basic rights.

Paradoxically, the condition of the working class in the organised sector is found to be drifting from resistance to hopelessness and less conflict in the context of the new economic policies. The new labour laws have diminished the space for class conflict in the organised sector of industrial India. There are three major events which have contributed towards the decline of the 'class power' of the organised workers in the last decade – i) disinvestment in the public sector, ii) retrenchment and contractualisation of the private industrial establishments, and iii) global recession in the industrial sector. An overview of the changing labour relations scenario may be presented by comparing the figures of industrial disputes in India in 1992 and 2002. It is seen that the figure has declined from 1714 to 413. There was also phenomenal decline in the number of workers involved in disputes and man days lost in the last decade. It needs further enquiry to be able to understand the implications of declining number of trade union strikes in an era of economic transition in favour of entrepreneurs.

On Caste Oriented Conflicts

Caste based conflicts are increasing in the context of enlargement of the capacity of two blocks - the political power of the dominant castes and political mobilisation of the Dalit castes or the Scheduled castes. It is causing conflict in the electoral arena, labour market, and civil society.

Table 2. Industrial Disputes in India since 1992

Years	*Disputes*	*Workers Involved*	*Man days Lost*
1992	1714	1252225	31259000
1993	1393	953867	20301000
1994	1201	846429	20983000
1995	1066	989695	16290000
1996	1166	939304	20285000
1997	1305	981267	16971000
1998	1097	1288923	22062000
1999	927	1310695	26787000
2000	771	1418299	28763000
2001	674	687778	23767000
2002	413	523594	15697000

The quest for political power among the Scheduled Castes around the provisions of 'Reserved seats' in legislature has been a major feature of Indian Democracy. They achieved a significant breakthrough with the growth of coalition politics in 1969-71. The making of OBC and Dalit Vote Banks was a singular contribution of socialist politics which contributed towards a 'Silent Revolution' in the era of "Green Revolution" At the same time there is marginal increase in the percentage of Dalits below the poverty line during the privatisation-globalisation regime from 44.7 per cent in 1987-88 to above 48 per cent in 1993-94, which is significantly higher than estimates for the general population (39 per cent). The literacy gap between the SCs and rest of the population has also remained more than 17 per cent between 1961 and 1991. According to the Census of 1991 more than 80 per cent rural Dalit women were found to be illiterate. They were also sufferers at the hands of the dominant castes in different parts of India. Between 1995 and 1997, a total of 90,925 cases were registered between with the police under different categories of crimes and atrocities against the Dalits. Nearly 70 per cent of all the offences were reported from the BIMARU states - Bihar, Madhya Pradesh, Rajasthan and Uttar Pradesh.

Mass murders of the Dalits by dominant castes in Andhra Pradesh and Bihar has underlined the depth of conflict between the castes in rural India over the last several years. According to an estimate, the period between 1990 and 1999 witnessed 35 instances of caste-based massacres, the total number of victims being about 400. More than 350 of those killed were from among the lower castes. In short the issue of caste-class convergence in the context of chronic poverty in an era of dominant caste democracy and liberalisation-globalisation is promoting anti-Dalit caste violence in rural areas and decline in the opportunities for the Dalits in the urban-industrial economy.

According to the Sixth Report of the National Commission for Scheduled Castes and Scheduled Tribes (1999-2001), the extent of crimes and atrocities on persons belonging to Scheduled Castes is much higher than those on Scheduled Tribe. The cases of atrocities on Scheduled Castes are about 6-7 times more than STs, though the population of SCs is only twice that of STs. Uttar Pradesh (6122), Rajasthan (5623), and Madhya Pradesh (4667) have reported highest incidence of crime against Scheduled Castes. These three states account for 65.4 per cent of the total cases of atrocities on SCs in the country during 1999.

One of the most obvious reasons for so many attacks on SC men and women is related to the refusal of the SCs to work without dignity and appropriate wages. The assertiveness of these castes for higher wages, freedom of choice of work and endeavour to achieve mobility as cultivators are among the most frequent reasons for atrocities against SCs.

Tribes and Conflicts

The Tribal dimension of chronic poverty is most pronounced in the context of conflicts and movements. They constitute 8 per cent of the population. 83 per cent of them live in the area between West-Bengal and Gujarat, 12 per cent in the North eastern region, 4 per cent in Nilgiri Hills and 1per cent in J&K and Himachal Pradesh. It is believed that confrontation has been the quintessence of the situation in the tribal areas after the rise of 'state' as a formal system of political and administrative authority. The ever-increasing exploitation of the tribals and elimination of their lands led to revolts and rebellion in many parts of India. 'Leave them alone' (or 'exclusion') as in the hills of North-East and 'light' administration (or 'partial exclusion') elsewhere was the response of the Imperial Regime in the face of determined resistance to their advancement and consolidation. The dawn of independence ushered in a new era of high hopes and soaring aspirations with an ebullient nation committed to the ideals of democracy, equity and social justice. The cause of weaker sections, particularly the tribal people, was accepted as a national task with clear premises and constitutional commitments. But the hopes were belied. The tribal people in fact faced regression as the personalised administration gave way to an amorphous faceless system. Influx of immigrants, alienation of their lands and underdevelopment are three major problems of the Tribal communities.

According to the Report of MPs and Experts (Bhuria Committee Report, 1995), "Notwithstanding the rhetoric of the past four decades, on account of absence of effective democratic decentralisation at even district levels, demands and agitations for separate states in the country have taken root in Jharkhand, Bodoland, Uttarakhand, etc. Iniquitous policies and actions and economic imbalance have led to resentment among the deprived regions. Assertions on the basis of region, ethnicity, languages, etc. Have been made. They have come to feel that without the political power of a state, they are not able to claim their rightful due".

In economic terms, the Scheduled Tribes (ST) have been found to receive a total household income of Rs. 19,556 and a per capita income of Rs. 3,504, which are 76 and 78 per cent respectively, of the national average. Both incidence and intensity of poverty are higher among the Scheduled Tribes in comparison with the national average. They have recorded a literacy level of about 40 per cent in comparison to an all India average of 54 per cent. Only about one-fourth of ST women are literate. Literacy levels are extremely low for STs in Bihar, Rajasthan, Uttar Pradesh, Madhya Pradesh and Orissa.

More than 87 per cent of the total population has been depending on agriculture for their livelihood, supplemented by collection and sale of minor forest products. However the percentage of cultivators has declined from 68 per cent to 54.5 per cent in 1991 and the proportion of agricultural labour is increasing correspondingly. Vast areas of tribal lands have been acquired under the Land Acquisition Act and still are being acquired for industrial and infrastructural development. Out of the total 213 lakh displaced persons (1951– 1990), 85.4 lakhs are Scheduled Tribes. They constitute about 40 per cent of the total number of displaced persons. From the total 83.8 lakh rehabilitated persons, 21.2 lakhs i.e. 39.4 per cent belong to STs. Dams (41 lakhs), mining (6.5 lakhs) and industries (3.8 lakhs) are the major causes of tribal displacements. A land mark judgement of Supreme Court in the case of Samatha vs. The State of Andhra Pradesh and others (11th July, 1997) has placed a check on this. The Supreme Court has ordered that government lands, forest lands and tribal lands in the Scheduled Areas cannot be leased out to non-tribals or to private companies for mining and industrial operations.

Social insecurity among the Scheduled Tribes, particularly the ST women, is also a cause of concern. Out of nearly 4000 cases of atrocities committed against Scheduled Tribes in 2000, there were 391 cases (9.8per cent) of rape. The incidents of atrocities on Scheduled Tribes were highest in Madhya Pradesh (1756), followed by Rajasthan (1221), Gujarat (367), Orissa (335), Andhra Pradesh (178), Maharashtra (171), Tamil Nadu (105) and Kerala (81). The direct and indirect relationships between the efforts of STs to move out of exploitative dependencies and the acts of atrocities is a relevant question for further systematic enquiry. At the same time, it may be concluded that the extreme forms of exploitation and violation of civil rights that exist in areas such as Chattishgarh and Jharkhand have turned them into places of long standing insurgency. Another reason for the rising violence in forest areas is encroachment by migrants who are taking over the land of the local people. This causes conflict over resource use.

Such a profile of tribal India makes it obvious that the tribals are the worst sufferers of resourcelessness and choicelessness as well as the most disenchanted section of the Indian population in post-colonial India. They are leading components in a variety of mobilisations in the last two decades including movements for environmental protection (Narmada Bachao), states reorganisation (Jharkhand, Uttarakhand, and Chattisgarh), political separation (the separatist movements of the North-Eastern Tribals), and resistance to globalisation (Kashipur). Such conflictual mobilisations have brought the issue of chronic poverty of tribal India to the attention of national media and policy analysts in recent years thereby prompting the governments to come forward with a variety of anti-poverty measures and development packages. Creation of three new provinces Jharkhand (out of Bihar), Chattisgarh (out of Madhya Pradesh) and Uttaranchal (out of Uttar Pradesh) is a major effort to address the challenge of tribal alienation and unrest. It also marks the beginning of assertiveness for tribal autonomy and dignity in the Hindi belt of India.

Trajectories of Poverty, Politics And Conflicts

India is a vast economic, cultural and political area with diversities. But the policy of the elimination of rural intermediaries and land reforms adopted after independence caused "reshuffling" of class relations in the countryside. The transformation initiative was a response to long peasant mobilisations during the freedom movement for addressing poverty. However, it performed a dual function: i) elevating the richer section of the tenants into owner class which broadened the base of the proprietary classes who take active interest in agricultural development for maximising profit, and ii) growth of marginal farmers, 'back door' tenants and proletarianised labour due to new tenurial system. The change has promoted intense competition among the newly emerging proprietary classes. They are also contending with the demands and struggles of the rural masses which are being steadily pauperised and marginalised.

On the other hand, evolution of democracy has contributed to the metamorphosis of major caste groups including the Dalits into competing associations beyond the ascriptive principles of the caste system. There has been eruption of caste organisations with intense activities in nearly all sectors of the emerging economy and in the political processes which is a response to the imperatives of the democratic political system. The changes in the caste system have the following characteristics: i) There is simultaneous weakening of the upper castes and strengthening of intermediary agrarian caste promoting a dominant caste coalitional complex in the political space, and ii) The lower caste who are also major occupants of the lowest economic labels, are getting regrouped to counteract the adverse effect of new economic and political processes. This section has been offered preferential facilities ('reservations') and opportunities in elections, education and government services. It has contributed to making the lower castes vocal.

The impact of new constitutional projects for the abolition of the caste system and restructuring the class system through affirmative action in response to the modern India has been uneven and complex. It has contained and resolved some of the most prominent issues causing conflict in the society. But it has also given rise to new competition and conflicts due to realignment of political, social and economic groups. Therefore it is relevant to provide a glimpse of the paradoxical relationship between economic, social and political structures and processes in the context of poverty and social conflict by presenting the cases of West Bengal and Bihar.

West Bengal

West Bengal and Bihar are neighbouring states which belonged to the Bengal Presidency in the colonial era. Their political economy was organised through zamindari system. Both had strong peasant movements, trade union activities and anti-poverty political formations. Both were sites of intense rural conflicts and urban movements in the post colonial decades. Both were ruled by the Congress Party between 1952 and 1967 and both got their first non-Congress governments in 1967. But they followed different trajectories in the last four decades since 1967 that resulted in major reforms in favour of poorer sections in West Bengal. Today, there is no major industrial or agrarian conflict in West Bengal.

First, we look at the politics and social change in West Bengal which along with Bihar and Orissa had the highest proportion of population below the poverty line. West Bengal has been plagued by high population density, industrial stagnation, rural conflict and economic decline in the 1980s. But these conditions were changed through reorientation of the government policies via social mobilisation and political alliances which was steered by a left front coalition in office since 1977.

High levels of unrest in rural areas for effective implementation of agrarian reforms, radical trade union movements for better wages, cheaper food items, education, health and transport facilities and emergence of a leftist political front were the outstanding features of West Bengal since late 1960s. The movement of the small and marginal farmers accelerated after the foundation of first United Front Government in 1967. It culminated into the famous Naxalbari revolt and the birth of Naxalism (or Maoism and Marxist-Leninist Communist Party). The United Front Government was removed by the centre and the peasant protests and 'Naxalite' activists were ruthlessly suppressed under President's Rule. But within a decade, there was Left Front Government in Kolkata after sweeping out the Congress regime at the centre and the state in 1977.

Agrarian reforms and organisation of local governance system were given top priority by the Left Front Government. This resulted in a sustained period of conflict containment and political stability for decades after 1977. For example, the number of riots came down from 11,702 (1977) to 3,899 (2000) whereas there was no substantial change in the scene of Bihar or All-India.

How was this accomplished? There was redistribution of more than 9,13,000 acres of land amongst 19,93,660 households which covered a large proportion of the rural population of the landless and land-poor households. Decades old demands of tenants-farmers organisations for higher crop shares, security of tenures and legal status of tenancy agreements were accepted through "Operation Barga". It gave relief and strength to the vulnerable and exploited sections of rural Bengal, which accounted for 1.44 million share croppers in the state.

West Bengal is an example of generating conducive setting for poverty eradication and conflict resolution through a combination of reforming production relations and instruments of local governance. It has been achieved on the basis of political mobilisation and electoral strength around 'peasant unity'. Now West Bengal is engaged in negotiating the path beyond the agrarian agenda for satisfactory progress in universalisation of health care and basic education. In other words the record of West Bengal shows positive correlation between poverty and conflict on one hand, and conflict, political change and economic reforms on the other.

Bihar

The history of rural unrest and agrarian movement in Bihar goes back to the Kol and Bhumiji insurrections of 1831-33 against the newly established colonial administration in Chota Nagpur and adjoining areas. The peasant movements in the regions to the north and south of the Ganges, from mid 19th century to the present day, have been regularly studied due to their significance for the peasants and agricultural workers of India. It proved to be the nucleus of All India Kisan Sabha as well as the Indian National Congress, Socialist movements and Communist movements in the twentieth century. But Bihar failed to institutionalise any change in the exploitative agrarian structure after independence. While the introduction of democracy with universal adult franchise, raised the expectations of poor peasantry, changeless agrarian system of Bihar soon became a victim of the dual failures -- continuity of extremely exploitative relations and growing stagnation in the agrarian economy.

The stagnation in agricultural production around 5 per cent annual compound rate of growth between 1969–70 and 1983–84; which was lowest in India, not only caused depeasantisation but also led to declining fortunes of the rich and middle peasants. It had widened the scope of conflict between the rich and middle peasants and the rural proletariat. The inability (as well as resistance) to pay minimum wages to the agricultural workers (most of whom belong to the Scheduled Castes) had turned them towards the new revolutionary leadership for their fight for wages. As a consequence violent clashes had become a general phenomenon in Central Bihar. According to official sources, there were 463 and 590 violent clashes in 1998 and 1999 respectively. It seems that the state machinery had become marginalised as most of these killings were carried out by armed groups belonging to peasant communities and the marginal and landless poor. These Senawars had become more prominent than the electoral and other institutional forms of conflicts and competition.

In short, Bihar is a case where politics has failed and there is absence of effective local governance apparatus, like Panchayats, Police Station and Block Development Offices.

The larger political system has been affected by corruption at high places. It has led to criminalisation of politics and politicisation of crime as a cumulative consequence which is indicated in the increasing number of kidnappings in Bihar. The incidents of kidnapping have increased from 580 in 1972 to 2711 in 2000 – a five-fold increase in the state of Bihar whereas it was 769 and 926 in 1972 and 2000 in West Bengal.

Bihar is also the state with the largest proportion of persons below the poverty line as 26 out of 37 districts are among the most backward districts in the country. Therefore, it should not be a surprise if Bihar is affected by increasingly violent settings of economy, polity and society as the state system has consistently failed to respond to poverty affected groups and social conflicts around poverty problems despite major changes in the governments between 1967 and 2002 at the provincial and central levels.

Limits of Planning and Reservation

It may be useful to have an overview of the relationship between poverty and politics, as articulated through the two processes of planning and reservation during the last five decades of post-colonial India. Poverty in India, whether it is measured in terms of income or nutritional levels, is concentrated among certain occupational classes and social categories in both the rural and urban sectors. Most of the rural poor are found among (i) peasant cultivators with very small holdings, and (ii) agricultural workers from the Scheduled Castes and the Scheduled Tribes. The causes of poverty in urban settings are mostly underemployment in various occupations with low productivity occupations such as porterage, insecure employment and low real wages in some industries. Migrant workers are prominent amongst the urban poor. Furthermore, as none of the urban poor are producers of food and have to buy a part of their total requirements in the open market, they are extremely susceptible to rising food prices. In addition, the urban poor suffer from extremely bad conditions of housing, water supply and sanitation.

There has been a steady decline in the proportion of people below poverty line from about 55 per cent in the mid-1970s to 36 per cent in 1993-94 and to around 30 per cent in 2001, but their actual numbers have been rising. At the same time it is true that food insecurity and income poverty have been brought on the state's agenda through series of mobilisations, as well as natural calamities, in the last five decades. It also shows that poverty continues to create severe adversities in the lives of the rural people, particularly the small and marginal farmers, agricultural labourers and artisans and has a high incidence among the Scheduled Castes and Scheduled Tribes in rural as well as urban areas. It is regional concentrated in seven states – Assam, Bihar, Orissa, Uttar Pradesh, Madhya Pradesh, Maharashtra, and West Bengal. But there are extremely poor districts in several other states as well.

As a consequence, food security and poverty eradication have been the key objectives of the Indian planning strategy. A number of direct poverty alleviation programmes were introduced from 1971-72 after the massive electoral success of the Congress led by Indira Gandhi in 1971-72. Integrated Rural Development Programme (IRDP) and Training for the Rural Youth for Self Employment (TRYSEM) were two key components of the poverty related programmes in this period.

Poverty was a major theme in politics and planning since 1971-72. But the crisis of implementation, non-viability of projects and slow economic growth created several weaknesses in it by the mid 1980s. It caused a shift from income generation to human development oriented schemes. It also exerted pressure for de-bureaucratisation of the poverty related programmes through peoples' participation via Panchayat Raj institutions and NGOs.

With a paradigm shift in the late 1980s to the early 1990s, the issue of poverty lost its significance in the political discourse of India. This decline in importance was reflected in the Election Manifestos of major Indian political parties where the idea of growth and governance found more prominence than poverty alleviation and expenditure on employment generation. Expectations from private sector activities were a new component of the planning strategy in the era of liberalisation.

Rise in the frequency of violent conflicts in the regions suffering from poverty is becoming a significant feature of the political landscape of India since the shift of political attention away from the challenge of poverty. Land reforms, removal of illiteracy and malnutrition, encouragement of shelter construction for the homeless, and social mobilisation for breaking down the caste barriers which have trapped the SC and ST population in rural areas are some of the neglected themes in the national politics of India since the inauguration of the phase of rolling back of the state from the economic sphere.

At the same time it may also be highlighted that the engagement with poverty alleviation through planning has experienced four kinds of limits- economic, administrative, political and international constraints. The Anti-Poverty Programme of today's India involves 1 percent of GDP or 6 per cent of the Central Budget, 55 per cent of which is allocated for food subsidy or Public Distribution System (PDS), 35 per cent is allocated for Rural Works Programme, and around 5 per cent is provided for Self Employment Programmes. But there are severe resource problems due to the compulsions of allocating 50 per cent of the available national resources for debt servicing and 25 per cent for defence needs. The challenge is compounded by the continuing mal-functioning of local self-governance mechanisms and bureaucratic inefficiencies in the poverty affected areas. Politically, the situation has worsened due to the rise of crime politics nexus and more importance being accorded to politics of identity over politics of 'common interests'. Internationally there are growing pressures upon the Indian state for 'rolling back'. It is further complicated by the presence of hostile neighbours who are not keen on promoting regionalisation in South Asia Economic Zone.

Reservation was the second most important political intervention in meeting the challenges of poverty and deprivation. But this has remained more symbolic than substantive. Let us first have a look at the constitutional provisions for safeguarding the interests of the SCs and STs. Article 17 (abolition of untouchability), Article 23 (prohibition of forced labour), Article 45 (universalisation of primary education), Article 46 (promotion of educational and economic interests of SCs and STs), Article 330 and 332 (proportionate reservation of seats in the Lok Sabha and the State assemblies) and Article 335 (appointment to services and posts in Union and State services), are the most important provisions of the constitution of India in the context of protective measures for the amelioration of the conditions of the weaker sections of Indian society.

In the case of the Other Backward Classes (OBCs), there has been the use of Article 16(4) of the Constitution of India to address the problem of inadequate access to representation in the services under the state. It was activated in 1990 on the basis of the recommendations of a Second National Commission on Backward Classes (also known as Mandal Commission) with the caution of the Supreme Court that the benefit of reservations will not be extended to persons/sections falling under the category of 'creamy layer'.

This system of special treatment to underprivileged sections involves three types of preferences.

1. Reservations, which provide easier access to valued positions within important social institutions like legislature, government services and academic institutions. It is also used in land allotments, housing and other scarce resources.

2. There are expenditures of government resources on behalf of the beneficiaries like scholarships, grants, loans, legal aids etc.

3. There are special protections, such as measures to protect "untouchables" from discriminatory treatment.

Given such an institutional approach, the policies of reservations have created a symbolic power for all those who belong to the SCs (16.7 percent of the population), STs (8 per cent) and OBCs (52 per cent). It has also given recognition to the need for national reorientation for such sections of the population who are found to be trapped in a 'web of poverty' due to conjunction of social, economic and political deprivations and discrimination over a period of time.

The reservation policy regime has promoted a progressive outlook in the society because it legitimises integrative representation and re-distributive mobilisation. Besides, it has to be recognised that the exclusive emphasis upon 'timeless' system of reservation in jobs and legislature has bypassed the poor of these categories. There has been evolution of blocks of vested interests in such category of the beneficiaries of reservation in the past five decades.

The majority of the Scheduled Castes and Scheduled Tribes are agricultural labourers. Because of economic compulsions, their children have to go to work when they should be in schools. Children who labour, lose education and therefore employment opportunities when they are adults. Without the means of income for want of education, they in turn may continue to send their children to work. It strengthens the vicious circle of poverty and this has not been addressed by 'job reservation'.

Similarly the question of number has played a crucial role in determining the chances of receiving attention of the state and gain of vote power. It has created cleavages between the large, medium and small groups of SCs, STs and OBCs. For example, the SCs are 21 per cent of the population in Uttar Pradesh. But chamars constitute 12.7 per cent and Pasis are 3 per cent. They have created a sub-category of empowered and mobile SCs. But there are 6.5 per cent other SCs, with a total share of only 2.8 per cent in population, who remain most depressed due to numerical marginality. The rise of dominant castes among the OBCs like Jats, Yadavas, Kurmis, Lodhis, Reddys, Kammars, Vokkaliggas, Lingayats, etc. Has led to marginalisation of the other OBCs who are recognised as Most Backward Castes (MBCs) in the discourse of power.

In short, the impact of reservation policies is visible in the political culture where the SCs the STs and the OBCs have emerged as new corporate identities with constitutional protection for representation and empowerment. But it has not contributed towards any qualitative shift in the lives of the poorer sections of these communities, where poverty is getting perpetuated in overwhelming numbers despite decades of freedom and democracy, planning and reservations.

Liberalisation, Poverty Alleviation and Conflicts

Opening the market of India to global companies and reducing the role of public sector have been two major components of the new economic policies. They are also associated with globalisation of capital mobility and ethnicisation of political mobilisation. It was found that there was i) a boom in the private sector, ii) stable growth in agricultural sector (3.6 per cent per annum), iii) declining rate of population growth (1.6 per cent per annum), and iv) improvement in social indicators (like literacy rate, infant mortality rate, gender related indicators etc.). In the early 1990's, poverty worsened following structural adjustments, a poor harvest and a decline in food availability. There was some decline in poverty and by 1993-94 it fell below the 1987 level. States in the north and east, that have 40 per cent of India's population have lagged in reducing poverty since the late 1970's. According to economic analysts, expenditure on social sector schemes as part of the welfare oriented programs of the Indian state has been increasing in real terms in the era of liberalisation. At the same time it has also been pointed out that it is mainly through increased expenditures of the Central government. The state governments are easing out of their constitutional commitment to sustain programmes in social sectors and it is a matter of concern. Here the social sector expenditure is defined as the total expenditure on social services and rural development. The social services include education, health and family welfare, water supply and sanitation. The rural development expenditure relates mostly to anti-poverty programmes and is presented as 'economic services' in the budget documents.

The realities of 'reforms' have created new challenges for India since: a) So far mostly the better off sections are able to respond to market signals and the rural population has benefited less. b) India is suffering marginalisation in a globalised world and loss of domestic market due to unfettered entry of the foreign companies under the WTO provisions. c) The role of government in economic and social matters is shrinking which has caused apprehensions about 'the future of the protective discrimination' for the weaker sections.

These challenges are being listed as tasks during the Second Generation Reforms. It is recognised by the policy makers that "Freedom from ignorance, diseases and fear, along with freedom from want, are the best guarantors of human development. But education, health care, water and sanitation services, which can ensure these freedom, are not accessible to all. To ensure easy accessibility, we need public action in these areas if human development has to gather momentum. Together, these facilities comprise a nation's social infrastructure that is as critical as physical infrastructure for a widely shared and inclusive development". These challenges have been integral in the making of the new approach to poverty.

A set of new goals has been adopted in the field of education, health, and safety nets. Ensuring 100 per cent literacy in the next five, if not three years; aim for 75 per cent enrolment in higher secondary schools of good quality with encouragement to private sector to provide good schools in every Taluka; raising college enrollment to 20 per cent in the age group 20-24 years; and revitalising the university system are the major goals in education. Healthcare policy goals include reducing the all-India infant and child mortality rate; expanding health care infrastructure to rural areas; ensuring access to clean drinking water; and encouragement to NGOs and private sector to engage in the health sector. The construction of social safety nets will be based on a) a model employment programme covering the whole country, b) Integrated child development services to reduce child mortality and poverty and c) group-based micro-credit schemes to cover the entire country. Thus, there are new tasks before India, in the context of Global Goals for moving further in the direction of construction of the welfare state after five decades of successful democratisation of the political culture and decolonisation of national economy.

The social sector expenditures have resulted in the decline of illiteracy from above 80 per cent in 1951 to less than 35 per cent in 2001. The longivity of the people of India has increased from less than 39 years in 1951 to above 65 years in 2001. Even the incidence of poverty has declined from over 50 per cent in 1950s to less than 30 per cent in 2001. But the new challenges are demanding a new interface between the nation-state and the modern world system at the global level and between the state and the market in Indian political economy. So far the shift of paradigm has been carefully utilised by dominant elite caste, the coastal zones of south and west, major industrial groups, and global financial firms. It has promoted consumerism among the middle classes and scans among the elite in power. At the same time a new wave of people's movements by political parties and non-party organisations has been created to demand freedom from illiteracy, hunger, diseases, environmental degradation, and unemployment.

The pressure groups for social justice and political empowerment are also becoming increasingly visible and assertive. The Dalit movement, the women's movement, the movement of local people (tribes) for control over land, forest, and water resources are some examples of it The movement for Right to Information and pressure for Electoral Reforms are becoming significant as the citizens are getting increasingly anguished about criminalistic of politics and increasing marginalisation of common people's concerns. It seems that the need of the hour is to drive India towards a system of participatory democracy through planning for decentralisation of power and empowerment of the marginal sections of the masses like women, the Scheduled Castes and the Scheduled Tribes, based upon the twin goals of rapid growth and elimination of poverty for the construction of a just and prosperous social order. It is likely that the heritage of Indian National Movement, the basic values of the Constitution of India and the continuous widening of the social base of democracy in India in the last five decades may provide the required support in the era of liberalisation and global market mediation.

It is important to take note of the roots of sluggishness in poverty reduction in the era of liberalisation and address the same. The World Bank approach attempts to argue that there are five interrelated compartments of problems which are contributing to the continuity of poverty:

1. Characteristics of agricultural growth in the 1990s,
2. The slow down of growth in the poorer states,
3. The problems of infrastructure, social services and poverty programmes (especially in the poorer states),
4. Poor incentive framework, and
5. Weakness in governance.

The World Bank analysis has also given content to the eradication of poverty in India in the new century:

a) up liftment of 300 million people concentrated in poorer states,
b) raising literacy rate from 62 per cent (50 per cent for females) by enrolling over 300 million children (mostly poor) who are out of school,
c) addressing the gender based inequalities faced by women in the political, legal and economic systems,
d) reversing the decline in infrastructure spending to meet urban needs and to increase the rate and spread of urbanisation.

It is arguing in favour of implementing "second phase of reforms" which involves – i) cuts in explicit and implicit subsidies together with privatisation of power, ii) government rolling back from infrastructure activities in favour of private sector, iii) more spending on health and elementary education, iv) improvement in government and governance, v) completion of deregulation of goods and factor markets, and vi) provision of high quality infrastructure services.

The critics of liberalisation are arguing that liberalisation has made the economy systematically "demand constrained". They indicate that the demand constrained nature of the Indian economy is manifested today as the combination of industrial recession and surplus stocks of foodgrains and foreign exchange. They argue that "withdrawal" by the state is the primary reason for the emergence of the demand constraint as it has created deflationary effects which are not offset by private investments. It has contributed negatively to the fields of employment and poverty. First of all employment in the organised sector has been virtually stagnant for some time; of late even rural employment expansion has begun to stagnate. According to the economic survey of 2003, there was a net 3 percent decline in rural employment in the preceding year which was a serious indicator of the crisis of employment. Secondly, the headcount ratio of rural poverty which had declined significantly during the eighties has ceased to decline over the nineties, and might have marginally increased.

This perspective points out that it is ironical that the government is claiming the existence of large foreign exchange reserves, massive food grain stocks and markedly low inflation, as achievements, while their simultaneous presence is indicative, on the contrary, of an unprecedented crisis in the Indian economy, a crisis of shrinking demand whose other manifestations are retrenchments, closures, and lay off in organised sector industrial units, a decimation of textile weavers leading to suicides, growing rural unemployment, and aggravation of rural poverty. The situation is more likely to deteriorate progressively.

8

Sociological Causes of Terrorism

The intellectual-political divide in defining terrorism as an analytical tool or policy-formation-abstract makes it a futile exercise to attempt a definition of terrorism in this chapter. The terrorist act, however, can be identified by the violent perpetrators and the organisation or social group (states, religious, ethane, sub-national groups or ideologies) behind them, the violent acts, the victims, the message the actors want to convey and the locus of authority where the message is intended. Terrorist acts are not much different from crime and suicide: they are the resultant of a sense of estrangement from the social milieu. These acts are intended to convey the existence of problems through spectacular violence, as other methods to broadcast the message are deemed ineffective. Blood and gore are presumed repulsive enough to public sensitivities to extend the resonance of the message to a wider audience.

Terrorist acts are committed against citizens (because of their vulnerability) in the country of the terrorist, in a neighbouring country or in the wider world, depending upon the audience. The assassination of leaders, politicians, decision-makers, opinion-formers and other high profile personalities, explosions (car bombs, IEDs, belt-bombers), massacres, hijackings, hostage taking, disruption of economic infrastructure, the destruction of high-value economic targets and attacks on a civilian populace are other examples of terrorism. The instruments of mega terror, with the diffusion of science and technology, are also accessible to terrorists. The danger of recourse to biological, chemical, radiological and nuclear weapons has made terrorism a threat to be dealt with swiftly in a coordinated manner.

Terrorism—A Sociological Perspective

Terrorist acts are not committed in a social vacuum. Terrorists are emergent of the social processes. A contextual, intuitive approach employing what was termed as 'the sociological imagination' by the redoubtable C. Wright Mills has been employed for this study. The level of abstraction has been extended from the individual to the interaction of two or more individuals, to larger social groups and ultimately to groups of nations.

Society is, in its simplest description, overlapping social groups composed of individuals with social roles, privileges and obligations implicit in their own cultural values and norms. Each social group undergoes the process of social integration and disintegration simultaneously. Social disintegration is the aggregate of personal disintegration. Disintegration causes three basic types of reactions: aggression, acquiescence or retreat. These reactions are not discrete and can combine in varying degrees in any covert or overt act. Terrorist acts are one such composite combination, as brought out in the following pages. Several factors, enumerated below, contribute to social disintegration

Social Structures, Change and Reaction

Social groups either adapt to environmental changes or perish. Adaptation leads to social change, which is a tension-ridden process. Change can be absorbed to the extent that management mechanisms and the elasticity of the group are developed. Members who perceive that the burden of adjustment is disproportionate to advantages either take to acquiescence, withdrawal or rebellion, depending upon their genetics and socialisation. Some such social processes are given below:

1. *Socialisation:* Social structures evolve over time. The stabilised structures, jolted by newer values, can upset the pattern of social ranking. Incumbent members perceiving slippage in their prestige take to either role-defence or acquiescence. Achievement, where the actor does not fit into the milieu and has either to move up the social scale or is pushed up, is elating, but is also depersonalising. The social traits of one class position may not be functional in another, causing social stress. This depersonalisation, consequent to mismatch of orientation, position in the social hierarchy, and extant expectations in the new setting causes social anomia – the pervasive feeling to both internalise and rebel from the norm. This less than optimal participation in society can lead to the quest for some supra-mundane activity, fulfilling some deeper psychological need of recognition, security and relationship

2. *Hiatus Between Social Provisions and Individual Needs:* Frustration is a natural product of mismatch of individual needs and social provisions. Those who are most deprived of need-satisfaction are also those most deprived of valued relationships that induce socially conforming behaviour. Deviance and violence is a plaintive call for deliberate action by authoritative roles for fulfilling these needs. Burton brings out this dilemma saying "If an attempt is made to subordinate individual values to social values, then, because it is not possible to enforce social values that are inconsistent with individual values, there will be

responses that are damaging both to the individual and through him, to the social system." Individuals either singly or in groups act deviant, sometimes despite themselves, to register their disaffection with the social group. Recourse to terrorism may appear to some to be a way to vent this 'structural conflict'–the gap between needs and provisions-possibility.

3. *Manifest and Latent Functions of the Social Structure:* Most social structures have both manifest functions and latent functions as brought out by Merton. Uprooting of such structures without social safety nets causes havoc (e.g. nuclear family efficient for social mobility displacing a joint family in rural India). This induces ambivalence towards both the new and old structures. Members displaced or dispossessed by this gap in fulfilment subconsciously take to social deviance.

4. *Mismatch Between Ideal and Reality:* The social ideal is an emergent of the social dynamic. Authority positions are expected to lead in attaining that ideal. If the elite, who are supposed to uphold the ideal, instead debase it, the lower echelons find themselves looking for either redefining the ideal or reviewing the prestige that they proffer on the elite. At the extreme stage of this skepticism comes the demand for removal of the elite or revolutionising of the structure so that the power wheel is turned upside down. The distancing of reality and the ideal is a cause of frustration. Deviance and disorganisation are its natural consequences.

5. *Ideal of Success:* Taking a cue from industrial societies, most developing societies now emphasise the ideal of success, forsaking the time-tested achievement of group goals. The pressures of modern production and consumption, underwritten by the rule of winner-take-all, create serious disequilibrium within societies, adjusting to the new industrial culture. The more

intense the pressures of success, the greater number of demoralised individuals it creates.

6. *Marginalisation:* Societies in flux tend to produce greater proportion of marginal individuals than stabilised societies. Marginalisation can be the resultant of diverse factors either by itself or in combination-genetic, environmental, faulty socialisation, lack of positions commensurate with the socialisation, intensity of competition for positions, etc. The flux in valued positions - due to changes in technology, levels of knowledge or rigours of training - leaves many newer entrants in each generation on the margins, unless newer opportunities open up, matching with the available social training. The modern labour-displacement technologies leave many seekers bereft of opportunities. The uprooting of some people, consequent to unsuitability for the new roles demanded by the milieu, throws them on the margins of acceptable behavioural patterns. This pool of marginalised people, under stress from the social group, but unable to adapt to newer structures, makes a fertile ground for the emergence of esoteric subgroups. Terrorism fills this need for conspicuous action and recognition. The greater the numbers of marginal people in society, the greater the danger of such deviant acts.

7. *No Safety Valves:* Each nation or social group has built-in safety valves for letting off stress. Religion, entertainment, expressive media, sports contests, gambling and prostitution are some of them. Authorities may have, at times, foreclosed these safety valves for some ulterior motive without taking into consideration the morale, habits and impulses of the people or without recognising their latent functions. Since the recourse to illegitimate wealth and

instruments of terrorism are necessarily a part of such operators of safety valves, terrorism becomes a proximate option.

Social Relationships as Integrative Mechanisms

(a) *Breakdown of Traditional Relationships:* Inter-generation social relationships have been continually changing. The latter day rapid pace of change and social flux upsets stabilised relationships, whether patriarchal, feudal or kinship, in most developing societies. Role models change rapidly. The most energetic elements in this dialectic seek emancipation from the internalised obligations, resulting in inter-generation friction. They cut themselves off from their groups of orientation or are thrown out by the milieu, for they cannot adapt to the greater flux of urban anonymity, ruthlessness, and open arena of intense competition. Such individuals and groups form a rich cache for future terrorists.

(b) *Transitory relationships:* By nature, the urban flux is depersonalising and transitory vocations cannot substitute for organic kinship. Life for the social animal that man is, in its metaphysical sense, is relationships. This floating is very disintegrated in the short run; there is a quest for the new and there is pining for the old with the present be fogged by both the future and the past. Some actors experience isolation for being far too above or below par of success in the given milieu. It is these individuals who gravitate towards delinquent gangs with their capability or inferiority pushing them to deviance. Most executors of terror acts come from this category offer of journalist Daniel Pearl in Karachi studied in London before taking to religiosity and terrorism.

Power Relations

Power relations in a society are the result of past power struggles and social accommodations. However, the tendency of the incumbents at authoritative roles to freeze social negotiation and perpetuate their legitimacy is a consistent cause of social mal-integration. The absence of mechanisms to de-freeze such a tendency forces recourse to deviance.

1. *Social Differentiation:* All societies have to move from the primitive mechanical solidarity, as in pre-literate societies, to organic solidarity with differentiation of functions, division of labour and prestige gradations in the modern world. Social differentiation is functional in case checks and balances are in place. In case accountability institutions are not available, authoritative roles can indulge in self-perpetuation causing social discontent, expressed in withdrawal of respect, privilege and subsequently aggressive acts to physically eliminate the depraved, devalued roles and the individuals holding them. Terrorism is one avenue to express this discontent.

2. *Relative Deprivation:* Deprivation and poverty *per se* do not cause disintegration. It is only when some individuals and subgroups perceive that the costs of change are being differentially apportioned and the allocation of resources are being inefficiently distributed that they experience relative deprivation even though they may be better-off from the *ex ante* position. Relative deprivation gradually coagulates into social resentment and loss of morale. It takes the form of regression, acquiescence or aggression, depending upon the strength of invidious experience.

3. *Creation of Power Positions:* Developing societies generally create far too few positions goods than could

assuage any significant number of entrants to the dynamic. Fewer power positions necessarily mean pride of ascension and its discretionary dispensation to favourites. The vicious circle of lack of empowerment leading to lack of morale and involvement, irresponsibility, malfeasance and sabotage, further concentrates power in fewer hands and operates with a vengeance in developing societies. Sabotage and malfeasance is social deviance.

4. *Legitimacy vs. External Support:* The breakdown of colonial rule has given rise to structures which hold and exercise power but which are not seen as legitimate by the various subgroups within the larger group - the nation. The lack of legitimacy is a potent source of dissent-suppression, frauds, opaque structures, nepotism and mis-governance. Depending upon the state of openness and tolerance for opposition and dissent, such subgroups either take to acquiescence, silent protests, strikes, demonstrations and even insurgencies. The lack of legitimacy is further exacerbated by wider power politics. Support to regimes patently illegitimate, partly representative or moving towards legitimacy evokes a sense of antipathy and resignation amongst the most vital of actors. The demoralisation amongst such individuals or subgroups leaves them flotsam in the power mart and they gravitate towards secretive, deviant organisations.

5. *Opposition and Religious Institutions:* The ambivalence of secular institutions (towards political participation by certain groups) hinders growth of functional opposition. This ambivalence opens a window for opposition groups that lack opportunities for expression, to channel their activities through the refuge of religion (e.g. Muslim Brotherhood, Islamic Jihad, etc). These groups lack available channels to disseminate their

ideas and thus, in order to gain acceptance from the wider mass, consolidate through public, religious charities, playing on the vulnerability of the state. The impulse to push forward an alternative then coagulates into reactionary activities, completing the vicious circle. The connection of terrorists with religious outfits, which in their nature cannot be democratic, allows the rise of religious autocracies - without dissent, discussions, compromise or consensus. Fundamentalism is a natural source of and only a step behind terrorism.

6. *Coercion as Major Form of Social Control:* Dissent is a natural concomitant of a living society. Progressive societies encourage it, but regressive regimes take to regulatory deterrence as the major and sometimes only means of social control. This is expensive, with large collateral damage on the morale of both sides, resulting in more acute deviance in new ways. This circularity of skepticism, its intolerance, coercion to suppress, loss of morale, overt defiance, and further suppression can culminate in leagues and networks, both overt and covert, to defy authority and garner adherents – the malcontents of the social group. Alternatively, the progressively waning social morale could lead to cynicism towards life. Withdrawal and suicide are symptoms of this process. Suicide *perse*, as a moral statement, is terrorism.

Management of Economy

1) *Alienation:* Social alienation is a typical reaction of the mass production-consumption social matrix. Alienated individuals seek means of adaptation and social stabilisation and to reach some equilibrium, though at a great emotional cost. But some individuals invariably slip outside the margins of sociability.

Similarly, modern education is a cause of typical alienation amongst the young. Most of them somehow adapt to mixed gender classes, new curricula, and new infrastructure. Some, however, cannot find their bearings until they drop out. Education dropouts, in almost all cases, have to settle for lower prestige, marginalisation and alienation, feeding the deviant networks.

Brutalisation and training in deviant activities (e.g. dropouts, returnees from jails convicted on minor offences) can lead to deviant networks. Ordinary criminality by such networks is sometimes transmuted into glorified deviance. Groups that start as criminals can transmute into social benefactors in case the milieu is willing to afford them legitimacy (Robin Hood type of gangs where the state has faltered). Such subgroups equipped with resources, training, and ideologies are a potent source of challenges to authority positions.

2. *Developmental Pressures:* Economic development, if not managed, causes social disruption. Development causes a strain on the physical environment, resulting in unforeseen sicknesses and disruptive absenteeism. Developmental pressures invariably give rise to centripetal forces. Sabotage, crime, rebellions, insurgencies are some common concomitants of developmental stress, especially if it is rapid and intense.

3. *Sectoral Grievances:* Social homogeneity is a matter of degree. Since the diverse actors vie for scarce resources, positions and need-filling mechanisms, there is competition amongst the contending subgroups. Sectoral grievances are expressed in the language of exploitation and can lead to noncooperation, withholding of consent, strikes, mobilisation, rebellion and insurgencies.

Culture

a) *Delinquency Subculture*: Most societies harbor a spectrum of social sanctions to outwit deviance. The allowance given to ideas (and their cultural manifestations - songs, dance, films, dress, body care, and general style of life) from the West in traditional societies wreaks havoc with the social morale there. This allows the growth of a delinquent subculture where the social signposts become blurred and ideals crumble to the warm, pink winds.

Successful individuals become the target of the masses (Foreign/American returned people in the local milieu in developing societies face derision if they vaunt the liberating values of the West and remain ever on the defensive; the expectation that people educated/ employed in the West would be bridges is misplaced). They either give-in, remaining maladapted and halfhearted social discontent, or openly defy the old order and perforce take to alien arenas. In either case it is a loss for the native milieu. The resultant anomia is a great source of deviance, often culminating into acceptance of questionable ideologies and ideal-constructs.

b) *Intensity of Communication:* The new technology ingress amidst traditional production, consumption and power relations, gives rise to the amorphous ubiquity of communication. Events, episodes, persons, ideals – totally alien in form and content, come to be internalised by distant and near actors. Symbols, whether suicide bombs or crashing planes, get embedded in the social ether. The communication mechanisms which are legitimately heralded as liberating influences can also become means of control, disinformation and coagulation of malcontents. Such mass dissemination, being impersonal, is generally out of the local context, and most of the times alienating. The skewed distribution of communications makes it a one-way affair, representing 'techniques of moral brokerage and encouragement to journalists to work on behalf of the established order.' As Erection says "it is the organisation of news, not events in the world that creates news." Terrorism is one way of communicating the reverse.

c) *Simplification of Reality:* In a society where anomie is pervasive, where relations and positions are in flux, intellectual leaders and opinion makers are atrophied with constricted imagination and intellectual sclerosis and the stage is set for the emergence of some normative patterns, intelligible to the atomic populace. Surrogates arise and propose simplification of reality into a series of pictures, images, and symbols, striking a chord amongst lethargic society -fatigued by the incessant flux of ideas and ideologies. These surrogates are essentially simple, impressionable people like children who lie and thereafter believe in the lies. They offer flimsy anchorage when the waters are choppy. Formation of cults is a logical progression in this simplification which gives meaning and content to lives made hollow otherwise. The failure of the intellectual leadership to adopt and channel the popular impulses into creative, productive and stabilising institutions is the sure sign of some messiah to emerge, some Moses bringing manna and the quest of the promised land. This is but the penultimate stage of social disintegration.

d) *Subculture of Violence:* Cultural traditions control behaviour patterns of individual members. Some subgroups emphasise violence (e.g. hunter groups) while others give acquiescence (e.g. agricultural societies) more weight in socialisation. The cultural traits of the subgroups, if not utilised in constructive ways, lead to anomie and less than optimal utilisation of their potential. Failure to recognise the potential of each subgroup can cause deviance and social dislocation resulting in violent protests.

e) *Non-rational Factors:* Non-rational factors play a great role in socialisation. Totems, myths, legends, however, can become a focus of rallying against the extant authorities if case avenues for expression of pent up frustrations are not available. Myths and totems become theatrical, raising the vision of an unrealised promised land, of the supposed 'grandeur' and 'justice' of the past. Apocalyptic groups which are but social failures can procure adherents by reverting to such episodes, symbols and myths which can neither be proved by empirical testing nor disproved because they are present in the social subconscious.

External Environment

The pervasive availability of ideas and cultures, artifacts and technologies, goods and wares is intense in a globalised world and has unintended, consequences. Technology can be imported but its appropriation calls for sustained social effort, which may not be forthcoming.

Similarly, the integration mechanisms such as entertainment and media make insidious ingress in social groups not ready for absorption and assimilation. The superstructure makes local culture inefficacious by what Gramsci called cultural hegemony. This subconscious hegemony is but a precursor of ideas coagulating towards repulsion and closing in. The skewed nature of ownership allows only a few to dictate what should be heard and seen, imbibed and referenced, rejected and consigned. These vulnerability are sustainable rallying points for terrorists – those who see that their life is being weaned away from its mooring. Material, intellectual and ideological aid, even if given with unadulterated benevolence, which is hardly the case with foreign aid anyway, can be a cause of demoralisation and disintegration unless reassuring mechanisms and social confidence have developed enough to counter the social demoralisation.

Terrorism in South Asia

South Asia, home to a fourth of the global population, is beset with serious problems of insurgencies, rebellions, militancy and movements giving occasion to several terrorist incidents, not allowing legitimate authorities time for consolidation and appropriate political dynamic to evolve. Terrorists of various hues—leftists, rightists, ethnic, religious, sub-national are active in the region, symbolising that the sociopolitical structures evolved during the past decades have not been able to satisfy major chunks of population.

Jihadi Terrorism

Jihad is a tenuous, perhaps expedient concept in Islamic theology. Muslim political ascendance during the seventh century called for *jihad* (righteous effort) and *fatah* (literally *opening* for the victory of the righteous). The cult of martyrs as the *shaheed* (witness, perhaps of God as he became the dearest of God) was for mass mobilisation in the essentially trading society. Jihad as a tenet of Islam, is defined, reviewed and redefined as per the predilection of the beholder. In the post-colonial, post-cold war period, with rampant demoralisation, Jihad transmuted from a guiding post to one of the pillars to the central pillar of Islam, and for some to be the basic of Islam, equal to the belief in Allah and his Prophet, with each Muslim obliged to do his duty to the religion and its dictates as interpreted by the pure and the learned (*ulema*). People in the sub-continent claim that though the Quoran descended in Arabia, it was interpreted in the sub-continent, decrying the Arabs as *jahils* (ignorant) and hailing the Deobandis as the rightful interpreters of Islam. This is hotly contested by the Arabs. Jihad came upon the subcontinent with a vengeance, with a combination of several sociopolitical factors. It is, however, a sociological puzzle that Indian Muslims did not find it expedient or even a teleological necessity to join the Jihadi movement, or even express solidarity with it.

1. *Similarities—Cultural Continuity:* The decadal census states that over 138 million citizens profess Muslim faith in India. Their growth rate of 2.93 percent over the decade 1991-2001 is comparable to growth rate in other parts of the Muslim world. Similarly the socioeconomic data on Pakistan, Bangladesh and India also reveals no wide diversity or difference in income levels. The per capita in dollar terms and PPP of the three countries, the HDI indexes and trends on economic growth and demographic profiles are roughly approximate. In addition, there are kinship ties among the Muslims across the borders in the subcontinent. The history of Islamic ingress and the adoption of Islam by the people at a certain socioeconomic level are common to all three peoples. All three countries share a common political background in terms of Arab-Turk-Mughal and colonial history. They also have commonality of languages and culture. Similarly the climate and topography, with regional variations, are similar. All three countries swear by democracy and tried to develop Westminster style of government.

2. *Differences in Political Evolution*: Muslims in India remain a significant minority, even if their relative percentage to the overall population is rather low—12.8 percent (a solid unitary group with a distinct identity, as opposed to the diffuse majority of Hindus

> as a residual category without any cohesive identity). Over 150 million Muslims today form the second biggest Muslim population in one single country after Indonesia. This bulk and influence can give Indian Muslims a significant say in the Islamic dynamic. But this has somehow not come about. Muslims in Bangladesh and Pakistan, in contrast, are the overwhelming majority and compose both the elite as well as masses.

This obvious difference, however, does not explain the indifference to the *Ummah* and the *Jihad.* If anything, the contrary effect is plausible with the minority (Muslims) seeking their inspiration from their land of orientation, the Arab world. This inspiration is evident in cultural manifestations like names, religious festivals, marriage rites or civil laws. Minorities have complexes bordering on paranoia - threats of assimilation, overt discrimination and social prejudice, even if not explicit in the political discourse, can be prefigured. Such complexes lead them to seek support and inspiration elsewhere. Hence, the endorsement of the supervening Ummah should be their first refuge in the expectation of political and moral aid and reassurance. The pressures of development, resource allocations and the invidious social and economic ascent could also be a source of frustration, forcing the minority to look beyond the immediate governance of the state.

Is it expedient acquiescence, what Turkish secularists deride as *takkiye*, from which most of the present Muslims trace their descent, or is it something deeper, a wider process? Social processes and social structures in India, their evolution and consolidation could possibly throw some light on the question under examination.

Pakistan, India and Bangladesh have a republican form of government with their constitutions swearing by democracy. But they all have taken different trajectories in their interpretation and ascent to democratic governance. This has given a peculiar hue to their form of State and the informing institutions. The plurality of institutions, their power, influence, independence and autonomy are a matter of degree. Some of them approximate the institutions established in developed countries while others are still in their infancy in the countries. Similarly, the reach and depth of the State vary.

Role of Political Institutions to Comabt Terrorism

The Indian State has progressively reached all corners of the land and has accomplished depth not visible in other countries – by way of accommodations, legitimisation, representation and co-option. Contra-movements have been dealt with politically rather than as law and order problems. Successive governments have engaged various insurgent groups, in attrition, in dialogue and in resolution. Similarly, the constitutional obligation to hold elections for installing popular, constitutional governments obtained legitimacy for the State. This accommodative depth has allowed India to focus on the developmental needs of its vast and ever-growing population. Democracy, even with all its imperfections, is seeped in the individual consciousness and there is a characteristic allergy to order, discipline, and diktat from outside of India. Chaos is preferred to discipline from without.

Institution Building

Institution building, even if inexpedient and causing tremendous strain on the paltry resources of time and material, is *sui generis* in India. The legislature, judiciary and the media being afforded unrestricted freedom to evolve their traditions, culture and functional ethics, expanded their space, even at the cost of the Executive. Any encroachment or transgressions has built-in resistance.

Pluralism

As institutions consolidate, newer institutions representing civil society emerge. The increasing civil society intervention in spheres affecting both public life and private interests is firmly embedded in social governance. Several institutions developed along the way: in economic management, cultural organisations, environmental groups, rights protection societies, clubs, fraternities, professional organisations and trade unions. The public space expanded to incorporate several overlooked individuals and groups, marginal outfits and peripheral constituencies. This expansion increased integration for the State and achieved strategic depth to contain all centripetal tendencies and forces. Pluralism was firmly established. Religion receded into the background with other mechanisms that have a lead role in frustration venting. Religion was progressively confined into the personal rather than the public domain. *iv) Military under Civilian Rule in India:* The military is only one of the several pillars of self-defence in India. The clear delineation of the privileges, role expectations, powers and chain of command is traceable directly to the President, who is advised by the Prime Minister. The military has a clear sphere of activity. It has never attempted to advice on governance, unlike in other countries where the military has actually assumed power. The strain of governance and defence duties generally contorts the military in these countries, insulating the institution from the currents of national life, and making it bureaucratic, bent on preserving itself and its privileges rather than serving the purpose it was established for or the responsibilities it took upon itself. People demoralised by military action take recourse to non-rational and sometimes irrational means and ends whereby - God and God's-Just-World become social aspirations with the individual self becomes an ephemeral, transitory reality. India has been spared of this anathema.

Channels of Communication

Communication is a *sine quinone* of development and empowerment. Representative institutions in India draw out the essence from the masses for national consideration. Violence is a reaction to indifference and maladaptation. Communication is a safe way to pre-empt it. Indian democracy has mature communicating channels. Dissent smothered by power instruments could hardly cover the social malaise. One of the best known Pakistani poets expressed it in a couplet. Aspirations and dissent never got channelled into the pulpits and mosques in India. Secular institutions, even in their bumbling way, fulfilled this role.

Political Parties

Political parties in India are omnibus organisations without explicit polarisation on religious lines. All parties solicit Muslim support since they have a swing-potential in elections. To give representation to this constituency is a prime electoral necessity for all parties. The structural necessity of omnibus coalitions of various religions, castes, and interests groups pre-empts polarisation. Compromises and negotiations in coalition building have given a stable equilibrium to the linguistic, religious, and ethnic minorities in addition to peripheral geographical groups. There is no disconnect between the polity and the state, no void of proscribed parties to be filled by unrepresentative interests.

Social Control Mechanisms

Social control in India is mostly endogenous through family, kinship, school, neighbourhood and community. Various mechanisms have pre-empted social frustrations from reaching their boiling point. Some of them are given below:

Secularism in India: India rejected the theory that a people following one religion constitute a nation, as is propagated in Pakistan. The ideal of a uniform civil code for all citizens, given a prominent place in the Directive Principles of the India Constitution though implementation of this article is suspended due to the sensitivities and vulnerability of the minority religions. Unless the minority community is ready for such a uniform code and willingly disposes itself to such change, it will not be brought into effect. The accommodation shown has tempered the fear psychosis in the minds of minorities. The freedom of practising and propagating religion has been guaranteed by the (stitution. It has successfully pre-empted a potential source of discontent and violence. In addition to foreclosing dissent and perpetual friction, this has given the Muslims a sense of reassurance about their future within the Indian nation – irrespective of the denomination to which they belong - Sunni, Shia, Ahmedi, Sufi or Bohri. This freedom has also been emphasised for Christians and Parsis. Freedom guaranteed by the constitution and enforced both by social dictates and law and order mechanisms has resulted in the withdrawal of religion into the personal domain, prevented polarisation on religious lines and split the monolithic religious traditions into several localised sects. Religion, confined to the personal domain, has become an effective tool for socialisation and social control. This cannot be said of other countries in the region, where religion occupies public-political space.

Counter-ideologies: Indian culture is catholic and eclecticism is the predominant reality in matters of faith - no book is considered definitive to guide social conduct or explain cosmology. All creeds are fused in this 'melting pot': from atheism to pantheism and strict monotheism. In such a diverse and pluralistic cultural flux, no particular ideology can reach an overarching position. The dialectic is not only tolerated but also encouraged. Puritanism is considered a public nuisance. It is this spirit of eclecticism which gives rise to innumerable practices and within which fundamentalism is scoffed at, derided, and ostracised. Indian society recognises the impossibility of converting terrorist impulses into productive and creative channels (e.g. into fighting elections and defeating the war of ideas) making it difficult to sustain terrorism within the state. Developing institutions in India have the obligation of co-opting diverse values and opinions into their functioning, thus blunting the edge of deviance. This has not been, unfortunately the case in other countries, where heterodox traditions, have been proscribed, with accompanying state or group violence.

Open Channels for Dissent: The right to freedom of expression and association has been vigorously exercised for organising groups and venting frustrations. Even if the disruptive potential of active dissent and protest movements borders on violent, the sinister nature of it brewing towards a dangerous eruption is pre-empted. Lack of channels for expression of dissent in other countries has fomented pressures, without curing any of the problems, and resulted in social dislocation and the retardation of desirable social structures.

Jihadism Usurped by Criminal Underworld: Judicium was pre-empted in its works by constitutional guarantees. The desideratum of fundamentalist elements, who continued with the pan-Islamic identity and proclivity to align themselves to the wider Islamic currents, did not find fertile ground in India. Social friction over material resources such as land, water, resource allocation and regional prejudice continue however, taking at times the communal colour. Clashes continue sporadically between Muslim and Hindu communities at the local level. This dialectic, however, is not oriented by Arabic influences. The Muslim leadership is already well entrenched in the Indian political system with privileged positions. The fallout of the Babri Mosque demolition was catastrophic and communal riots were ubiquitous. However, the drift towards the Ummah was not seen even during the height of these clashes. Frustrated elements, which saw some "ethnological defeat" in this apathy, transmuted their rage, with the help of criminals and mafia dons in Bombay, into high blown bomb blasts in 1993. This criminalistics of what could have been an ideological rallying point was taken care of by law and order agencies (e.g. Dawood Ibrahim, Chota Shaqeel, etc and were given refuge in Pakistan). Criminals-on-the-run who take up the mantle of ideological purity enshrined in the *Ummah or Jihad* made it repulsive for ordinarily religious Muslims to follow suit.

Islamist terrorist events in India, even if occurring with regularity, invariably have the footprints of external support, instigation or execution, even if there is voluble denial. It follows from the ideological basis of a low-cost, covert war to 'complete the unfinished agenda' of partition. The native Muslims find it repulsive to identify and align themselves with Pakistan and its actions. Support to Kashmiri nationalism by Pakistan is considered an excuse to divert the Jihad-turned-upon-itself after finding no outlet following the Afghan war. This insurgency suits the oligarchy in Pakistan to both vindicate its *raison deter* as well as to deflect the Jihadi energy from challenging the position and privileges of the establishment. The partition of the country is considered in India to be a manipulation of historical currents for personal ambition and a sense of failure of leadership is pervasive amidst the Muslims in India, in hindsight.

Effect of External Influences: India has been the recipient of aid for some decades but its social and economic depth, its inward-looking orientation and its emphasis on self-sufficiency has never allowed external factors to play any major, determining role. Its political process was determined by its genius and neither the dictates of cold war nor the 'clash of civilisations' had any perceptible influence. What emerged in India was a broad moral consensus within which all processes and ideas had the space to play, consolidate, and eliminate the dysfunctional. Foreign influences always remained peripheral. Jihad, which is a foreign ideology, did not strike a chord within the Muslim community. This cannot be said of other countries where aid penetrated deeper into the popular psyche – through midtarsal schools, civic projects or religious fraternities. Demoralisation by external aid-effort is less apparent in India and Muslims remained insulated from the external, fundamentalist currents.

International Cooperation in Countering Terrorism

Terrorism is causing tremendous strain on the developmental process in the sub-continent, and elsewhere, resulting in the curbing of freedom otherwise taken for granted. Since terrorism transcends boundaries, international cooperation is an imperative. Terrorism has to be countered simultaneously at four levels: global, regional, national, and local. In the short run, terrorism should be tackled through a convergent approach using instruments of power, diplomacy, pre-emptive intelligence and covert action to pre-empt terrorist acts. This approach, however, cannot eliminate terrorism. A terrorist cannot be defeated but only made irrelevant. A divergent, holistic approach is therefore necessary to relegate terrorism to redundancy. Intensive cooperation between India and the United States in the following ways could help in addressing this problem.

At the international level, India and US could work closely to secure final agreement on a Comprehensive Convention on International Terrorism, which endeavours to close gaps in international laws to counter terrorism. Similarly, the tightening of controls on financial operations, without dislocating legitimate financial transfers, is an imperative where functional cooperation is possible and desirable. Cooperation in controlling narcotics and arms running, which together finance much of terrorism, may be prove decisive in curbing terrorism in the short run.

At the regional level, where US and Indian interests coalesce, cooperation could be intensified (e.g. stability and development of the region). The ambivalence displayed towards Judicium earlier has paroled the region. The US can, with its influence, steer the regional dynamics away from terrorism. Ambivalence towards terrorism, in the name of 'moral support' to 'freedom fighters,' should be progressively nailed by diplomatic pressure. Military/Police cooperation could be tried to overreach the 'minimum satisfied' type of actions in Afghanistan. Similarly, the emerging fundamentalist nurseries in Bangladesh need to be eliminated through moral and diplomatic pressures and cooperative action.

The Indian State has depth to counter its national and local terrorism with both accommodation and pre-emption by political and policing means respectively. Interference by foreign powers would heighten national sensitivity. However, cooperation in capacity building like training, equipment, etc. Could be helpful.

Indo-US cooperation to combat terrorism, crime and trafficking is covered under the Indo-U.S. Joint Working Group on Terrorism, the Extradition Treaty and the Mutual Legal Assistance Treaty. The Defence Framework Agreement, *inter alia* sets out cooperation in "areas of common interest of both countries in maintaining security and stability, defeating terrorism and violent religious extremism, protecting the free flow of commerce via land, air and sea lanes and preventing the spread of weapons of mass destruction and associated materials, data and technologies." Other legal instruments to combat new challenges like proliferation of nuclear and chemical weapons, delivery vehicles to non-state actors, digital and bio-piracy, maritime piracy, cyber crime, money laundering, etc. Could be negotiated to counter emerging terrorist threats.

Functional co-operation of the intelligence agencies is an imperative. All ways should be explored to intensify cooperation and exchange in information sharing and identification of: trends in terrorism, terrorist infrastructure, cadres, nurseries, new recruits, and returnees from areas affected by insurgencies to prevent their rejoining terrorist nets. Joint development of anti- terrorist equipment such as devices for intrusion-detection, x-ray screening, alarms, non-lethal weapons, body-armour, explosive detection portals and developing software and hardware for integrating data on terrorism and forensic facilities may be some areas to focus on. Joint training on tactical combat skills for urban warfare, post-terrorist-attack disaster management, etc. Could also be fruitful areas for cooperation. US technological intelligence could be combined with Indian human intelligence for optimal results.

A divergent, all-inclusive, heuristic approach, focused on problem solving, in addition to the convergent approach of the intelligence agencies, is indispensable to eliminate this threat in the long run. As Singer says: 'some systematic research which can simultaneously think big and think small and which embraces in a rigorous synthesis both the lone individual and all of mankind,' is necessary. The problem needs to be addressed by the civil society – academics, social scientists, bureaucrats, development planners, writers, journalists, politicians and public personalities. Exchanges at various levels, both structured and unstructured, can fill the gap and should be encouraged. The disintegrating factors need to be examined with all thoroughness and dexterity available in the non-ideological, secular and intellectual universe. Extensive, inter-disciplinary work needs to be carried out for chalking out relevant strategies. It is necessary to examine socialisation, social control, and social morale and tension management subsystems in the region. Comparative analysis on the causes of democratic attenuation or expansion in countries of the same region, ambivalence of states towards religious fanaticism, and ways and means to delegitimise 'non-state actors' in popular perceptions could also be helpful. The negative rôle of media and information technology in facilitating terrorism needs extensive examination. Broadening the mechanisms for dialogue between governments, academics and think tanks should be encouraged. There is a necessity to create more social space for various tiers of society. It is not impossible to create this space with accommodations, adjustments and negotiations. At the same time, it is necessary that geographic space (state sponsors of terrorism, failing states, ungoverned areas where terrorists can train and organise) and cyber space (internet-based means for communication, planning, resource transfer and intelligence collection) available to the terrorists is constricted and eliminated.

The United States as the oldest democracy and India as the largest democracy, both with their peculiarities, can work towards creation of an irreversible broad framework of democratisation, not only as a principle but also as an expedient. The South Asian region is on the cusp and needs very mature consideration. It has to be steered towards a course that guarantees security, development and recognition of the native genius. The US could, with its unlimited power and influence in the region, adopt policy initiatives similar to the EU's policies towards Turkey. India, with its civilisations linkage, political insight and as a social-intellectual repository of the region, can be of great help in this endeavour. This coalescence of interests could be built upon.

US power in the global context and Indian power in the regional context plays on the negative psychology of peoples. They derive vicarious sense of empowerment in opposition. US and Indian soft-power, films, media spread, academic, and digital depth, could be cooperatively utilised to create reassurance for the region in an inclusive manner, working in tandem with the comfort levels acceptable to the various countries. Joint projects in some high visible areas like film and print media, with the active involvement of local genius could be tried.

Regional economic consolidation is desirable and almost imperative in co-opting the forces which give rise to terrorism. India as a regional economic engine and the US as a global engine can help steer the region to greater exchange, towards the building of linkages and the development of cooperative constituencies. India cannot afford to move ahead with weak states surrounding it, for it will cause an unavoidable demographic strain on her development. It needs to develop all of its neighbours along the way and this endeavour requires assistance. India's intellectual and political depth has generated the capability to absorb help from external sources without dentine morale. Exploitation of regional asynergy could help in the development of organic linkages within the region. The United States, as the largest market for products from the region, could assist India. Increased regional economic interaction through institutional arrangements with SAFTA could be attempted. Business constituencies, having a vested interest in stability, could reduce dislocation by engendering maximum employment opportunities.

The development of Jihadist ideologies and their accompanying movements can only be countered by coherent alternative ideologies. Unorthodox but tried ideologies in the region—Pacifist, Gandhian Non-Violence, Buddhist Tempering, etc.—though outdated could be encouraged to revive and update their relevance to present conditions. Paucity of intellectual efforts should not be allowed to give space to simplifies of reality. This will reduce the ideological space of terrorists.

Terrorism is a global problem that transcends national boundaries, but does not emerge from a social vacuum. It is influenced, encouraged, and caused by interaction between the individual, society, and the state. Social disintegration can alienate individuals and groups to such an extent that terrorism is seen as an available and expedient recourse to address their grievances. For this reason, terrorism cannot be addressed exclusively as a military or political problem, but rather must be confronted on a socialite level as well. Indian society, shaped by India's unique history and commitment to democracy, has succeeded in deterring its Muslim population from turning towards the Islamic jihadist movement, unlike many of its regional neighbours. This success, while tenuous, should be seized upon as a lesson for other states combating terrorism. India and the United States, in particular, can enhance their already blossoming relationship by capitalising on India's success and cooperating with one another to combat terrorism.

9

Sociology of Women in Local Politics

India is a federal system of government with 25 states and 7 union territories. It has a population of about 1 billion out of which 26 percent live in urban areas. The per capita GDP of India is about US$ 370. Agriculture accounts for 31.1 percent of the economy, while industry and services account for 23 percent and 45.9 percent respectively, of the economy. The sex ratio of the population is 48.1 percent and is rather skewed in favour of males. The most favourable sex ratio in the country is in the state of Kerala at 50.9 percent, while the Union Territory of Lakshadweep has the worst sex ratio at 40 percent. Life expectancy at birth for women is 58.7 years and for men it is 57.7 per cent. The overall literacy rate is 52.2 percent. Literacy among men is 64.1 percent and among women it is 39.3 percent. Women make up about 28 percent of the labour force.

The political and administrative structure of the country is largely inherited from the British. The British introduced local democracy in India by constituting municipal councils and the municipal corporations in the last quarter of the nineteenth century. They also provided a federal structure to the country with the Government of India Act, 1935.

The country today has a quasi-federal structure. Apart from the Government of India in New Delhi, there are twenty-five States with their own state governments. The

Seventh Schedule to the Constitution of India divides the subjects of State activity between the Union and state governments. The Union (Centre) as well as State governments in India both have a parliamentary form of government based on the Westminster pattern. The executive powers of the central government are vested in the Council of Ministers with the Prime Minister at its head. Similarly, the executive powers in the State governments are vested in its Council of Ministers with the Chief Minister at its head. However, following the Westminster pattern, the Head of the State. is not the Prime Minister but an indirectly elected President, who broadly performs the role as the Head of State. India has a bicameral parliament, with the Lower House directly elected by the people on the lines of the House of Commons in the U.K. or the House of Representatives in the U.S.A. The Upper House is more like the U.S. Senate. It is a permanent house with one-third members retiring every two years. Like in the U.S.A. The Vice President of the country presides on the Upper House.

Although local government in India is a subject of the State governments, the seventy-third and the seventy-fourth amendments to the Constitution of India now make it obligatory for the State governments to organise local bodies, to hold regular elections to them and to give them appropriate finances.

The urban local bodies are of three grades; municipal corporations for cities with a population of more than (0.3 million), municipal councils for towns smaller than this population limit and nagar panchayats for villages in transition to becoming towns. These bodies are elected on a universal suffrage basis, with all citizens above the age of eighteen years of age having a right to vote.

The rural local bodies are organised in three tiers, the village panchayat at the village level, the block panchayat samiti for about 100 villages and a district council for a district comprising about 1000 villages. The rural local bodies do not have many resources of their own. They actually spend the state government funds as implementing agencies.

The civil service in India is a closed system, with a very limited scope for lateral entry at senior level. Most permanent officials join the service as a lifetime career through an entrance examination/ interview conducted by the Public Service Commission. The age of entry is usually 21 to 30 years and the age of retirement either 58 or 60 years of age.

The subject matter of the Government of India is divided between the Union Government and the State Governments. The respective governments recruit most of their employees independently. However, a unique feature of the Indian system is the existence of three All India Services, the Indian Administrative Service, the Indian Police Service and the Indian Forest Service. The Government of India recruits the members of these services although they work with the States where they are allotted (their cadres) for most of their career. However, the Government of India obtains the services of these officers at higher and middle management levels through deputation for a period of about five years. This enables a regular exchange of officers between the field and the central levels. Senior Indian Administrative Service Officers who have had their initial grounding in different States of India thus man the top secretariat posts in most ministries of the Government of India.

India is a democratic republic and full freedom of speech and religion is allowed to all its citizens. The Constitution of India guarantees the following Fundamental Rights to the citizens of India.

Right to Equality: This includes equality before law (Article 14), prohibition of discrimination on grounds of religion, race, caste, sex or place of birth (Article 15) and equality of opportunity in matters of employment (Article 16).

Right to Freedom: This includes protection of certain rights regarding freedom of speech etc. (Article 19), protection of life and personal liberty (Article 21) and protection against arrest and detention in certain cases (Article 22).

Right against Exploitation: This includes prohibition of traffic in human beings and forced labour (Article 23) and prohibition of employment of children in factories etc.

Right to Freedom of Religion: This includes freedom of conscience and free profession, practice and propagation of religion (Article 25), freedom to manage religious affairs (Article 26), freedom as to payment of taxes for promotion of any particular religion (Article 27) and freedom as to attendance at religious instruction or religious worship in certain educational institutions (Article 28).

Cultural and Educational Rights: These include protection of interests of minorities (Article 29) and the right of minorities to establish and administer educational institutions (Article 30).

The Constitution of India further guarantees the right to move to the Supreme Court for enforcement of the above rights.

India has a multitude of political parties; some organised on economic ideology, some on religious ideology while some on local and linguistic aspirations. However, only three or four parties really have a presence at the National level; the Congress Party that was the ruling party for more than forty years, the Bharatiya Janata Party (the present ruling party with its allies), the Janata Dal and the Communists. There are many religion-based parties like the Akali Dal (Sikhs in Punjab), the Muslim League etc. The regional parties like the DMK and AIADMK (Tamil Nadu), Shiv Sena (Maharashtra), Telugu Desam (Andhra Pradesh) and some parties in the smaller North-Eastern States have been contenders of powers in the State governments of their respective states. However, at the National level, only three parties have been able to provide the Prime Minister i.e. the Congress, the BJP and the Janata Party/Janata Dal in alliance with smaller parties.

An independent body called the Election Commission of India conducts elections to the parliament and the state legislatures in India. The elections are based on a universal adult suffrage with voting rights to all citizens above eighteen years of age. The lower houses of the national and the state legislatures have a five-year term although elections are regularly held before this term expires.

The elections to the local bodies have been brought under the purview of a similarly constituted body called the State Election Commission. These bodies also usually have a five-year term. It is statutory not possible to supersede the local bodies for long periods or to keep them under Government-appointed Administrators.

An age of more than twenty-one years is usually an eligibility condition for getting elected to an elective post in a local body. The eligibility for being a member of the Lower House of the National or state legislatures similarly prescribes the minimum age of twenty-five years. A minimum age-limit of thirty years is similarly a qualification for membership of the Upper Houses of the National and State legislatures. A minimum age-limit of thirty-five years is prescribed as a qualification for holding the post of the President or Vice-President of the Indian Republic.

The elections to both the urban and rural local bodies in India are ward based. The local area is divided into wards of more or less equal population. Each ward sends one representative to the concerned local body. After the

Seventy-third and Seventy-fourth Amendments to the Constitution of India, one-third of the wards are reserved for women candidates and only women candidates can contest elections from these wards. Apart from the reservation for women candidates, some other wards are reserved for candidates from socially underprivileged sections.

Political parties are allowed to take part in elections to all local bodies except the village panchayats in India. It is, however, not uncommon for locally influential politicians to form local fronts to contest and win elections to municipal councils and the smaller municipal corporations in the country.

India became independent in the year 1947. In all the elections held since independence, women had the voting rights. The pattern of participation by women in the national elections.

The percentage of seats won against the seats contested is showing a declining trend only because the number of women contesting elections has increased sharply. However, it may be seen that voting for women in all tiers of Government has always been a feature of the Indian polity since 1947.

Representation of Women in Politics

Women play a dual role in politics—as voters and political representatives. On the voting front, though adult franchise was granted in 1937, it was the progressive spirit that pervaded the making of the constitution that made it a reality. The Constitution of India guarantees equal rights to men and women as voters and citizens. Generally, in India, registration and participation of women as contestants is less than that of men. In recent past, records show that there has been an increase in the percentage of women who vote. Such participation is also contingent on the mobilisation efforts made by political parties, NGOs, Action Groups and the general awareness among the community of the importance of women exercising their franchise. Again, a note of caution is required, lest it be assumed that political participation always indicates political awareness on the part of the woman voter. Usually, however, countries that do hold regular elections show an improved recognition of women as a political constituency and parties and candidates tend to adopt pro-women stances and appeal specifically to women's votes, especially at the time of elections.

Since Independence, due to exercise of their franchise, Indian women have been exposed to the political processes and are showing increasing awareness about not only lack of rights but also their utility. A majority of illiterate rural women are also politically sensitive and aware of the various issues confronting them. Women get easily mobilised in the political processes by the political parties who approach women very often for party issues and for short-term goals by winning elections, but not for long-term goals of bringing about social changes and gender equality in political power-sharing.

In all the elections held since independence, women had the voting rights. The percentage of seats won against the seats contested is showing a declining trend only because the number of women contesting elections has increased sharply. However, it may be seen that voting by women in all tiers of Government has always been a feature of the Indian Polity since 1947. Due to the parternalistic family and male dominated political structures which do not provide space for women in decision-making bodies, women constituted 3.1% of the total contestants in 1996 election and did not occupy more than 6.10% of the total seats in the state legislative assemblies and Parliament.

The number of women contestants in Parliamentary elections has not increased significantly over the years.

Political parties are still reluctant to field women candidates at national level.

In the early days of the Indian republic, the number of women representatives was a mere 22, which was a lowly 4.4% of the total seats in the Lok Sabha. The sixth Loksabha in the year 1977 saw an all time low of just 19 woman representatives. The twelfth Lok Sabha had 44 women i.e. 8.8% of the total.

Even as early as the 19th century Indian women had begun to appear on the national scene in public and political activity. Women were not only being accepted in public activity but were organising themselves to fight for their rights in different walks of life.

Though women constitute nearly half of the population of the country, it was only after Independence that efforts were made to promote women's participation in public life. Though the Constitution of India provides for the Government to make special provisions to safeguard the interests of women as detailed in Article 15 (3) and Article 39, it has not made any provision for reservation for women in respect of jobs and political offices. However the 73rd and 74th Constitional Amendment Act mandated reservation of one-third seats in the village, block, districts, municipal elected bodies in India. As a consequence, women had not advanced much politically and economically. From the records available of the past 50 years, since the independence, it is seen that the strength of women in the political field as reflected in State legislatures remained at an average of 3 % to 5% of those elected. At the level of Parlaiment, the position of women members has varied between 5 to 7%.

It is seen that women in large numbers have come out against atrocities on women, in defence of their traditional control over crucial resources, water, forests, and land, mass literacy drives and other issues. They are also coming out in large numbers over ecological degradation, price rise or protests against police repression, etc. While there is the increased participation in grass root political movements, it is not getting translated into a growing share of women in the formal political structure of the country.

Amongst the several reasons for such a situation is the growing money power and muscle power required to contest even the smallest of elections in India, the intimidation, violence and slander that a woman candidate has to face combined with the traditional male domination that seeks to keep her indoors. Narrow electoral arthmetic and the necessity of fielding a winning candidate makes most political parties shy away from fielding more than a token number of women candidates. And if they are fielded at all, kinship and affinity factors play a major role. It is very common to observe that the relatives of politicians are promoted and supported to emerge as politicians.

Increasingly, women have stood for elections and got elected as members of State Legislative Assemblies and the Parliament. However, at the national level there is only one woman Cabinet Minister and 8 Ministers of State in a Cabinet of 70. There is only one woman Governor and one woman Chief Minister.

Some studies of Parliamentary participation indicate that women members participate more actively in 'women's issues' – health, welfare, atrocities against women, crimes like dowry and violations of human rights. This participation is confined to the more articulate women. In issues such as defence, finance, politics, etc. Their participation is relatively limited. Analysis of trends of women' participation to contest elections to the State Legislatures indicate that there is a gender discrimination which is responsible for poor representation of women in India.

Women's role in decision making is one of the most important questions for consideration in the movement for their empowerment. The 73rd and 74th Amendments(1992) to the Indian Constitution have served as a major break through towards ensuring women's equal access and increased participation in political power structures. This Amendment provided for reservation of one third of seats for women at level of local governance in urban areas. There is also a one-third reservation for women for posts of chairpersons of these local bodies. This amendment has initiated a powerful strategy of affirmative action for providing the structural framework for women's participation in political decision-making and provided an opportunity to bring women to be forefront and centre of city development and develop new grass-root level leadership. There are about 1 million elected women representatives in Panchayats and Municipal Bodies in India.

After 1993, women's participation in local governments increased quite radically, with the enactment of the legislation providing 33 percent reservation of seats for women in local bodies. The legislation and its implementation has added another level in political participation. The previous table indicates the total number of urban local bodies as well as elected representatives in India.

In Governments too, there has been limited representatives of women. A few eminent women have no doubt, occupied important administrative positions, such as Secretaries of Departments in the National Government as well as in State Governments. It is only 5.71% of the total number of persons in administrative services are women. It is noteworthy that within the premier civil services of India, the representation of women is not that encouraging.

Since relatively few women enter the civil services. several efforts have been made to improve the situation. The

Department of Personnel and Administrative Reforms of the Government of India has also provided, wherever possible, women officers on the selection boards for posts and services.

Women's Participation in Local Governance

The 74th Amendment to the Indian Constitution, 1992 has served as a major breakthrough towards ensuring women's equal access and increased participation in local government. The Constitution (74th Amendment) Act, 1992 aims at Constitutional guarantees to safeguard the interests of urban local self government to enable them to function as effective democratic and self governing institutions at the grass root level. This Amendment provides for reservation of 33 1/3 percent of elected seats for women at local government level in urban and rural areas. There is also a one-third reservation for women of posts of chairpersons of these local bodies. A very active role for women in local governance is envisaged as compared to governance at the state and national levels in India. These provisions have provided great opportunities and challenges to women in India, particularly in the local government field. This is of great significance, since this grass-root level participation has considerably broadened the base of women's participation in politics at city level.

Limits and Constraints

Involvement of women in the political arena and in decision-making roles is an important tool for empowerment as well as monitoring standards of political performance at local level. However, in the present political process of entry into decision making political institutions, there is growing influence of money and muscle power, backroom dealings, communalisation and criminalisation. In many respects women and men elected representatives face similar problems on election to office. Above all there is a need to understand just how to be a good local politician. The role of political representatives at local level is demanding and all new 'recruits' need time to gain experience and to understand the rules, regulations and procedures governing the administrative bureaucracy with which they now have to work – often quite closely in the urban service delivery system.

Some of the major constraints that prevent women from effective participation at local level are as follows:

1. Lack of orientation / training in urban development issues and municipal administration.
2. No proper knowledge / orientation about municipal acts and rules and regulations.
3. No prior experience about dealing with multidimensional urban development issues / civic issues and its complexities.
4. Lack of knowledge about technical inputs related to urban service delivery system.
5. Lack of support from senior male / female colleagues in the party / municipal body.
6. Less co-operation from municipal officials understanding about various facets of the budget, such as allocation of budget at ward level (at central / ward level).
7. Lack of party support and poor organisational structure.
8. Lack of money and resources to sustain the electoral campaigns (inspite of code of conduct by election commission).
9. Discrimination in decision making at party level.
10. Specific notions towards politics and political atmosphere.

11. Fear and insecurity.
12. Lack of confidence in public speaking.
13. Criminalisation of politics and use of money power.
14. Family responsibilities.

Civil Society Initiatives

Political system in India works through political parties who contend for power by invoking popular support. Therefore it is necessary that if women want to share power they have to make a place for themselves within the political parties through which the Indian democratic system operates. The experience of the last 52 years show an inability to create 'this space' and recent studies show that there has been no significant change in either the nature of women's functioning or in the political parties' approach to women and women's issues. If we examine women's participation (prior to 1993) it is seen that the political parties have given less importance to women's issues in terms of ideology, either in priority in their party manifesto or in terms of the number and importance of the position that women occupied in individual political parties. Women are not seen as a vote bank to be approached, and once the men are mobilised, women will merely endorse their choice of party and candidate. Male candidates rarely have access to the female electorate and there are not enough women involved in political campaigns to be able to reach out to a large section of women even in big cities. As a result, the exposure of women to political debates and issues has always remained indirect. According to women from all parties the political environment was not conducive to women's participation in politics. The analysis made by Kumari and Kidwai stated that political parties have dominated the conservative 'cultural' perspective and no conscious attempt has been made to increase active participation of women.

Women in India today are agitating at the doors of Parliament, demanding reservation for 33 per cent of the seats. The issue at stake here is more complex than it may seem. It is not only a question of a few more or a few less women in the corridors of Parliament and legislatures but also a response to the fact that a large section of society has historically been denied its legitimate share in the exercise of political power, that ultimately determines its destiny. In this demand for reservation, women are also raising their voice against a system, which has consistently denied them space by harnessing the forces of tradition in order to marginalise and travails their role. Reservation of seats for women in Panchayats/Municipal bodies have shown that it has tremendous implications, not merely in terms of the number of women entering the public arena and holding public office, but also in terms of the social, economic and political impact that these reservations have had for the total system.

It is for these reasons that women are increasingly demanding political roles for themselves. They recognise that constitutional guarantees do not ensure effective participation and that these cannot ensure political equality. Hence the need to gain entry into political institutions and in the functioning of the state, and to share control over the power the state exercises. This alone would lead to a situation where women are able to reverse the existing situation, which has consistently been against their interests, and bring about the necessary changes in policy and the social structure so as to ensure a more equitable and humane order.

The role of women's participation in elected bodies should not be undervalued. Elections are after all a forum for self government and democracy, they are significant in drawing the attention of the nation to the problems and needs of disadvantaged sections; the manifestos, campaigns, promises made by individual candidates, track record and future course of action of political parties are indicative of national concerns as well as mandates for action. Proper selection of candidates in an election is vital if this representative democracy is to function in the interests of a majority of the population that is depressed and disadvantaged. Hence, opportunities for participation at this level are significant for the adoption of politics and measures for women's development.

Strong and dynamic women who would not dream of appropriating privilege are today talking of reservation because they have come to recognise that they will not give "easy entry" in the corridors of power without reservation. This hierarchy is so rigid that the natural processes of democracy and constitutional guarantees have not been able to make a dent in these fortresses of power. The demand for reservation should not therefore be seen as either a gift or a privilege that women are seeking. For most women it is the last straw and a desperate measure to ensure their coming into the political mainstream. Their participation becomes vital in the context of the adoption of development strategies that are negative and harmful to women. Today most of the political parties in India have initiated some initiatives to activate political participation of women and develop their capacities. However, most of the political parties have not yet developed any special programmes to meet the special requirements of women in urban or rural areas, despite the fact that most of the women activists felt that if planned efforts were made, they could be easily mobilised. Different debates concerning struggles of women as well as various actions by women's groups and NGOs on local as well as national problems have forced the mainstream political parties to accept women's concerns in their political programmes. The political parties started changing their attitude towards women which is reflected in their election manifestos, their attitudes towards women candidates, speeches and slogans.

Statistics on women's participation in the electoral process are not very encouraging. It is important not only to pressurise the political parties but also to make the leaders understand the significance of organising systematic training of women's possessing leadership qualities, of carefully selecting women candidates and ensuring financial, technical and human resources for affirmative action.

The need to strengthen womens's participation and leadership is constantly emphasised by various institutions viz, All India Institute of Local Self Government, NIUA, HSMI, Rambhau Mhalaji Prabhodini, etc and several NGOs and Women's groups like SEWA, Working Women' Forum, YUVA, Disha, Prayas, Astha, Winavani, SNDT University, Aalochana, Agni, FASDSP (Forum Against Sex-determination and Sex Preselection), Stree Mukti Sanghathana, etc.

Many NGOs / CBOs, Women' groups have provided some training, however systematic training of women possessing leadership qualities is not enough and more concentrated efforts are required to facilitate the process of women's ascent to key positions in political field. It is essential that the women's groups and movement recognise the importance of women as a constitutency and ensure their participation and representation in policy formulation. The movement must provide a support system for women who enter political processes to win elections. As stated by Nath Kamale 'The women's movement has been a powerful agent of empowerment and has provided an alternative perspective for fundamental structural changes. The movement has created organisational strength of women, has focussed on women's issues and mobilised them around these issues. The women in the movement, however, have shied away from active participation in politics.

The women's groups and women activists thus aim to bring about a change in the women's perceptions, but not necessarily in the structures which subordinate women. If we want to bring about change in the lives of women and transform mainstream politics, there is no other way than to get involved in politics and transform it.

The women's movement and groups have to recognise the importance of women as a constituency and ensure their participation and representation in policy formulation. This can be achieved through reorienting existing structures for entry into decision-making including the political party system and introduce quotas or reservation as a temporary means of women's representation. The movement should also provide a support system (women's groups) for women who enter political processes to win elections.

The women's groups working at the grassroots level are small and scattered and have diverse ways of empowering women. There are no infrastructure facilities of networking available that could bring them together and strengthen them while allowing autonomy in their functioning. It is important to create unity in diversity between women's groups, organisations and individuals involved with women's empowerment. They need to adopt a common strategy, informed by a common vision, to be able to bring about changes in the policies and structures that perpetuate their subordinate status.

Encouraging Women to Participate in Local Governance

Reservation for women in local government is not just a question of getting a certain number 'in'; it also develops their capacities to play their rightful roles in the development process and makes an important difference as the local governments deals mostly with the quality of life for citizens. Municipal responsibilities relate both to women's practical needs and their strategic needs. The better we meet women's strategic needs, the better they are able to contribute to good city governance. Good Local Governance, in turn, enables a better response to women's practical needs.

Most local governments have initiated orientation / training programmes to encourage women to participate in local governance by organising city-specific induction or theme-based training programmes, wherein intensive training is given in various subject areas, such as, municipal acts and its implementation, laws of meetings, municipal budgeting, budgeting at ward lèvel, municipal taxation, mobilisation of resources, urban service delivery systems (solid waste management, water supply, sewerage, health care services, traffic and transportation), poverty alleviation schemes, community management, environment management, shelter programmes, new reforms in municipal administration, functioning of ward committees, motivation techniques, communication skills, women and development, handling the media etc.

The Ministry of Urban Development, Government of India and Urban Development Department of State Governments organise a number of training programmes, workshops, seminars for women elected representatives at local level through various training institutions. Many municipal bodies have initiated a series of in-house training in m unicipal administration and urban development, in collaboration with premier training institutions in India. State governments through their State Training Centres organise capacity building programmes for women elected members from municipal bodies in their States. Special training / orientation programmes are organised by Ministry of Urban Development and Poverty Alleviation, Government of India under the UNICEF assistance and government's funds in the area of poverty alleviation schemes and its implementation in urban areas (e.g. SJSRY, NSDP, etc.)

Gender Sensitising of Local Government

Local governments are using sex-desegregated data for policy and programme formulation. It is an obligatory duty of municipal governments in India to collect, compile and maintain vital statistics in their city limits. Sex-disaggregated data is in use in many cities of the States in India for policy programme formulation and implementation of some special programmes and projects at local city level.

The Government of India regularly collects, analyses and disseminates quantitative and qualitative data on the number of women and men employed at various levels in government on an annual basis and many mechanisms have been set up within governmental structures for monitoring progress in this field.

The Department of Women and Child Development, Government of India is collecting and using gender-disaggregated data to evaluate development from a gender perspective. The Department is also developing a Gender Development Index (GDI) for the construction of EDI and Gender Empowerment Measure (GEM).

Bringing women to positions of political power in local government is just the first step in social transformation. Gender sensitisation of those in power, be they men or women, is of critical importance. Influencing the choices of those at decision – making levels and bringing gender issues to the political agenda are important factors. Over the years, this perspective has gained acceptance within organisations, action groups and political parties.

Government departments, other institutions, non-governmental organisations, and women's organisations have undertaken several programmes to sensitise local governments about the issues and needs of women in their cities.

It is recognised that law enforcement is a critical factor for bringing about enduring changes in gender perceptions. Several initiatives have been taken by the Government of India and the voluntary sector to sensitise law enforcement personnel and policy makers. Gender sensitisation of police personnel and urban administrators in the National and State level training centres is now a regular programme. A National Centre for Gender Training and Research has set up in the National Academy of Administration in Mussourie with the objective of sensitising young administrators and policy makers on gender issues.

The Election Commission of India maintains updated information on women representatives in each Parliament, including categorised information on the number of scheduled castes women representatives. With the recent revolution in information technology, the entire information is available not only in print but also on the Internet in the Parliament and Election Commission websites. This increases out-reach and access of this information to the general public.

The Ministry of Rural Development, Government of India maintains updated information on the representation of women in local self-government or Panchayati Raj. The Department of Women and Child Development, Government of India also has come out with publications like 'Women in India – A Statistical Profile' in 1997, which compiled information on all aspects related to women in India. The Planning Commission, which is mooting the process of collection of gender desegregated data by all concerned departments in various Ministers, has included information on women's representation in power and decision-making in its Ninth Five Year Plan Document.

Besides these, several independent organisations are carrying out their own research and surveys that provide updated information on the same. These are also widely used and are quoted in different public documents. Sensitising the leadership of people's movements in the country to gender issues need to be prioritised.

Women's Representation In Local Government

Legal and Political Initiatives

The number of women in politics at the local level had been very small, and their influence negligible. As stated by Kumari and Kidwai, "Prior to 1990, the women in local politics were generally either politicians who had lost membership of higher institutions, and those who were given such an opportunity to serve the purpose of publicity. In many cases, the motive was partially also to satisfy the aspirations of these few women, since they could be kept under virtual control and denied higher aspirations. The insignificant presence of women at these levels was an important indicator of two basic facts: one that women who are planted at the top often lacked the kind of training required for effective participation, secondly, the society was unable to accept women in politics, particularly at the grass-root level.

If we examine the reasons for low participation, as stated by Nath, Kamle 'down the ages women have always been treated as subordinate to men in every aspect of life. Their place of work was confined to the domain of the household with household chores and rearing of children. Her identity was attached to that of her father, husband or son, i.e. she was given a status in accordance with that of her male partner. It is not that women in the past have not contributed substantially in politics, but because of their secondary status and low esteem, most of them were denied entry in political decision-making.

The 74th Amendment of the Indian Constitution in 1992 ushered in a new era in the democratic process of the country as it not only provided constitutional status to the municipal bodies but also provided an enabling environment for women to a direct part in the local self government and brought women to the forefront and centre of local development. Sharing power and responsibilities with immense control over resources for development and social change will be an empowering instrument for women.

Article 243 T (I) of Constitution Amendment (1992) states as follows: "Reservation of Seats:

1. Seats shall be reserved for the Scheduled Castes and the Scheduled Tribes in every Municipality and the number of seats so reserved shall bear, as nearly as may be, the same proportion to the total number of seats to be filled by direct election in that Municipality as the population of the Scheduled Castes in the Municipal area or of the Scheduled Tribes in the Municipal area bears to the total population of that area and such seats may be allotted by rotation to different constitutions in a Municipality.
2. Not less than one-third of the total number of seats reserved under clause (1) shall be reserved for women belonging to the Scheduled Castes or, as the case may be, the Scheduled Tribes.
3. Not less than one-third (including the number of seats reserved for women belonging to the Scheduled Castes and the Scheduled Tribes) of the total number of seats to be filled by direct election in every Municipality shall be reserved for women and such seats may be allotted by rotation to different constituencies in a Municipality.
4. The office of Chairpersons in the Municipalities shall be reserved for the Scheduled Castes, the Scheduled Tribes and common in such manner as the Legislature of a State may by law, provide.

5. The reservation of seats under clauses (1) and (2) and the reservation of office of Chairpersons (other than the reservation for women) under clause (4) shall cease to have effect on the expiration of the period specified in article 334.
6. Nothing in this Part shall prevent the Legislature of a State from making any provision for reservation of seats in any Municipality or office of Chairpersons in the Municipalities in favour of backward class of citizens."

Different political parties in India have shown great reluctance to field women candidates. Reservation of seats at Municipal level has put pressure on political parties to identify and field more women candidates.

Training and Support Mechanisms

Attention is being given to the training and capacity developing skills and capacities of all elected representatives in local government, including women. They are trained to acquire skills, knowledge and orientation needed to carry out the onerous responsibilities given to them. A time bound, systematic and comprehensive training programme has been drawn up which will be funded by the Central Government. The Indira Gandhi National Open University has been associated with the preparation of a syllabus on women and development. The Government of India is also committed to capacity building efforts by organising and funding training programmes for women elected to municipal bodies in India. A large number of such kind of training programmes for elected members are handled by All India Institute of Local Self Government which is a premier training institution in local government field in India. Ministry of Urban Development (MUD) supports several such kind of training programmes through Regional Centre for Urban and Environmental Studies (RCUES) which are functioning in all the regions of India. Apart from this, some of the theme-based training programmes are organised by State Training Institutions in several States for women elected members in municipal bodies.

Support Groups and Forums

Women elected to local governments have not formed any formal associations, groups and forums. However, all women mayors meet during meetings organised by All India Council of Mayors (AICM), which is an association of mayors representing all cities in India. These meetings give women mayors an opportunity to interact with each other and with other male Mayors and exchange ideas, information about effective urban service delivery, good governance and also provide issue based support. Similarly, various seminars, workshops, training programmes organised by Government of India, State Governments and National and Regional institutions provide wide opportunities for women elected members to meet and interact with elected women members from different municipal bodies in India. Similarly, events organised by political parties, women's groups, non-governmental organisations also provide an opportunity for women elected members for experience sharing, networking and sometimes lobbying for some specific purpose in urban development and good governance.It is also observed that in many cities women elected members have close links with local NGOs, CBOs or Residents' Associations or action groups and through such networking women members support each other and initiate networking among themselves about governance at local level or any issues related to women and development.

Training of Women in Local Government and Civil Service

The following institutions undertake training of appointed officials:

1. Urban Development Department, Government of India and Urban Development Departments of various State Governments in India have initiated several capacity building or training initiatives to train women working at various levels of municipal administration.
2. National Academy of Administration in Missouri is actively involved in training senior government officers from Indian Administrative Services in India. The Academy has set up a National Centre for Gender Training and Research to further issues related to women and development. Apart from this, several State Training Centres in various states organise training-cum -orientation and workshops for women appointed in local government.

It is observed that women officers from the Indian Administrative Service (IAS), Police (IPS), and Foreign Services (IFS) have their associations in all the States of India. These associations organise periodic meetings and 'get together' which provide an opportunity for the women officials to interact with each other. The City Managers' Association of Gujarat State also provides opportunities for women officials in local government in Gujarat State. 'Metro Forum' an association of Municipal Commissioners of Metro Cities will also provide an opportunity for women municipal commissioners to meet and interact on issues related to civic governance and any other issues related to women and development. Similar efforts are underway to establish an association of women officials in all municipal bodies in India.

All India Institute of Local Self Government, through its various Centres in India imparts training in the field of municipal administration. Besides short-term specialised programmes, it also organises full time diploma courses on various aspects of municipal administration for junior and middle level municipal personnel. These courses are attended by large number of women employed at junior and middle and senior levels in municipal bodies in India. The following main institutions also offer several need-based or tailor-made specialised programmes for women working at different levels of municipal administration in India.

The main purpose of urban management training is to develop capacities of officials to deal with the complex urban problems in a holistic manner to achieve efficiently the aim of municipal bodies and of the urban sector as a whole. These institutions cover the main areas for orientation / training or capacity building in urban development and municipal administration field.

Special Measures to Recruit Women in the Civil Service

One of the variables that go into the Gender Empowerment Measure, as depicted in the Human Development Report, is the proportion of men and women at senior levels of government. In this context the study initiated in 1996 by the Department of Personnel and Training (DoPT), as part of a project 'Capacity Building for Civil Services', was a significant step. In order to crystallise the problems faced by women in Civil Services as well as to isolate areas which needed to be addressed through policy guidelines, a survey was carried out across a cross section of the services, among men and women officers, to ascertain the issues on which guidelines would have to focus. The survey questionnarie was formulated keeping in mind different areas of concern for women officers like Gender Image in workplace and in the family to stress factors.

Various government studies have been undertaken in the past on problems and issues related to the various individual services that constitute the Indian Administration. But this survey broke new ground in terms of coverage of services and levels of both women and men, as well as the range of related issues. Many issues, such as stress and motivation and sexual harassment, that persist across the services were touched upon for the first time. A national level Project Steering Committee was set up for carrying out the Capacity Building project, and a Focal Point was identified in the DoPT for examining the sphere of "Women's Issues in the Civil Service".

The Lal Bahadur Shastri National Academy of Administration (LBSNAA) was appointed as consultant for developing a curriculum for Gender Sensitisation Programmes and ten Regional Seminars were conducted at nine State Administrative Training Institutes.

The Focal Point identified in the DoPT will begin work towards framing guidelines on women's issues by reviewing existing rules / regulations of various services. The task that has emerged for the Focal Point is as follows :

> Review of existing rules and regulations for possible gender bias and discrimination against women and suggest corrective action.

Co-ordinate output flowing from various activities of the project related to the issues requiring policy formulation.

In the Civil Services, the overall percentage of women in 1997 was 7.5%, the highest being 12.3% in the Indian Foreign Service. Women are increasing their presence in other sectors such as the Revenue Services, the Railway Management Cadres, Telecommunication etc. On the whole, women in 1997 represented 13.8% of the employee strength in the public sector, as against only 8.6% in 1971.

Women's Organisation or other civil society organisation have taken some initiatives in some states of India to encourage women to stand in local government elections, however, these groups or organisations are small and scattered and have diverse ways of empowering women. There are no infrastructure facilities of networking that could bring them together and strengthen them while allowing autonomy in their functioning. It is important to create unity in diversity between women's groups and civil society organisations involved with women's empowerment.

Political participation would make a significant different if it came from those who are at the helm of affairs of political parties, and if women are there wielding power, the situation can improve to a great extent and political participation would give every woman a sense of dignity as a individual.

The women's movement and groups have to recognise the importance of women as a constituency and ensure their participation and representation in policy formulation. This can be achieved through reorienting existing structures for entry into decision-making including the political party system and introduce quotas or reservation as a temporary means of women's representation. The movement should also provide a support system (women's groups) for women who enter political processes to win elections.

The women's groups working at the grassroots level are small and scattered and have diverse ways of empowering women. There are no infrastructure facilities of networking available that could bring them together and strengthen them while allowing autonomy in their functioning. It is important to create unity in diversity between women's groups, organisations and individuals involved with women's empowerment. They need to adopt a common strategy, informed by a common vision, to be able to bring about changes in the policies and structures that perpetuate their subordinate status.

Non-partisan women's groups should provide necessary moral and advisory support to women candidates to increase their chances of being elected to political offices. They should work towards enhancing the capacity of women candidates to win the elections by providing them with a forum whereby they could exchange ideas and experiences and learn from experts on electoral laws and politics and evolve issues and strategies to win elections.

Special Civil Society Initiatives

The 33 per cent for women in municipal bodies has brought into focus the fact that there is a need to bring more and more women into the party. But the problem is that many women are often not equipped to become members of the political parties, as the party expects a certain level of consciousness for membership – not everybody can become a member. Also, women have difficulty in attending party meetings, study circles or demonstrations because of their timings and the pressure of housework. Most of the parties have not yet developed any special tailor – made programme to meet the special requirements of women in urban areas, despite the fact that most women activists felt that if such an effort was made, they could easily be mobilised.

The party's ideology itself may be discriminatory, on the other hand its ambiguity in a traditional society may leave adequate space for discrimination. Party workers at times exhibit a sense of lack of gender equality because they carry with them their traditional value systems which are often feudal and patriarchal, into the party. Much of the discrimination against women in the party is because of the attitudes of these individuals. But at the same time women assert that the party does not try to change the attitude of both men and women who come to the party or make them more gender sensitive.

The nature of electoral politics in India also marginalises women and women's issues from the political agenda. Many women feel that electoral politics, at times limits the kind of support women politicians would like to extend to members of their own sex, since they realise that they cannot win elections on women's issues alone. Most of them are still assistant to identify themselves with women's issues, claiming that women form only one section of their constituency and till recently not the determining section. Also, elections are largely conducted by men and with men's support. Electoral expediency requires women participants to compromise to survive in the man's world of politics. All parties recognise the need to win women's votes, but often seem unsure of the best way to gain support among women.

The type of leadership required is of transformational type. Women's entry into processes of governance should create change in the very institutions of governance. In order to effect such change, leaders have to emerge which can occur only through participatory processes. The participation allows empowerment, which then generates leadership. It is only through their leadership, and their implied changes in the hierarchy of party and power that they may provide that they can justifiably participate in governance as representing something 'different'. This leadership can emerge only through active participation. Therein lies the role of the political parties in creating an enabling environment for active leadership generating participation. Prior to 1992, political parties have not been initiating any special initiatives or programmes to encourage women to stand in local government elections. The number of women in politics at the local level has been very small, and their influence negligible. After 1993, women's participation in local governments increased quite radically with the enactment of the legislation providing one-third reservation of seats for women in local bodies. The effective implementation of this legislation has added another level in political participation. According to women from all parties the one third reservation for women in local governments has brought into focus the fact that there is a need to bring more and more women into the local government field and develop their capacities.

This particular 74th Amendment of the Indian Constitution ushered in a new era in the democratic process in India as it not only provided constitutional status to the municipal bodies but also provided an enabling environment for women to take direct part in the process of local self government and brought women to the forefront of city development.

The 74th Amendment mandated reservation of one – third seats in municipal bodies for women. There is also one third reservations for women in position of chairpersons of these local bodies in India.

A very active role for women in local governance is envisaged as compared to governance at the state and national levels in India. These provisions have provided great opportunities and challenges to women in India.

The challenge now is to transfer this large presence of women at local government level supported by the real delegation of power and responsibilities.

Women's role in decision making is one of the most important questions for consideration in the movement for their empowerment. Reservation of seats for women in local bodies has shown that it has tremendous implications, not merely in terms of the number of women entering the public arena and holding public office, but also in terms of the social, economic and political impact that these reservations have had for the total system.

Recognising various constraints such as present day politics, elements of criminalistics, corruption, muscle power, violence, lack of awareness of political participation, preparation to fulfil the role and responsibilities as elected representative, etc, the Government, NGOs, Women Groups and activist's have been actively involved in providing necessary inputs to women. Women have been mobilised to participate in elections as candidates and voters, and to be vigilant citizens where elections are held. Communities have received gender sensitisation to facilitate acceptance of the new roles assigned to women. Leadership and organisational training of women has been conducted to enable them to be dynamic change agents. Networks have been interacting, to influence mass based political structures to prove more space to women.

Bibliography

Alford, Robert and Roger Friedland. 1985. *Powers of Theory: Capitalism, the State, and Democracy*. Cambridge: Cambridge University Press.

Block, Fred L. 1977. "The Ruling Class Does Not Rule: Notes on the Marxist Theory of the State" in *Socialist Review* 33:6-27.

Bourdieu, Pierre. 1984a. *Distinction: a Social Critique of the Judgement of Taste*. Cambridge, MA: Harvard University Press.

Burton, M., & Higley, J. 1998. "Political Crises and Elite Settlements." In M. Dogan & J. Higley (Eds.), *Elites, crises, and the origins of regimes* (pp. 47-70). Lanham MD: Rowman & Littlefield.

Chadha, G.K. and Sharma, Alakh (eds.) 1997. *Growth, Employment and Poverty: Change and Continuity in Rural India*. Delhi: Vikas Publishing House.

Cox, Robert. 1987. *Production, Power, and World Order: Social Forces in the Making of History*. New York: Columbia University Press.

Dahl, Robert. 1961. *Who Governs? Democracy and Power in an American City*. New Haven: Yale University Press.

De Tocqueville, Alèxis. *Democracy in America*. Anchor Books edition, 1969.

Domhoff, William G. 1998. *Who Rules America? Power and Politics in the Year 2000, Third Edition*. Mountain View: Mayfield Publishing Company.

Fukuyama, Francis. 1989. "The End of History?" in *The National Interest* (Summer): 3-18. Gramsci, Antonio 1971. *Selections From the Prison Notebooks*. London: New Left Books.

Hegel, Georg Wilhelm Friedrich. 1830/1956. *The Philosophy of History*. New York: Dover Publications.

Held, D., A. McGrew, D. Goldblatt, and J. Perraton. (1999). *Global Transformations: Politics, Economics and Culture*. Polity and Stanford University Press.

Higley, J., & Burton, M. 2006. *Elite foundations of liberal democracy*. Lanham MD: Rowman & Littlefield.

Hirst, P and G. Thompson, 1996, "Globalization: A Necessary Myth?" in Hirst and Thompson, *Globalization in Question*, Cambridge: Polity Press, 1-17.

Huntington, Samuel. 1993. *The Third Wave: Democratization in the Later Twentieth Century*. Oklahoma: University of Oklahoma Press.

Inglehart, Ronald. 1977. *The Silent Revolution: Changing Values and Political Styles Among Western Publics*. Princeton: Princeton University Press

Jessop, Bob. 1990. *State Theory: Putting the Capitalist State in Its Place*, Cambridge: Polity Press.

Jessop, Bob. 2002. Globalization and the National State, in S. Aaronwitz and P. Bratsis, éd., *Rethinking the State: Miliband, Poulantzas and State Theory*, Minneapolis: *Alternatives: Turkish Journal of International Relations, Vol. 5, No.1&2, Spring & Summer 2006* 19 University of Minnesota Press, pp. 185-220.

Lenin, Vladimir. 1932. *State and Revolution*. New York: International Publishers

Lukes, Steven. 1974. *Power: A Radical View*. London: Macmillan.

Marx, Karl. 1848. "The Communist Manifesto" in *Karl Marx: Selected Writings* (ed.) David McLellan (1977). New York: Oxford University Press.

Michels, Robert. 1915. *Political Parties: A Sociological Study of the Oligarchical Tendencies of Modern Democracy*. New York: Hearst's International Library.

Mills, C. Wright. 1956. *The Power Elite*. New York: Oxford University Press.

Mosca, Gaetano. 1896/1939. *The Ruling Class*. New York: McGraw-Hill.

Pareto, Vilfredo. 1901/1968. *The Rise and Fall of Elites*. New Jersey: Bedminister Press.

Polanyi, Karl. 1944. *The Great Transformation*. Boston: Beacon Press.

Poulantzas, Nicos. 1969. "The Problem of the Capitalist State." New Left Review 58: 67-78.

Reich, Robert. 1991. *The Work of Nations: Preparing Ourselves for 21st Century Capitalism*. New York: Alfred A. Knopf.

Robinson, William I. 1996. *Promoting Polyarchy: Globalization, US Intervention, and Hegemony*. Cambridge: Cambridge University Press.

Robinson, William I. 2004. *A Theory of Global Capitalism: Production, Class and State in a Transnational World*. Baltimore: Johns Hopkins University Press.

Smith, J, Chatfied, C, and Pagnucco, R. 1997. *Transnational Social Movements and Politics and World Politics: Solidarity Beyond State*. Syracuse: Syracuse University Press.

Index